CANOEING

The Chicagoland Canoe Base, Inc.
RALPH C. FRESE
4019 N. NARRAGANSETT
CHICAGO, ILLINOIS 60634
CHICAGO AREA
CANOEING INFO. SP 7-1489

AMERICAN NATIONAL RED CROSS

WASHINGTON, D.C.

THE MISSION OF THE RED CROSS

The American Red Cross is the instrument chosen by the Congress to help carry out the obligations assumed by the United States under certain international treaties known as the Geneva or Red Cross Conventions. Specifically, its Congressional charter imposes on the American Red Cross the duties to act as the medium of voluntary relief and communication between the American people and their armed forces, and to carry on a system of national and international relief to prevent and mitigate suffering caused by disasters.

All the activities of the American Red Cross and its chapters support these duties.

Nationally and locally the American Red Cross is governed by volunteers, most of its duties are performed by volunteers and it is financed by voluntary contributions.

❦

The Small Craft program of the American National Red Cross, for which this book is a teaching text, stems from the Congressional charter provision that the organization shall devise and carry on measures for relieving and preventing suffering.

AMERICAN RED CROSS

CANOEING

Prepared by the American National Red Cross

First Edition 1956
With 411 Illustrations

Fourth Printing
December 1969

DOUBLEDAY & COMPANY, INC.
GARDEN CITY, NEW YORK

Library of Congress Catalog Card Number: 56-3327
Printed in the United States of America
8

PREFACE

For many years the American Red Cross has included canoeing instruction in its water safety program. This has been done at national aquatic schools since the early 1920's. There, water safety instructor candidates have received instruction in safe canoe handling, self-rescue, and ways to help others in or on the water. The amount of time devoted to the subject at these schools is limited but is sufficient to enable the water safety instructor to include canoe-safety instruction in his junior and senior lifesaving courses and in other appropriate circumstances.

Since 1948 the Red Cross has conducted national small craft schools, where canoeing instruction is one of the major subjects, offered primarily to prepare canoeing instructors to teach the Red Cross Basic Canoeing Course. Instruction is also given in methods of conducting canoe-safety demonstrations. Thousands of these demonstrations have been conducted through the years, reaching large numbers of people with canoe-safety information. Canoeing instructors are also trained in Red Cross chapters and at selected national aquatic schools.

The American Red Cross has prepared this canoeing textbook in response to a popular demand and in knowledge of the need for it as support for the programs described above. It should strengthen them and greatly further the aim of preventing loss of life in canoeing activity throughout the country. The text contains all the information required for Red Cross canoeing programs on both the basic and instructor levels.

To make a greater contribution to safety, the book also extends into broader areas of canoeing activity. It therefore contains information on specialized forms of activity such as

v

trips, racing, canoeing on swift rivers, contests, and other activities. There is information on how to take care of canoes and equipment and how to make repairs to the various types. The first two chapters explain the historical development of canoes. Chapter III contains a variety of information including such subjects as making paddles, building canoe docks, canoe racks, paddle racks, and rigging canoes for special purposes. For all, from the beginning canoeist to the very proficient, there is information of value in accordance with individual need or special interest. As knowledge and skill increase, safety is increased. The end result will be fewer drownings, not only among beginners but also among those who possess special skills but have lacked essential safety and self-rescue information.

ACKNOWLEDGMENTS

This textbook has been written for the American Red Cross by Joseph L. Hasenfus, formerly assistant director of Safety Services for Small Craft Safety.

The American Red Cross wishes to acknowledge with deep appreciation the contribution made by Waldemar Van Brunt Claussen to the small-craft phase of its Water Safety program. His efforts for the advancement of safe and skilled canoe-handling contributed greatly to the preparation of this book.

Special acknowledgment and thanks are extended to a review committee, comprised of Mr. Claussen, Thomas Costello, Ruth Elvedt, Roy Kneip, and Charles Barnes. Their findings and recommendations, made in a conference when the manuscript was thoroughly examined, have been incorporated into the text, and represent a great contribution.

Gratitude is further expressed to the many first aid and water safety volunteers, chapter directors, and representatives whose experience and assistance in the program through the years contributed in innumerable ways; the staff at national headquarters for their careful and assiduous assistance in the planning, research, photography, art work, editing, and other tasks; and to the many organizations, agencies, and individuals who helped in the research, making of photographs, and in providing authentic material on various activities.

CONTENTS

AMERICAN RED CROSS

CANOEING

CHAPTER I

OUT OF THE PAST

The canoe is an incredibly significant product of human workmanship. In the earliest ages of man, there was a time when he had neither the mentality nor the skill to make any object or to use any tool more refined than a club. Then gradually over a very long period of time he developed the simplest of tools and made the simplest of objects useful in his struggle to survive. If he lived near water, one of these objects was a dugout canoe.

This first vessel wasn't much of a craft, but its contribution to and its influence on the course of the history of man is immeasurable. From it evolved all the vessels that man has used on the waters of the earth through the countless centuries to our time. It is fascinating to compare the parent craft with its evolving descendants, galley to modern liner and warship, but greater meaning lies in the fact that there would be no civilization as we know it today without water transportation, which started with the dugout canoe. Added to this, and making it all the more remarkable, is the paradox that in some areas of the earth the dugout never evolved to higher types of craft. It exists today as it did in the beginning, serving its essential role in the lives of contemporary primitive people.

How man first got afloat is, to a degree, a matter of supposition. However, based upon accumulated knowledge of early man and contemporary primitive people, it is generally agreed that primordial man probably ventured in and on the water merely because of his proximity to it. His adventure in this direction may have been hastened or intensified by the need to get food for himself and his family or to escape from a predatory enemy.

A log was probably the first floating support man used. At first he held onto it, supporting himself and "swimming" it along wherever he wished to go. Later he lay on it and hand-paddled it, and then sat up astride the log and poled it in shallow water areas. These latter two skills were rather difficult; so when members of his family group on other logs came close to his, he welcomed the greater stability resulting when they held the logs together. It was then a natural step to lash the logs together with vines or root fibers to make a raft. When getting out of shallow water, at first accidentally, poling the raft had to give way to paddling it with the pole until the bottom could be reached again. This activity suggested flattening a stick for better purchase in the water. This was the birth of the paddle, which permitted trips far from shore.

The Dugout Canoe.—Then the dugout—a product of man's development of primitive tools and discovery of fire-making —came on the scene. This first vessel may have been suggested by nature. Surely lightning caused fires then as now, and logs partially burned out could have been found, experimented with, and further hollowed with fire and stone tools, revealing greater stability and increasingly shallower draft as the hollowing deepened and extended fore and aft. The next step was shaping the ends to lessen resistance and make the craft speedier and more maneuverable. Afterward, suitably sized logs were deliberately selected and hollowed, and a "home industry" of canoe-building was inaugurated (see Figs. 1 and 1A).

Felling trees by burning and chopping with a stone axe.

A Dugout Canoe was made by shaping a Log, charring the inside, and then scraping it with sharp stones.

FIG. 1—Making a dugout canoe. (Courtesy of C. W. Jefferys Imperial Oil Collection)

Since this explanation of log, raft, hollow log, and dugout canoe suggests such a natural evolutionary process probably taking a very long time, it is logical to presume that it took place independently in many places over the earth, at the same time, and at different times. In some instances, of course, primitive people who had developed canoes may have migrated over land or water and taught their new art to others.

As the art of making dugout canoes developed, regional

The manner of makinge their boates. XII

FIG. 1A—When the first settlers came to the coast of Virginia, they encountered Indians making dugout canoes. (This picture and narrative are from Thomas Hariot's *Narrative of the First English Plantation of Virginia*. (Courtesy of the Smithsonian Institution)

XII.

The manner of makinge their boates.

THE manner of makinge their boates in Virginia is verye wonderfull. For wheras they want Instruments of yron, or other like vnto ours, yet they knowe howe to make them as handsomelye, to saile with whear they liste in their Riuers, and to fishe withall, as ours. First they choose some longe, and thicke tree, accordinge to the bignes of the boate which they would frame, and make a fyre on the grownd abowt the Roote therof, kindlinge the same by little, and little with drie mosse of trees, and chipps of woode that the flame should not mounte opp to highe, and burne to muche of the lengte of the tree. When yt is almost burnt thorough, and readye to fall they make a new fyre, which they suffer to burne vntill the tree fall of yts owne accord. Then burninge of the topp, and bowghs of the tree in suche wyse that the bodie of the same may Retayne his iust lengthe, they raise yt vppon potes laid ouer cross wise vppon forked posts, at suche a reasonable heighte as they may handsomlye worke vppon yt. Then take they of the barke with certayne shells : they reserue the innermost parte of the lennke,* for the nethermost parte of the boate. On the other side they make a fyre accordinge to the lengthe of the bodye of the tree, sauinge at both the endes. That which they thinke is sufficientlye burned they quenche and scrape away with shells, and makinge a new fyre they burne yt agayne, and soe they continne somtymes burninge and sometymes scrap- inge, vntill the boate haue sufficient bothowmes. Thus God indueth thise sauage people with sufficient reason to make thinges necessarie to serue their turnes.

---

* Probably a typographical error for " barke."

FIG. 2—Pamunkey dugout canoe, made by the Pamunkey Indians of Eastern Virginia and used by them on the Pamunkey River and elsewhere. It measures 8 feet 10 inches long, 18 inches abeam, and 9 inches deep. It is round bottomed, keelless, and has full convex raking ends. It was made by the burning and scraping process. (Courtesy of the Smithsonian Institution)

FIG. 3—A dugout being poled by a native on a river in Panama. (From: Black Star, New York)

FIG. 4—Seminole Indian dugout canoe: length 20 feet, beam 16 inches, depth 7 inches, weight 94 lbs. (Courtesy of W. Van B. Claussen)

variety in sizes and designs resulted. Some were small and simple in construction like that of the Pamunkey Indians of eastern Virginia (Fig. 2). Simple dugouts of this type are used today in parts of Africa[1] and elsewhere. At the present time a much longer and more graceful dugout is used by natives in Central America (Fig. 3) and by Seminole Indians in Florida

[1] *Terence T. Quirke*, Canoes the World Over (*Urbana, The University of Illinois Press*, 1952), Chap. 4.

FIG. 4A—Seminole Indian dugout canoe being poled by a present-day Seminole Indian. Its estimated measurements are: length 24 feet, beam 27 inches, depth 10 inches, weight 210 lbs. (Courtesy of W. Van B. Claussen)

FIG. 5—Futuna dugout canoe from Futuna Island, a French possession north of the Fiji Islands. Paddled by hand and used for fishing, it is 9 feet 2 inches long, 24½ inches wide, and 17½ inches deep. The bottom extension is used to lift the canoe on shore and empty it of water. (Courtesy of The Mariners' Museum, Newport News, Virginia)

FIG. 6—Bushnegro dugout canoe, built by a native at Ganzie (Surinam River), Dutch Guiana. In their native waters these canoes are equipped with a palm-leaf-thatched shelter. It measures 15 feet 7 inches long, 35½ inches wide, and 12½ inches deep. Note the style of paddles. (Courtesy of The Mariners' Museum, Newport News, Virginia)

FIG. 7—Bonito canoe, ceremonial and sacred, from the Santa Cruz Islands of British Solomon Islands. The decorations are mother-of-pearl inlay. It was built in the Island of Santa Anna in the Solomons for The Mariners' Museum in 1940. (Courtesy of The Mariners' Museum, Newport News, Virginia)

(Figs. 4 and 4A). A crude but rather unique dugout (Fig. 5) is that from Fortuna Island, a French possession north of the Fiji Islands. The dugout of the Bushnegro of Dutch Guiana (Fig. 6) combines good design with decorative carving. Decorative pattern is carried to a high degree of excellence in the ceremonial and sacred canoe of the Santa Cruz Islands of the British Solomons (Fig. 7). Canoes used in the Pacific Islands have outriggers (Fig. 8) to provide stability. Sizes range from small ones for children to large war canoes. Many are equipped with sails.

Indian tribes of the Northwestern coastal regions of North America made dugouts of excellent design and of elaborate totemic decoration (Figs. 9 and 10). They were made of cedar logs, some of giant sizes, often as long as sixty feet, for use on the ocean, and sometimes for hunting whales (Fig. 11), a

FIG. 8—Outrigger dugout of the Papuans of New Guinea represents types found among many islands of the Pacific Ocean. The cloth canopy protects from the hot tropical sun. The platform is built on a very narrow hull and the outrigger provides stability. (Photograph by Ewing Galloway, New York)

FIG. 9—Tlinkit Indian canoe (a model). This is a North Pacific coast Indian canoe, hollowed and carved out of a cedar log. The ornamentations are totemic designs that were once put on all canoes but now are seen mostly on models. The high ends of this canoe and those in Figs. 10 and 11 are carved out of separate pieces of wood attached to the main hull. They provide greater seaworthiness to the canoe and have totemic significance. The canoe is a small one, built for two or three people. (Courtesy of the Smithsonian Institution)

FIG. 10—A Northwest Pacific coast dugout made by the Haida Indians, inhabitants of the Queen Charlotte Island of British Columbia, noted for their seamanship and their carvings. This craft measured 36 feet long, 6 feet at the beam, and 25 inches deep. *A model* (Courtesy of the Smithsonian Institution)

remarkably courageous canoeing adventure. Canoes of very large sizes have been used on nearly every continent and in the Pacific Islands. An interesting and elaborately decorated one is that formerly used by the King of Siam in state processions (Fig. 12).

A rather rare primitive canoe is that made by sewing thinly hewed planks together with root fibers or rawhide (Fig. 13).

The dugout canoe is the type that evolved into larger craft. As men progressed with canoe-building, some of them enlarged the canoes to transport goods for trade with neighboring tribes or groups. To get more freeboard than the dugout could provide, boards were added to extend above the normal gunwale level. Progressive people continued this process until the original dugout became little more than the keel. The planks, first added for extra freeboard to keep out the slop of waves, became the planking of the hull. During this time, oars and sails were invented for use with the larger craft. The latter evolved into the galleys of earliest history, which in turn led to larger ships of subsequent centuries.

Frame-and-Skin Canoes.—Where trees were scarce, frame-and-skin canoes were made. One interesting type is the *bull boat,* or circular canoe (Fig. 14). A circular framework of sticks was covered with animal skin. In the early days of the West, the Plains Indians made these craft with buffalo hides. After about 1885, cowhide was used. In the British Isles, a craft

Fig. 11—*Kwakiutl Whale Hunting*, painted in 1934 by George Peter, hangs in the Milwaukee Public Museum. The Kwakiutl are a tribe of Indians of northwestern Vancouver Island. These large canoes they hollowed and carved out of a single cedar log. A width greater than the diameter of the log was achieved by softening the hollowed log with water kept hot with heated stones. The desired width was maintained by carefully placed thwarts. These giant log canoes were sometimes made as long as 60 feet, with a beam of about 8 feet, and a depth of 5 feet. Whale hunting from canoes required hard work and much bravery. Apparently, whaling parties were led only by great chiefs. (Courtesy of the Milwaukee Public Museum)

FIG. 12—Royal Siamese barge, a very long, elaborately decorated, gilded canoe used about the middle of the nineteenth century by the King of Siam in state processions. It was 65 feet long, 4½ feet at the beam, and 15 inches deep, and was propelled by thirty-two men with paddles. The gilded and decorated pagoda amidships was the throne, upon which the king sat during the procession. *A model* (Courtesy of the Smithsonian Institution)

FIG. 13—Yukaghir canoe of the people of northeastern Siberia having some language relationship to the North American Indian. This is their hunter canoe built of three thinly hewn poplar boards stitched together. It could be regarded as a prototype of modern plank canoes and planked pirogues. The original measured about 16 feet 3 inches long, 24 inches wide, and 7½ inches deep. *A model* (Courtesy of the E. T. Adney Collection, The Mariners' Museum, Newport News, Virginia)

FIG. 14—Bull boat, or circular canoe, is covered with buffalo hide and was made by an Indian named Crow's Heart at the Fort Berthold Reservation in North Dakota. Prior to about 1885 bull boats were covered with buffalo hide; after that, cowhide was used. Measurements of this canoe are 49 inches beam and 14½ inches deep. (Courtesy of The Mariners' Museum, Newport News, Virginia)

of this type is called a *coracle*. In the region of the Tigris and Euphrates rivers, a craft of the same shape is woven of basket material and made watertight with pitch. Another unusual type of craft propelled by paddles or poles is the balsa raft, or grass boat, which could also be called a grass canoe (Fig. 15).

A type of primitive craft about which few people have heard is a moose-hide canoe made by Indian hunters of northeastern America out of the hides of the moose they killed. They built a frame consisting of gunwales, keel, and ribs; sewed two or more moose hides together, and shaped and secured them

FIG. 15—Grass boat of Senegambia, Africa, measured 18 feet 10 inches long, 37 inches wide. It is double-ended and propelled by paddle or pole and hence could be called a grass canoe. The body is made of two cigar-shaped bundles of rushes bound together with two-stranded rope and curved up at the ends. Above the outer edges of these are two smaller bundles so lashed as to increase the beam and height of the craft and form a hollow inside. This grass balsa resembles grass balsas of South America and elsewhere. *A model* (Courtesy of the Smithsonian Institution)

tightly over the frame. After the seams were waterproofed with pitch and melted moose tallow, the canoe was ready to load with moose meat to be taken downriver to the home village. Speck gives a detailed description of one he saw made.[2]

The Eskimos, inhabiting the Arctic coasts of the North American continent, mainly Alaska and Greenland, made frame-and-skin canoes, the kayak and the umiak. Both of these words are spelled in several ways, but the currently preferred spelling is as given here. In parts of Alaska the kayak is called a bidarka, bidarkee, or baidarka and the umiak is called a bidar,

[2] *Frank G. Speck*, Penobscot Man (*Philadelphia, University of Pennsylvania Press, 1940*), *pp.* 65–67.

FIG. 16—Eskimo kayak, side view, with the skin covering removed from one-half of the craft to show that it is constructed of a wooden framework over which sealskin is stretched and secured in place. This kayak from Nunivak Island in Alaska is used for hunting and fishing. Note the 7-inch diameter hole for hand-grasping at the bow and the curved projection at the stern, presumably for the same purpose. (Courtesy of the Smithsonian Institution)

FIG. 17—Eskimo kayak from Nunivak Island, Alaska, top view. Length, 15 feet 3 inches; beam, 30 inches; depth, 18 inches. Many kayaks are much narrower and shallower than this one. (Courtesy of the Smithsonian Institution)

bidarra, or biadara, but *kayak* and *umiak* are more widely used.

The kayak is made by constructing a wooden framework and stretching sealskin over the frame, bottom and top, leaving only the cockpit opening (Figs. 16 and 17). The wooden framework is usually made of driftwood pieces held together with rawhide thong lacings and ties. The skin covering is similarly held in place with rawhide.

The umiak is also constructed of a framework of driftwood pieces or other wood covered with the skin of seals or walruses. The upper edges of the covering are stretched tightly

FIG. 18—Umiak from Kodiak Island, Alaska, measured 29½ feet long, 8 feet 9 inches at the beam, and 3 feet 5 inches deep. The single-blade paddles, which Eskimo women used, were over 7 feet long. Umiaks of the Hudson Bay and Greenland regions have blunter ends, do not have the disk-like projection at the bow. *A model* (Courtesy of the Smithsonian Institution)

over the gunwales and held in place by a rawhide lacing passing through holes in the skin covering and over and under, or around a riband (longitudinal strip of wood) a few inches below the gunwale (Fig. 18). The typical size is about 30 feet long by 8 feet at the beam.

The kayak is usually manned by a male, paddling with a double-blade paddle. Although typically a one-place craft, larger ones for two or three persons are sometimes made (Fig. 19). The umiak, a large craft, is usually manned by several women who paddle it with single-blade paddles often more than 7 feet long.

FIG. 19—A three-hatched Eskimo kayak made in modern times in Alaska. (Courtesy of the Smithsonian Institution)

The Birchbark Canoe.—Primitive canoe-building reached its highest form in the birchbark canoe made by the North American Indians inhabiting the forest regions of the United States and Canada where the *paper birch* tree (also called *canoe birch* and *white birch of the North*) grew in great numbers. This remarkable canoe of frame-and-bark construction (Fig. 20) deserves special consideration for the reason given above and because it has a very special place in American and Canadian history.

When the discoverers, explorers, missionaries, merchants, and settlers from Europe and the British Isles came to Canada

MAKING CANOES

Building a Birch Bark Canoe

Stripping Birch Bark

FIG. 20—Making a birchbark canoe. (Courtesy of the C. W. Jefferys Imperial Oil Collection)

and the United States, they found the greatest primeval forest area on earth—literally impenetrable except on foot or afloat on the countless thousands of rivers, lakes, and streams. The American Indian had a remarkable craft, a birchbark canoe, to facilitate his travel in regions to be known as Canada and northern parts of the United States. In fact, so many of the Indian's activities depended upon the birchbark canoe that

FIG. 21—Dogrib birchbark kayak. The original was made by the Edge-of-the-Woods Dogrib Indians of Great Slave Lake. It is now in the National Museum of Canada, Ottawa. It measures about 12½ feet long, 26 inches wide, and 8½ inches deep. A *model* (Courtesy of the E. T. Adney Collection, The Mariners' Museum, Newport News, Virginia)

FIG. 22—Abnaki-type birchbark canoe. The original was about 12¾ feet long, 34 inches wide, and 13 inches deep. The Abnaki name signifies "Those living at the sunrise" or "with the East." They were part of a confederacy of 13 Algonquin tribes. Note: the frame lying on the canoe thwarts is a "canoe form" used in making the canoe. See Chapter XIV. A *model* (Courtesy of the E. T. Adney Collection, The Mariners' Museum, Newport News, Virginia)

FIG. 23—Tete-de-Boule birchbark canoe was of the region of the St. Maurice River, Quebec. The gunwales are root-sewed in ancient Indian manner. The canoe measured a little less than 13 feet long, was 30½ inches wide, and 13 inches deep. The Tete-de-Boule Indians, a detached branch of the Wood Cree, were located near the St. Maurice River (Quebec) and along the upper Ottawa River. A *model* (Courtesy of the E. T. Adney Collection, The Mariners' Museum, Newport News, Virginia)

some people have called his a "canoe culture." His canoe was of good lines for speed and maneuverability on the water and light of weight for ease in carrying it between bodies of water. It was made of a size to suit its owner in accordance with the use for which it was being built. Some one-man birchbark canoes were as short as 12 or 13 feet, with beams ranging from 26 to 35 inches (Figs. 21, 22, 23). Variations of design in these

and larger canoes were relatively minor for the most part, but
included shape of ends, amount of sheer, depth of craft in
respect to length and beam, tribal decorations, and quality of

Fig. 24—Ojibway birchbark canoe from the locality of Lake Superior. It
measured 13 ½ feet long, 35 inches wide, and 16 inches deep. The Ojibway
(or Ojibwa or Chippewa) Indians were one of the two largest divisions of
the Algonquian linguistic family. From earliest times they were one of those
tribes most often in the minds of writers on the American Indians: for
example, their mythology inspired Longfellow's Hiawatha. They are proficient in mat weaving and as canoe builders. In the region of the Great
Lakes over 30,000 still live on reservations in the United States and Canada.
A model (Courtesy of the E. T. Adney Collection, The Mariners' Museum,
Newport News, Virginia)

Fig. 25—Ancient Algonquin-type birchbark. The original measured 15 ½
feet in length, 38 ¾ inches at the beam, and 12 ½ inches in depth. The
Algonquin were a division of the Algonquian linguistic family of North
American Indians, located in the region of the Ottawa River in Canada.
A model (Courtesy of the E. T. Adney Collection, The Mariners' Museum,
Newport News, Virginia)

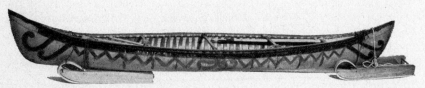

Fig. 26—Malecite canoe mounted on toboggans has decorations in red and
black paint of protective spirals and "camps." It is mounted on toboggans
for transport over ice. The original measured 17 ½ feet long and 34 inches
wide. The Malecite, frequently classed under the general name of Abnaki, are
a tribe of Algonquian Indians. Some of them live partly in New Brunswick,
others in Quebec, and quite a few in Maine. A model (Courtesy of the
E. T. Adney Collection, The Mariners' Museum, Newport News, Virginia)

FIG. 27—Dogrib birchbark canoe, a family canoe of the Dogrib Indians of Great Slave Lake, in Northwestern Canada. The original measured about 20 feet long, 47½ inches wide, and 15½ inches deep amidships. "Dogrib" is a popular English term for their "Thlingchadinne," meaning "dog-flank people." They were located between Great Slave Lake and Great Bear Lake. A *model* (Courtesy of the E. T. Adney Collection, The Mariners' Museum, Newport News, Virginia)

FIG. 28—Hudson Bay fur-trade canoe. The original was 30 feet 9 inches long, 62 inches wide, and 27 inches deep. It has full equipment aboard. With full equipment and carrying high officers of the Hudson's Bay Co., during the period 1860–1870, with a crew of eight paddlers and a guide, it was called a Canot Leger, or light canoe, meaning one lighter-laden for fast travel. A *model* (Courtesy of the E. T. Adney Collection, The Mariners' Museum, Newport News, Virginia)

workmanship. Many were of a size similar to the popular canoes of the present day for which they were, of course, the prototypes. These ranged in length from about 14 feet to about 20 feet, with beams varying from 32 inches to about 47 inches (Figs. 24, 25, 26, 27). Some very large canoes were built for war; later, in times of the white man, for trade. They ranged up to 30 feet and longer (Fig. 28). It is probable that the very longest were made after the coming of the white man and that the typical war canoe of the Indian was somewhat less than 30 feet.

Other Frame-and-Bark Canoes.—In areas where the birch tree did not grow, other barks were used in the making of bark canoes. Basswood-bark canoes (Fig. 29) and elmbark canoes (Fig. 30) were made by the Iroquois in regions south of the birch forests.

FIG. 29—Iroquois-type basswood-bark canoe, made by the Iroquois and often used by white men in the settlement period in Kentucky. The original measured 14 feet long, 39 inches wide, and 14 inches deep. *A model* (Courtesy of the E. T. Adney Collection, The Mariners' Museum, Newport News, Virginia)

FIG. 30—Small Iroquois elmbark canoe. The original measured 14 feet long, 38¾ inches wide, and 15 inches deep. The Iroquois Indians were located first in the upper and central part of the Mohawk Valley and the lake region of central New York, but later were important from Maine to the Mississippi and from the Ottawa to the Cumberland rivers. Obtaining guns from the Dutch helped them attain this dominance. *A model* (Courtesy of the E. T. Adney Collection, The Mariners' Museum, Newport News, Virginia)

FIG. 31—Goldi birchbark canoe, made by the Goldi tribe of the Lower Amur River in easternmost part of Asia. The original measured about 15 feet long, 27½ inches wide, and 13 inches deep. Canoes of this unusual construction were also common in the Kootenay region of British Columbia and in the northwestern United States. *A model* (Courtesy of the E. T. Adney Collection, The Mariners' Museum, Newport News, Virginia)

Interestingly enough, frame-and-bark canoes have been made in other parts of the world also. One is of special interest because of its monitor, or ram-style, ends. It is the *Goldi Birchbark Canoe* (Fig. 31), made by the Goldi Tribe of the Lower Amur River in Asia. Canoes of bark, usually pine or spruce, closely resembling this design, were found in the Kootenay region of British Columbia and in Northwestern U.S. In view of the fact that aboriginal Americans are known to have

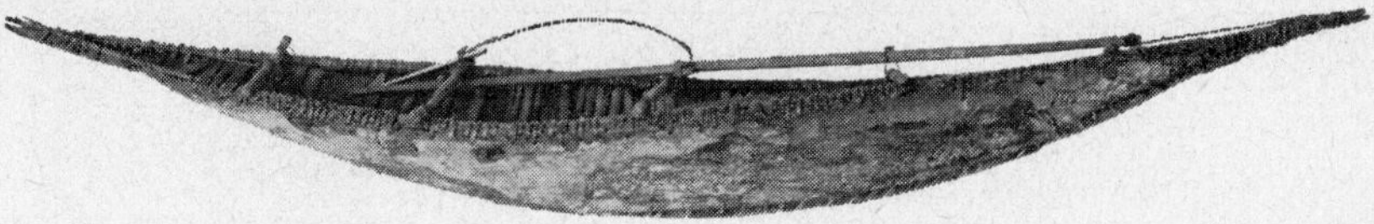

FIG. 32—Fuegian canoe, a bark canoe made and used by the Indians of Tierra del Fuego in the region of the Straits of Magellan. It is made of coarse bark and sewed together with thin, tough, flexible strips of whalebone, which also secure the bark to the gunwales and bind the converging gunwales together at the ends. The crude ribs are made of split saplings or branches of trees bent to the required shape. Five crossbars are lashed to gunwales to serve the purpose of thwarts. The canoe is 25 feet long, 6 feet at the beam, and 20 inches deep. A *model* (Courtesy of the Smithsonian Institution)

migrated from Asia to this continent, we can assume a relationship between the canoes of these two groups. Another bark canoe (Fig. 32) of interest is that of the Indians of Tierra del Fuego at the extreme southern projection of the continent of South America. It is of frame-and-bark construction, rather large, 25 feet long, but of less refinement of workmanship than the birchbark canoes of the North American Indians.

The white man upon his arrival on the North American continent made almost immediate use of the birchbark canoe in his exploration, missionary work, fur trading, and settlement. Every schoolchild reads of the explorers and missionaries using birchbark canoes and employing Indians to help them. In fact, it was the chief means of travel to unexplored areas for a couple of centuries.

Perhaps the most romantic of all the chapters in the story of canoes is that of the *coureur de bois* and *voyageur*. During the early period of the settlement of Canada many of the French found that clearing the land and farming it was less inviting than the more adventurous life of hunting and trapping for fur. Canoes were essential in this occupation and were obtained on short notice from the Indian canoe builders. The mobility involved in the work brought these men the romantic name

FIG. 33—*Voyageurs* paddling Simon Fraser down the Fraser River, which he discovered and explored in 1808 in British Columbia. The other canoes in his expedition are seen in the background. All are birchbark and about 25 feet long. Canoes of greater length and larger crews were used in eastern Canada (Fig. 28). (Courtesy of the C. W. Jefferys Imperial Oil Collection)

of *coureurs de bois,* or bushrangers. They came in close contact with the Indians, and many married Indian women. A
great amount of their activity involved transporting by canoe
large quantities of merchandise into remote areas of the wilderness to trade with Indian tribes for beaver and other furs.
This was during the 17th century. By the 18th century most
of the *coureurs de bois* had changed from independent hunters, trappers, and traders to hired canoemen called *voyageurs.*
They were French Canadians, half-breeds, and sometimes
pure-blooded Indians. They worked for merchants licensed
to trade in fur and for explorers famous in history (Fig. 33).
Gibbon[3] has much interesting information about these men,
including quotations from the writings of explorers and other
leading men of those periods. The prowess of the *voyageur* as
a canoeman and a *portageur* apparently reached an extremely
high level—especially in terms of his ability to paddle rapidly
for hours on end and to carry very heavy loads on portages.
His character is legendary in Canadian folklore and history.
The Canadian poet William Henry Drummond has immor-
talized the *voyageur* in poems including "The Voyageur."[4]
This poem like much of his work is written in the French-
Canadian dialect. Some selected lines are:

* * *

Gone he is now, an' de beeg canoe

* * *

Ax' heem de nort' win' w'at he see
Of de Voyageur long ago,
An' he'll say to you w'at he say to me,

[3]*John Murray Gibbon,* The Romance of the Canadian Canoe (*Toronto
The Ryerson Press, 1951*).

[4]The Poetical Works of William Henry Drummond (*New York, G. P.
Putnam's Sons, The Knickerbocker Press, 1912*), *p. 259.*

* * *

"I see de track of hees botte sau-vage
On many a hill an' long portage
Far, far away from hees own vill-age

* * *

. . . I meet heem singin' hees lonely way
De happies' man I know—
I cool hees face as he's sleepin' dere
Under de star of de Red Riviere,

* * *

De blaze of hees camp on de snow, I see
An' I lissen hees 'En Roulant'
On de lan' w'ere de reindeer travel free,
Ringin' out strong an' clear—
Offen de grey wolf sit before
De light is come from hees open door,
An' caribou foller along de shore
De song of de Voyageur."

So dat's de reason I drink tonight
To de man of de Grand Nor' Wes',
For hees heart was young, an' hees heart was light

* * *

I'm proud of de sam' blood in my vein
I'm a son of de Nort' Win' wance again.

Be- | hind our lit - tle | cab- in and lake, A- | Ro- ly Po- lo- ly My
The | son of the king, | Three white ducks a bath- ing go; | the king his son;

Row - lie Bow - lie, Two | ducks go bath - ing and a drake, A
The prince he comes with a gun and bow.
He comes to hunt with a sil- ver gun.

Ro - ly Po - lo - ly En | Roul - ant Ma Boule | Row - lie Bow- lie A-

Roll- ing my bowl, | Row- lie Bow- lie En | Roul - ant Ma Boule.

With his gun of silver bright
Took aim at the black and killed the white.

You are wicked, oh son of the king;
Killing my duck was a wicked thing!

My duck you've killed; my duck was white;
His eyes were agleam with diamonds bright.

And from his eyes the diamonds leak
And gold and silver from his beak.

His beak is dripping golden rings
And blood is rippling from his wings.

The white duck's wings are dripping blood;
The wind is white with his feather-flood.

Three ladies gather the feather yield
And soon we shall make us a bed in the field.

A feather-bed we'll gather and keep
In which to snuggle, in which to sleep.

From AMERICANS AND THEIR SONGS by Frank Luther. Copyright,
1942. McGraw-Hill Book Company, Inc. By permission of the author.

Voyageur Song

Old French folk melody "La Rose Blanche" mentioned by R. M. Ballantyne in "Hudson Bay" as a favourite paddling song with the voyageurs of the fur brigades in Western Canada.

John Murray Gibbon

Tune- "La Rose Blanche"
French Canadian Folksong

Key Ab

1. Ho! for the life of a voy - a - geur!
2. Ho! for the tumb - ling— rap - id's roar!
3. Ho! for the land of the Ind - ian brave,
4. Hard is our la - bour and low the wage;

Ho! for the haunts of __ game and fur! We
Ho! for the rest on __ lone lake shore! We
Hun - ter and trap - per and no man's slave; His
Heav - y the pack on the long port - age; But

drive a - long the old can - oe, And
lie be - neath the old can - oe, And
squaw is in his bark can - oe, His
o - ver - head we swing can - oe With

comb the bank for __ beav - er.
sleep be - side the __ riv - er.
ar - rows in his __ quiv - er.
brawn - y arm as __ lev - er.

From NORTHLAND SONGS No. 1
Copyright Gordon V. Thompson Limited, Toronto, Canada
Used by permission.

CHAPTER II
MODERN CANOES

It was inevitable that the superior tools and materials of white men would be used to produce canoes of better quality than those of the Indians, while at the same time retaining their best features. The period of transition from the birchbark to the all-wood and the canvas-covered canoe is not well recorded; therefore, an explanation of it will have to be partially assumptive. For example, the Indian no doubt used the white man's tools, as he did his weapons, as soon as they were made available. This could have resulted in some improvement in the birchbark canoes. This probability has been mentioned by some writers. An occasional effort was made by an individual, either Indian or white man, to use materials other than bark, roots, and pitch or hollowed log, to make a canoe. Two famous examples are those of John McGregor who, about 1865, made the famous *Rob Roy*, a decked canoe patterned somewhat after the Eskimo kayak, and Nathaniel H. Bishop who, a few years later, had a canoe made for him out of paper pulp mixed with glue. Both of these sportsmen took voyages in their canoes and wrote accounts of them.[1] Other efforts of this sort were no doubt made in many more utilitarian and unpublicized circumstances.

In Peterborough, Ontario, about 1870, John Stevenson made an all-wood canoe of rib-and-plank construction. Stevenson worked with Colonel J. Z. Rogers in the perfection of this canoe and in the year 1879 a canoe company was founded in Peterborough for its production. It is still in production. Only

---

[1] *N. H. Bishop*, Voyage of the Paper Canoe (*Boston, Lee & Shepard, 1878*). *This book is out of print.*
See also McGregor's Rob Roy series of books, sometimes available from dealers in old books.

a few years later in Old Town, Maine, men were considering the possibility of making canoes of rib, plank, and canvas construction. This was the result of known success in patching birchbark canoes with canvas or cloth. Beginning in the 1880's canoe companies were founded in Old Town and elsewhere for building canvas-covered canoes, which ultimately became famous throughout the world.

A later development was a canoe of double-plank construction with a waterproof cloth lining between the layers of planking. In recent times canoes of molded plywood have been made; a few in this country, but most of them in Europe. In common with other watercraft of molded plywood they combine strength, lightness, and easy upkeep.

The aluminum canoe also has come on the market. It has achieved popularity because of its relative ruggedness combined with light weight and easy upkeep.

On the following pages, the well-known types of canoes currently being manufactured are described. This information is given to provide a general understanding of canoe construction and an appreciation of canoe qualities and features. The purpose is not to give instruction in how to make these canoes.

Note: A dominant feature of the white man's canoeing activity is that in modern times it has been largely recreational. In some instances this led to the establishment of canoe clubs, outing clubs with special interest in some form of canoeing, and canoeing programs within various organizations. A pioneer and leading organization in canoeing has been the American Canoe Association established (August 3, 1880, at Crosbyside Park, Lake George, New York) to unite canoeists for the advancement of the various forms of recreational canoeing. This organization still gives leadership to canoeing activity in the forms of *canoe racing, canoe cruising, canoe sailing,* and other related activities. It issues to members a quarterly publication entitled *The American Canoeist*, which contains information for members and articles of interest to canoeists.

The Canvas-Covered Canoe.—The canvas-covered canoe is the traditional canoe of the white man, as its forerunner, the birchbark canoe, was of the Indian. There is expert craftsmanship in its construction as there so often was in the making of the birchbark canoe. In some instances the Indian and the white man work side by side at the present time making the canvas canoe. The general procedure is as follows:

1. A form is built. It is a permanent, relatively solid mold designed to the inside measurements of the canoe to be put in production. It will last for years and through the making of many canoes.

2. The inwales are laid in the canoe form (Fig. 1).

3. The inside stems, preshaped, are put in place in the same manner (Fig. 1).

4. After being softened by steam, the ribs are bent around the form and fastened to the inwales (Fig. 1).

5. The ribs and stems are then faired up (smoothed) by plane, and the planking laid on (Fig. 2).

6. Only the bottom planks are fastened to the inside stem while the canoe is still on the form. This allows the canoe to be spread enough to take it off the form (Fig. 3). This is necessary because of the tumblehome in the canoe at the sides and of the curve at the ends.

7. When the canoe is taken off the form, the decks are attached to the inwales and the stems. The ends of the planking also are attached to the stems (Fig. 4).

8. The rest of the planking is put on and the thwarts are put in place to give the canoe strength and maintain its shape (Fig. 5).

9. The canvas is applied (see Chapter XIII), filled, and finished. Then the outwales, outside stems and keel (if any), and

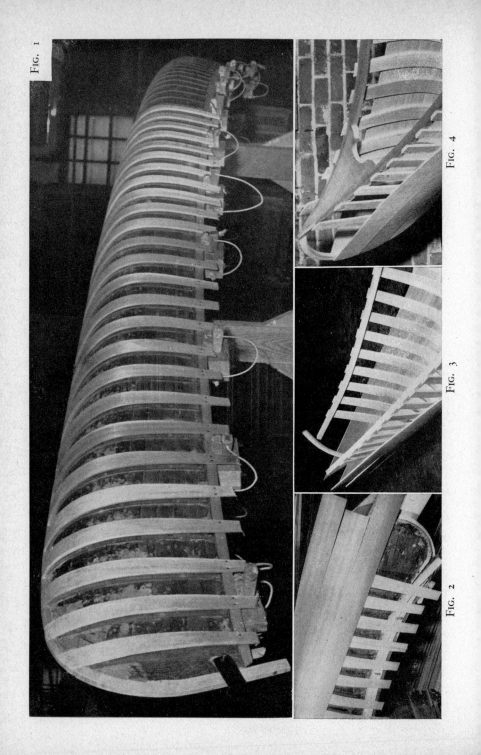

FIG. 1

FIG. 2

FIG. 3

FIG. 4

FIG. 1—Making the traditional canvas-covered canoe. Inwales and inside stems are in place and the steam-softened ribs are being bent around the form and fastened to the inwales (Courtesy of Thompson Bros. Boat Manufacturing Co.)

FIG. 2—After the ribs are in place, the planking is nailed to them with small brass nails that clinch over against metal strips on the form beneath each rib. (Courtesy of Old Town Canoe Co.)

FIG. 3—The canoe has been removed from the form before the planking is nailed to the stems at the ends of the canoe; otherwise, it would not come off because of the curve of the ends and the tumblehome of the sides. (Courtesy of Old Town Canoe Co.)

FIG. 4—After the canoe is off the form, the decks and thwarts are put in place and the planking nailed to the stems at the ends of the canoe. (Courtesy of Old Town Canoe Co.)

stem bands are put on and all wooden parts finished with varnish.

Some characteristics of the canvas-covered canoe are:

Ribs are nearly always made of white cedar, $\frac{5}{16}$ inch thick (sometimes $\frac{1}{4}$ inch thick on lightweight canoes), $1\frac{1}{2}$ inches to $2\frac{1}{4}$ inches wide, and spaced from $1\frac{1}{2}$ to $2\frac{1}{4}$ inches apart. On freight canoes the ribs are wider, thicker, and closer together.

Planking is generally made of red cedar, from $\frac{5}{32}$ to $\frac{3}{16}$ inch thick and $3\frac{3}{4}$ to 4 inches wide. On lightweight canoes the planking is sometimes $\frac{1}{8}$ inch thick.

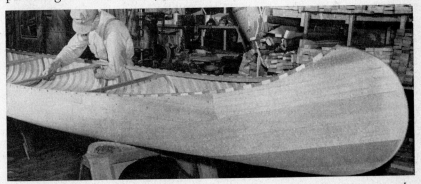

FIG. 5—Putting thwarts in the canoe. All that now remains is to put the canvas on, fill it, and do the over-all finishing job. (Courtesy of Old Town Canoe Co.)

Gunwales are made of mahogany, spruce, oak, or ash.

Decks are made of mahogany or oak.

Stems are made of oak or ash.

Thwarts are made of mahogany, oak, ash, or spruce.

Keels. Canoes come with or without keels, as specified. The conventional keel is a tapered one measuring from ⅞ inch to 1 inch wide where it is attached to the canoe bottom and the same in depth. It is on the median line of the canoe. Often shoe keels are used in place of the tapered keel. The shoe keel is ⅜ to ½ inch thick, and 2 to 2¼ inches wide. Large heavy canoes, especially the freight canoes, have one to three bilge keels on each side of the main keel.

Canvas of medium texture (for example, No. 8 or No. 10) is commonly used. On very large canoes No. 6 is common, with No. 4 used in exceptional cases. On very lightweight canoes which are to have careful handling, finer canvas up to No. 15 is used.

Filler is a mixture of products whose exact nature is not usually specified. Some fillers are mostly white lead. Some more recently developed are plastics (see Chapter XIII, Canoe Repair).

Canoe of Double-Plank Construction.—In a double-plank construction canoe currently manufactured (Fig. 6) the inside planks run crosswise from gunwale to gunwale, taking the place of ribs. The outside planks are narrow and run lengthwise on the canoe. Between these two layers of planking is a waterproof cloth lining made of high-grade, closely woven muslin treated with a waterproof marine glue. The two layers of planking are held together with over 7,000 copper nails, driven from the outside and clinched on the inside. The canoe has both inside and outside stems, a keel, seats, thwarts, and decks. The gunwales, of one-piece construction, are attached

FIG. 6—This is a canoe of double-plank construction. It is 17 feet long, 34 inches at the beam, 12½ inches deep amidships, 23 inches deep at the bow and stern, and weighs 75 pounds. Its mahogany decks are 2 feet long. The thwarts, gunwales, and keel are also made of mahogany. The stems are of white oak and the seats are spruce. The planking is selected vertical-grain cedar of combined thickness of ⁵⁄₁₆ inch. The canoe has four coats of highest grade spar varnish carefully applied to get the smooth finish apparent. (Courtesy of Willits Bros., and Pierce County Chapter, ARC, Tacoma, Washington)

outside the hull, thus making a flush finish to the inside from deck to deck. All the bent parts of the canoe are formed by steaming selected pieces on special forms and holding them in place until they dry, after which they are released to fit perfectly in their respective places in the canoe.

Molded Plywood Canoes.—With the introduction of modern waterproof plastic resin glues, it became practical to mold watercraft hulls of plywood. Such craft are light and strong—in fact, the great strength of the molded plywood makes ribs unnecessary, thus eliminating much weight.

The molded mahogany plywood canoe used in so many of the illustrations in this book (for example, Figs. 13 and 28 in Chapter IV) was made as follows:

1. The form was covered with a layer of cellophane to prevent the canoe from sticking to it.

2. Inside stems were fitted into recesses on the form.

3. The ¹⁄₁₆ inch thick strips of mahogany veneer were coated on both sides with the plastic resin adhesive, except for those strips to be used as face veneer on the inside and the outside

of the canoe. These were coated on only one side. All were laid aside to dry for a day.

4. The first layer of veneer was then stapled to the form, with the strips lying all the way across at a 45-degree angle to the keel line. When the layer was completely on, all the staples were removed except those beyond the trim line at each gunwale.

5. The remaining three layers of veneer were similarly applied each at right angles to the preceding one, with the strips arranged so that they overlapped the seams beneath.

6. The bonding process of getting the four layers of veneer permanently glued to each other and molded into the shape of the form was done by placing the whole thing into an autoclave after first wrapping it in canvas and inserting it in a rubber vacuum-bag. The door of the autoclave was bolted shut and the air withdrawn from the rubber bag through a special vacuum line. Steam was turned on to produce the heat and pressure needed. For 45 minutes the temperature was kept at 270° F. During this time the resin melted and flowed into all openings and pores, then hardened and set, producing a permanently waterproof, one-piece hull.

7. Then the form was withdrawn from the autoclave, the rubber bag and canvas cover removed, and the hull lifted and pried free of the form.

8. The remaining steps are the obvious ones of trimming, sanding, finishing, and putting in gunwales, decks, and thwarts.

Molded plywood canoes are especially popular in Europe. Some excellent ones are used in this country for canoe racing (Figs. 1, 3, and 5 in Chapter X).

All-Wood Canoe of Rib-and-Plank Construction.—The all-wood canoe (Fig. 7), quite rare now in this country, is still manufactured in Canada. It has been manufactured continuously since its development in the 1870's by John Stevenson and Colonel J. Z. Rogers. The maker now calls it a canoe of *longitudinal strip construction*. Its ribs are of hardwood, ⅝-inch half round, spaced 2 inches apart center to center. Its planking is of selected cedar not over 2 inches wide, and ⁵⁄₁₆-inch thick. The planking is of shiplap cut; that is, a portion of each plank's width is cut away at each edge, but on opposite sides, so that it will make an overlapping but flush joint with planks similarly cut. The joints are given a coat of a special waterproof-gum compound and the planking pulled together under pressure and nailed to the ribs by large-headed copper nails, clinched on the inside of the ribs. Brass bolts and screws are also used, namely in attaching the reinforcing parts, such as thwarts, decks, outside stems, and keel. Lightweight floor boards are screwed to the ribs on the inside so that the paddler's weight will be borne by the ribs, not by the planking.

FIG. 7—An all-wood canoe of *longitudinal-strip construction*. It is 16 feet long, 32 inches at the beam, 12 inches deep amidships, and weighs 80 pounds. Its planking is cedar and its ribs, gunwales, stems, and thwarts are oak. (Courtesy of Peterborough Canoe Co., Limited)

Canoes of this type were made for canoe racing in this country until quite recently. Several of them are shown in Chapter X, "Canoe Racing" (Figs. 7, 8, 10).

The Aluminum Canoe.—Aluminum-alloy canoes, especially noted for their relative durability, have achieved popularity in recent years.

An aluminum canoe is formed in two longitudinal halves, riveted together. A leading manufacturer makes it as follows: The process starts with a rectangular sheet of aluminum alloy several feet longer than the finished canoe. The ends of this sheet are clamped in hydraulically operated jaws, which stretch the sheet longitudinally over a solid die. The machine is capable

Fig. 8—Making an aluminum canoe. After the canoe-half is removed from the die, drilled, and trimmed to shape, it is placed in an oven and baked for 8 hours at 360° F. to toughen and temper it. This whole load of canoe-halves, or "skins," is being put in the oven. (Courtesy of Metal Boat Co., Marathon, N.Y.)

of exerting pressure up to 140,000 pounds during this operation. The formed "half-canoe" is then removed from the die and placed in an elaborate fixture where it is drilled and trimmed to shape. It is then baked in an oven (Fig. 8) for 8 hours at a temperature of 360 degrees to temper and toughen it. Gunwales, thwarts, seats, decks, and other reinforcing parts are also made on special dies, which eliminate most hand forming. All parts are cleaned and given a protective coating before assembly. If a canoe is to be painted (for use in salt water), all parts go through additional preparations, including a coat of corrosion-inhibiting zinc chromate primer. When the two halves are prepared, they and the reinforcing parts are put together with about 2,000 rivets (Figs. 9 and 10). Each rivet goes through from 2 to 4 holes. The seams are made permanently watertight with neoprene (synthetic rubber) tape and a special compound. The canoe is then tested under pressure for leaks. Finally, a flotation material called styrofoam is in-

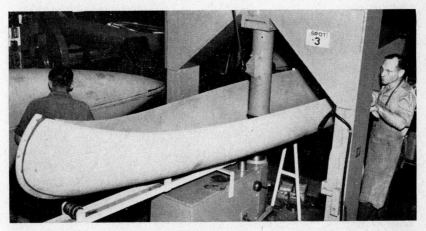

FIG. 9—Making an aluminum canoe. After the two canoe-halves are prepared, they and their reinforcing parts are put together with about 2,000 rivets. This is a keel riveting machine in operation. Twelve rivets are pressed at once—not only a good production feature but, more importantly, it assures a waterproof joint because all rivets are set up with the same amount of pressure. (Courtesy of Metal Boat Co., Marathon, N.Y.)

stalled in each end of the canoe and held in place by bulkheads. The styrofoam is permanent and should not have to be replaced unless attacked by turpentine, paint thinners, or gas. Early models, however, did not have the styrofoam material. Instead, they depended upon the buoyancy chambers being watertight. Canoes of this type should be tested for buoyancy in the swamped condition or have their air compartments filled with styrofoam to assure permanent buoyancy.

Some specific details of this canoe are as follows:

1. Standard models have hulls made of aluminum alloy .051 inch thick, and the lightweight models .032 inch thick.

2. The manufacturer recommends the standard models for camps, liveries, and general use where rough handling may prevail; and the lightweight models for experienced canoeists and those who have much portaging to do.

3. These canoes are available in lengths ranging from 13 to 20 feet. The 17-foot canoe, for example, measures as follows for the two types:

Fig. 10—Making an aluminum canoe. The ribs are riveted in place. The keel (left) and keel batten (right), previously riveted (Fig. 9), are clearly shown. (Courtesy of Metal Boat Co., Marathon, N.Y.)

	Weight	Beam	Depth
Lightweight	59 lbs.	36⅛"	13⅛"
Standard weight	73 lbs.	36⅛"	13⅛"

Pirogues.—Due to the influence of other languages, in some regions the name *pirogue* has been applied and maintained for canoes that were originally dugouts, but which now nearly

FIG. 11—A modern pirogue. It is made of ¼ inch marine plywood. Its overall length is 13 feet 10 inches. Its bottom length, outside, is 12 feet 10½ inches. Its depth amidships is approximately 9 inches. Its stem posts are 13½ inches long. (Courtesy of New Orleans, La., Chapter, ARC)

FIG. 12—Same pirogue; view of the inside. The beam at the top of the gunwales is approximately 3 feet; at the bottom, approximately 2 feet 2 inches. Most pirogues do not have these heavy gunwales. They were designed for mass practice-sessions by splitting 2 by 4's down the middle, making one piece the outwale and the other the inwale on each side, and then rounding them off. (Courtesy of New Orleans, La., Chapter, ARC)

always are made of boards in the manner of making a typical small flat-bottomed rowboat or skiff. These are popular craft in southern parts of the United States, and for the most part are homemade. The New Orleans Chapter, American Red Cross, has had several constructed (Figs. 11 and 12) for use in its small-craft safety program. The design used is patterned after a type of pirogue in common use in that region. The

FIG. 13—Folding kayak with a set of double-blade paddles lying along its deck. It is 14 feet long, 30 inches at the beam, and weighs 45 lbs. Its cockpit measures 18 by 48 inches. (Courtesy of Dorothy Claussen)

FIG. 14—Same kayak being paddled on smooth, clear water in Florida. (Courtesy of Dorothy Claussen)

message "Hang On I'll Float" has been painted on the sides and bottom of the craft so that it will at all times convey a safety message, whether resting on a rack, being carried on a car top or trailer, or being used in a small-craft safety demonstration.

Modern Kayaks.—The modern version of the Eskimo kayak is of two types, the rigid and the collapsible. The rigid kayak reaches a point of maximum refinement of design in the models illustrated and described in Chapter X, "Canoe Racing."

The collapsible kayak (Figs. 13 and 14) consists of a wooden framework that is assembled at the water's edge and a rubberized canvas envelope into which the frame is inserted. It is well decked over fore and aft and along the sides amidships. A popular feature of this craft is that it may be carried collapsed in the trunk of an automobile. Another feature is its suitability for running rapids without swamping or incurring hull damage.

Measurements of Modern Canoes (kayaks not included).— Typical measurements of the common contemporary canoes are as follows:

A canoe 15 feet long has 33 inches beam and is 12 inches deep.

A canoe 16 feet long has 34 inches beam and is 12 inches deep.

A canoe 17 feet long has 35 inches beam and is 12 inches deep.

A canoe 18 feet long has 36 inches beam and is 12 inches deep.

There are, however, canoes of numerous lengths and of considerable variation among their other measurements. Canoes of great depth and beam and weight are called freight, or commercial, canoes. Those that are narrower than is typical are generally regarded as for use by experts. Lightweight canoes are liked by anyone who has to portage the canoe much and are very suitable for children's programs. The following table gives the range of measurements for lengths of canoes now being manufactured.

Length	Beam	Depth Amidships	Weight
11 feet	34" to 36"	11¾" to 12½"	35 to 50 lbs.
12 feet	32" to 34"	12" to 14"	50 to 55 lbs.
13 feet	26" to 36"	11¾" to 12⅞"	45 to 55 lbs.
14 feet	32" to 34"	11¼" to 13"	55 to 60 lbs.
15 feet	28" to 37½"	11" to 15"	45 to 70 lbs.
16 feet	30" to 36"	11¾" to 16"	50 to 80 lbs.
17 feet	35" to 45"	12" to 17"	55 to 115 lbs.
18 feet	33" to 46"	12" to 18"	60 to 130 lbs.
18½ feet	36"	12"	80 lbs.
19 feet	51"	19"	150 lbs.
20 feet	36" to 52"	13" to 20"	95 to 180 lbs.
22 feet	38" to 62"	14" to 24"	130 to 260 lbs.
24 feet	40" to 41"	14" to 15"	150 to 160 lbs.
25 feet	44" to 50"	14½" to 23"	180 to 250 lbs.
26 feet	40"	14"	160 lbs.

Selecting a Canoe.—There is no uniform opinion regarding relative merits of the various canoes available on today's market any more than there is in the area of automobile selection. All the canoes currently made are good. It would be a misfortune if opinion should become too standardized, for then discrimination would prevail against some products in favor of others. Consequently, this book will not make precise recommendations regarding selection of canoes, but the reader will be able to make up his own mind on the basis of the fundamental information below, the over-all content of the text, and other information available to him.

This chapter has pointed out the variations among canoes—in their sizes, types of construction, and materials. Obviously these varying canoes have proved satisfactory to users. Otherwise, lack of demand for some of them would have led to discontinuance of their production. Such diversification is based on the variety of activities and conditions in which canoes are used; for example, evening or Sunday paddling on quiet water near centers of population, fishing on local waters, day cruising, canoe camping trips, running river rapids ("white-water canoeing"), summer camp canoeing, canoe racing, wilderness canoe trips. All these activities are recreational. In addition, in northern Canada, the canoe is still used for freighting and water transportation in wild, undeveloped regions.

Men who use canoes commercially for transportation and hauling goods select them on the basis of the size load that is practical to haul in the regions in which they operate. If no portages are involved, they may wisely use large canoes. Furthermore, if the canoe does not have to be carried, excessive weight is not a disadvantage; therefore, greater strength may be built into it with thicker planking and wider and thicker ribs spaced closer together. If portages are involved, smaller canoes of lighter construction are preferred.

Men who participate in formalized canoe racing use canoes that conform to specific measurements agreed upon by the American Canoe Association and similar organizations in other countries. Canoes of this type are shown and described in the chapter entitled "Canoe Racing."

Many of the people who engage in the sport of running "white water" prefer aluminum canoes because of their quality of withstanding bumping and scraping against rocks without being punctured and developing leaks. However, a great number of canoeists prefer other types, stressing the importance of exercising greater carefulness in negotiating rapids and pointing out such factors as the toughness of modern canvas fillers. It is consequently a matter of individual opinion and viewpoint and not one that needs resolving by determining a majority opinion. The activity is enjoyable in a metal canoe or other types. There is quite uniform agreement, however, that all-wood canoes of rib-and-plank construction should not be used where they may hit rocks because of their unquestionable vulnerability to serious damage.

People engaged in other forms of recreational canoeing look for canoes that embody strength and lightness. Some persons place lightness in the position of first importance; others prefer sacrificing a degree of lightness to attain desired features of strength in construction. It is a good plan for a prospective buyer to request catalogues from canoe makers in order to study the features of specific canoes and to learn of alternatives in construction. For example, manufacturers of canvas-covered canoes usually have standard-weight construction and lightweight construction. Often they will offer hardwood gunwales in place of softwood, at a small extra cost. A popular combination is lightweight construction combined with hardwood gunwales, thwarts, and decks. Aluminum canoes are also available in lightweight and standard-weight construction.

The size of a canoe for general recreational use is an important consideration. If too big, it will be hard to carry and launch, and in some cases difficult to handle on the water. The 16-foot canoe is regarded as the most suitable size for all-around use, either solo or tandem. If, however, a canoe is to be used far more often for tandem paddling than for solo paddling, especially on trips where gear is taken, a 17-foot canoe would be preferred by many canoeists. If the trips were extended, requiring added weight of food and gear, or if a third person were added, some canoeists would elect to use an 18-foot canoe for ease of handling with the added load. In certain regions 20-foot canoes are popular in the latter circumstances. Canoes 17 and 18 feet long may comfortably carry three and four average adults respectively and are sometimes misjudged as being too large for good solo-handling. This is not entirely true. For example, if a man is a good paddler, he can probably paddle a narrow 17- or 18-foot canoe faster than he can paddle one of any other size, other factors being equal. This is particularly true if he is a large man. Fifteen-foot canoes are popular for adult solo paddling and for either solo or tandem paddling for youngsters. Their lightness makes them desirable for children's programs. Canoes of even shorter length, especially when of good proportions, are easy for children to carry, launch, and paddle.

The canoeist has a choice of selecting a canoe without a keel, or with a standard tapered keel, or with a shoe keel. Because the keelless canoe is very maneuverable owing to its smooth bottom, it is excellent for use in a fast stream and for smart handling, as when among other craft or coming alongside a dock. The same canoe with a standard keel will be less maneuverable, but on open water will hold a steadier course because the keel projecting down into the water tends to prevent the canoe from swinging off course in response to the paddling strokes and from being blown sideward by the wind. The keel also is a great protection to the bottom of the canoe in the event of accidentally running aground or onto an underwater obstruction such as a rock. This type of protection is most needed when paddling on rivers, but it is often sacrificed for the greater maneuverability possible without it. The shoe keel is the ideal compromise for a river canoe. It provides protection to the bottom of the canoe; but because of its flatness and the rounded bevel of its edges, the shoe keel does not noticeably lessen maneuverability.

These are some of the items of a practical nature relating to design that might be considered in selecting a canoe:

1. A canoe that is wide and consequently quite flat-bottomed is relatively very stable. The farther forward and aft the fullness of the bottom is carried, the more stable the canoe will be. Such a canoe will not be fast; and although it will

handle nicely with a tandem crew, it will be relatively cumbersome for solo paddling.

2. Any canoe that has the fullness of the bottom carried well fore-and-aft toward the ends will rise with the waves of a lake or river rather than knife dangerously into them as a canoe with more pointed ends would do. (See Chapter V, "Positions," for information on the importance of the locations of paddlers in respect to paddling conditions.)

3. A canoe that has a slight, longitudinal, rocker-like curve to its bottom will be more maneuverable than a canoe with a straighter bottom line. This feature will also help its ends to rise and fall with the waves, especially in solo paddling, and also somewhat in tandem paddling when the crew members move closer together near amidships.

4. Narrow canoes are also rounder of bottom. Their narrowness makes them easier to paddle solo. If the longitudinal bottom line of a narrow canoe is straight, the canoe will be fast. If it is a long canoe, it will be still faster; if in addition, it has nicely shaped, narrow knife-like ends, it will be the fastest of its type. It will, however, be the least maneuverable of canoes and will tend to knife into waves rather than rise with them; it will be gripped firmly by currents rather than slide over.

5. Canoes with higher than typical sides (deeper) and high ends will be noticeably more affected by the wind, but in high waves will be less likely to take in water.

6. Hardwood gunwales are extremely important if the canoe is to be paddled solo, and desirable in any case.

7. If you plan to learn to paddle after the manner of skilled paddlers, order your canoe without seats. (See Chapter III for a formula for placement of thwarts for efficient paddling.) Canoe makers will locate thwarts according to your wishes. On the other hand, canoes with thwarts placed otherwise may also be paddled skillfully.

CHAPTER III

ACCESSORIES AND FACILITIES

TERMINOLOGY

As is true with other special activities, some words and phrases are used in canoeing that are not used in general conversation or writing. These comprise names of the parts of the canoe and terminology relating to its use. Figs. 1 and 2 illustrate in detail the names of canoe parts. Many of them are not employed in ordinary use of the canoe, but would be used when discussing construction or describing various details of the canoe.

Fig. 3 illustrates additional terminology often used by the canoeist. Some of it may be unfamiliar to many good canoeists who are remote from coastal areas, where terminology of larger craft influences terminology applied to small craft. When there is conflict in terminology, there is no reason why local tradition and usage should not prevail.

Figs. 1 and 2 should make clear most of the parts labeled. For further clarification, some are defined below.

Ribs—The transverse framework of the canoe.

Planking—The longitudinal boarding nailed to the ribs and to the stems.

Stem—Curved piece of wood at extreme end to which planking, ribs, gunwales, and deck attach. All traditional types of canoes have inside stems. Some also have outside stems.

Stemband—Piece of brass screwed to stem as a protective device.

Gunwales—The uppermost portion of the sides of the canoe, all around.

Deck—Triangular piece of wood to which the gunwales at-

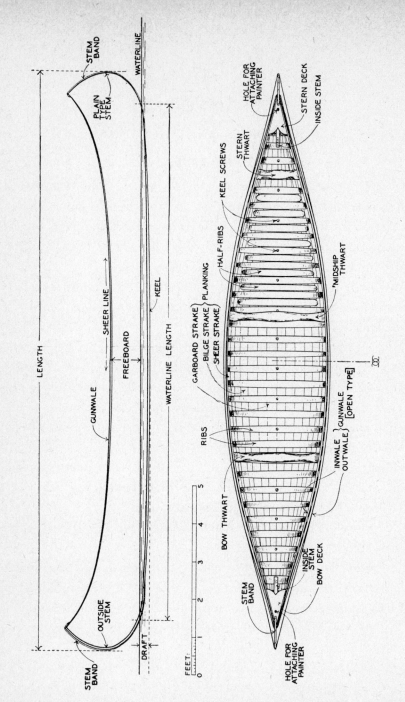

FIG. 1—Canoe nomenclature and details (part of drawing, ARC 1065-10).

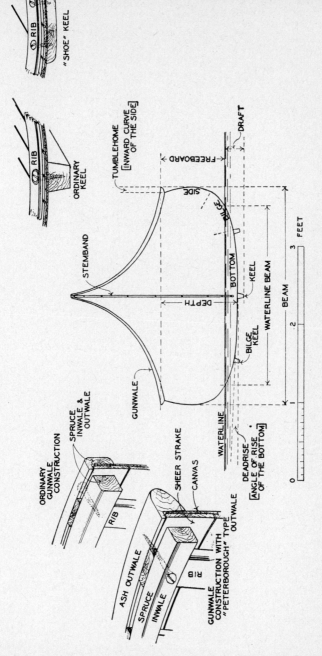

Fig. 2—Canoe nomenclature and details (part of drawing, ARC 1065–10).

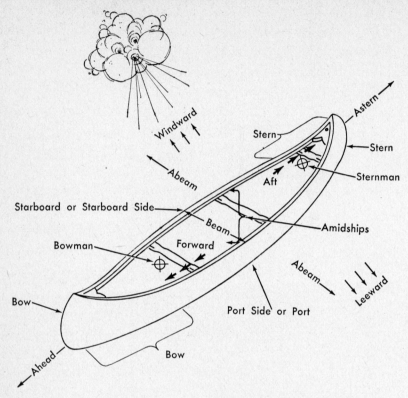

FIG. 3—Commonly used terminology:

Ahead—ahead of the canoe
Astern—behind the canoe
Amidships—the middle of the canoe
Forward—toward the bow
Aft—toward the stern
Bow—the forward part of the canoe (also the extreme end of forward part)
Bowman—person who paddles in the forward position
Stern—the rear portion of the canoe (also the extreme after end)
Sternman—person who paddles in the rear position

Beam—width of canoe at widest part
Abeam—at right angles to the centerline of the canoe
Windward—the direction from which the wind is blowing
Leeward—downwind side (direction toward which the wind is blowing)
Port—to the left
Portside—left side of canoe, facing forward
Starboard—to the right
Starboard side—right side of canoe, facing forward

tach at their places of convergence, at both ends of the canoe.

Canvas—The covering stretched over the planking.

Thwarts—Transverse braces, from gunwale to gunwale.

Beam—Transverse measurement, at the canoe's widest part.

Depth—Height of canoe measured from the bottom, inside and over the keel, to a line across the top edge of the gunwales at the beam.

Keel—A strip of wood along the bottom of the canoe from end to end, and centered, on the outside.

Sheer—The upward curve of the sides from amidships to the ends.

Trim—The angle to the surface of the water at which the canoe rides, e.g., down at the stern, down at the bow, or trimmed even.

PADDLES: GENERAL DESCRIPTION

Single-Blade Paddles.—*Length of Paddle.* A common rule for selecting a paddle of proper length is that with the tip resting on the ground, the grip should reach about eye level. It is probably not wise to use a paddle very much shorter than this. Sometimes, however, a longer paddle may be used. A short man with strong shoulders and arms usually prefers a paddle his own height. When very light paddles, much lighter than the commercial varieties, are available, youngsters will be able to use paddles longer than their height with enjoyment and effectiveness, so long as the bent upper-arm method of paddling is employed.

Another method of determining a paddle of suitable length for average use is based on the length of the paddler's arms. With the second joints of the fingers of one hand curled around the grip, the second joints of the fingers of the other hand should curl around the tip of the blade. For the average person this is equivalent to the eye-level measurement, and is more convenient to apply when kneeling in a canoe. It would be helpful for each paddler to measure the length of his paddle both ways to discover his own equivalents since the relationship of height to arm span will vary among individuals.

Description of Softwood Paddles. Spruce is commonly used to make softwood paddles. These paddles are light for their size and consequently easy and pleasant to use. Those of three-piece construction (sometimes five-piece) are commonly used in canoe racing and, though more expensive, are superior to those made of one piece of wood. It is best not to use softwood paddles in shallow water or where rocks or stumps are apt to be hit, for they split rather easily. Those constructed of three or more pieces are less likely to split than the others, and almost never break in the shaft or at the throat. This is because the center piece running from tip to grip has straight edge grain throughout its length, facing in the direction of the flat surfaces of the blade where pressure is applied. The side pieces have the flat grain facing on the surfaces of the blade to resist splitting at the tip and edges of the blade. There should be no knots anywhere in the paddle, particularly in the shaft. When paddles are made of several pieces, usually they are made largely by handwork, with considerable care given to the features mentioned. Paddles made of one-piece construction are often mass-produced, consequently the purchaser should examine such a paddle to be sure the grain in the shaft is straight and faced correctly, and that it has no knots. Other soft woods (fir, cedar, basswood) are sometimes used, but not often. Paddles of great beauty and extreme lightness can be made from cedar, but they require unusually careful handling.

Description of Hardwood Paddles. Hardwood paddles are commonly made of ash or maple, and occasionally of other hardwoods. They are heavier than the softwood paddles and consequently usually not preferred when softwood paddles are available. The added weight may be partially reduced by thinning down the blade and, in many cases, the shaft as well. They resist splitting and breaking—even with hard or careless use. This does not mean that they resist outright abuse. They warp rather easily, especially if left lying in the sun. On long trips, or on any trip where shallows, gravel bottom, rocks, and fast water are to be encountered, hardwood paddles should be taken along for intermittent use so that the softwood paddle may thus be protected from otherwise almost inevitable damage. Hardwood paddles are almost always made of one-piece construction, in view of the fact that their natural strength makes special construction unnecessary.

Double-Blade Paddles.—Double-blade paddles are usually made of spruce. The spoon-blade type is most common and is superior to the straight-blade type. The over-all length of a double-blade paddle depends upon the width of the canoe with which it will be used. For use with a canvas-covered canoe a double-blade paddle 9 to 10 feet long is desirable. Nine feet has been fairly standard for use with racing canoes, which have a beam of about 30 inches. For narrow-beamed kayaks, the length of paddle is less—7½ feet being common. Racing blades usually are made in one piece. Types for cruising have a ferrule joint in the middle of the shaft. Fig. 4A gives details.

PADDLE CARE AND REPAIR

Properly used and cared for, a well-selected paddle will last for many years. Few ready-made paddles "feel" just right to the experienced canoeist and some balancing is usually necessary. Most are found to be too heavy in the blade for proper balance. These can be improved by thinning the blade. Work for a paddle that, when held and used properly, does not give an awareness of weight in the blade. The paddle should also be

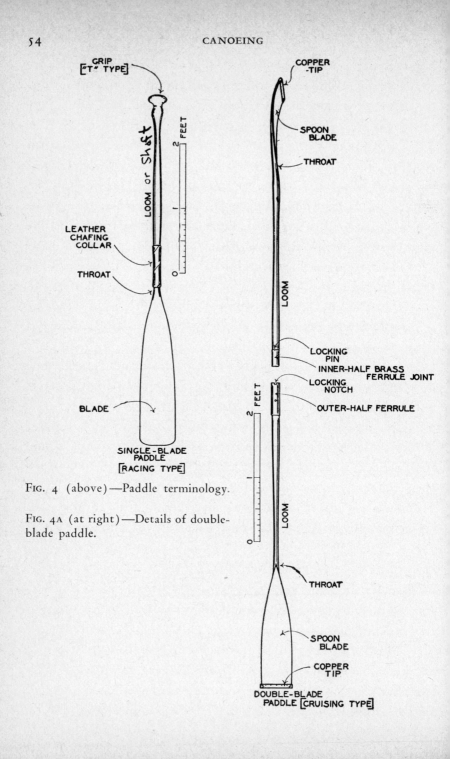

GRIP
["T" TYPE]

LOOM or SHAFT

2 FEET

1

0

LEATHER
CHAFING
COLLAR

THROAT

BLADE

SINGLE-BLADE
PADDLE
[RACING TYPE]

COPPER
-TIP

SPOON
BLADE

THROAT

LOOM

LOCKING
PIN
INNER-HALF BRASS
FERRULE JOINT

LOCKING
NOTCH

OUTER-HALF FERRULE

2 FEET

1

0

LOOM

THROAT

SPOON
BLADE

COPPER
TIP

DOUBLE-BLADE
PADDLE [CRUISING TYPE]

Fig. 4 (above)—Paddle terminology.

Fig. 4A (at right)—Details of double-blade paddle.

fitted with a leather collar (see Fig. 11C) around the shaft immediately above the throat to protect it from chafing from contact with the gunwale.

Keep the paddle well-varnished, especially the tip and edges of the blade, with a good grade of marine spar. If the tip is allowed to wear, moisture absorption will soon add excess weight and general deterioration will set in. The blade may be painted before varnishing, if color is desired, or enamel may be used instead. Usually it is not necessary to revarnish the entire paddle, sometimes not for several years if good quality varnish was originally used. Some canoeists prefer that the grip not be varnished, but worked down to fit the hand and sanded smoothly. The absorption of moisture and oil from the hand by the bare wood will prevent softening of the skin and will lessen the danger of blisters. Too, there is better control of the blade with a less slippery grip. To some canoeists these factors seem trivial and they interchangeably use paddles with the grip either varnished or not varnished.

Some Specific Guideposts for Care of Paddles.

1. Store the paddles in the shade outdoors, or in a ventilated place indoors. Hang them up. (See Figs. 15 and 16.)
2. Avoid laying the paddle down where it might be stepped on during launching or landing operations.
3. Avoid using the paddle as a pole in shallow water, or for fending off. This does not refer to an old hardwood paddle purposely used for poling, nor does it mean that the paddle ought not be used to fend off in an emergency situation.
4. Avoid leaning the paddle against a tree or other support in a manner that would make it easily blown down or knocked down.
5. Limit the use of the paddle to the purpose for which it was made.

6. Breaking a paddle while paddling is an experience a skilled canoeist almost never has. A muscular beginner sometimes breaks a paddle because he failed to recognize the poor grain in the shaft and applied power too suddenly rather than smoothly and steadily.

Paddle Repairs.—Broken shafts and blades can be repaired, but, unless the paddle is a favorite one or a large number are involved, it is probably better to replace it. Long paddles, if they are broken rather cleanly across the shaft, and not too close to the throat, can be repaired with a lap joint. The length of the lap joints should be at least six times the diameter of the shaft, and for best results the surfaces should be prepared on a jointer and at right angles to the blade and grip. Use only waterproof glue on the joint and bind until the glue has set. Of course, the repaired paddle will be considerably shorter than before but will be usable for a smaller person.

Shafts that split in a "green stick" sort of break are glued back without too much trouble. Some projecting splinters may have to be carefully cut out to enable the fractured ends to mesh properly. Most of these breaks occur near the throat. The repair should be further strengthened by putting on the leather chafing collar previously mentioned. A shortwhipping to cover the fractured ends can also be applied if it doesn't interfere with the proper grip of the lower hand.

Split and broken blades are repaired with waterproof glue. Trim out any splinters necessary to get a good fit, and bind the blade until the glue has dried. Avoid applying too much pressure that could "starve" the joint by squeezing out all the glue. Rubber bands cut from inner tubes as well as strips of adhesive tape are used for binding purposes. After the glue has set, the paddle is further protected and improved by adding a few laminations (thin strips of wood) around the edges of the blades in the following manner:

1. Plane the rounded edges and tip of the blade down to a flat, smooth surface (round the corners of modified square blades to some degree), and carry the flat edge up into the throat.

2. Prepare a thin strip of a tough hardwood, such as ash, approximately $\frac{1}{32}$ inch thick and wide enough to extend slightly over the edges of the blade. It must be long enough to encircle the blade and extend a few inches up the shaft beyond the throat. (Fig. 5.)

3. If the blade is a modified square (Sugar Island) type, steam or soak the strip of wood in hot water before fitting and gluing. Coat the edges of the blade and one side of the strip with glue. Center the strip along the tip of the blade, and tape tightly with strips of adhesive. Next, carefully bend the strip around the blade and bind to the edges as you work up to the

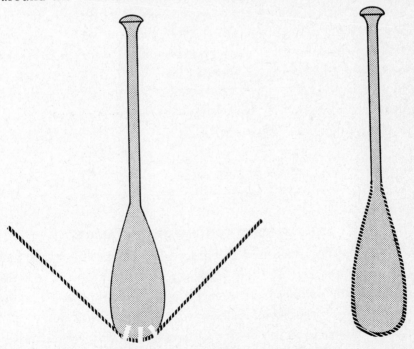

FIG. 5—Protect and repair blades with laminations.

throat. When the glue has set, a second lamination can be added if desired.

4. Plane and sand the edge of the lamination to a smooth roundness and "feather" the ends into the throat. Several coats of varnish are then applied to complete the job.

Repairing a split blade or protecting a new one, as illustrated in Fig. 5, strengthens and preserves the blade without increasing its weight. Fiber-glassing the tip and edges of the blade would produce the same desirable results.

Sometimes an otherwise perfectly good paddle will develop one or more short splits at the tip of a type difficult to press together so that glue alone will not be enough to effect the repair. A split of this type may be repaired and prevented from getting worse by sawing on the split, with a small saw, from the tip of the blade in as far as the split goes and filling the opening with a small piece of wood shaped to fit and glued in place with a waterproof glue. After the glue is dry, any unevenness may be filled with plastic wood. Later, the area can be sanded and varnished. (See Fig. 6.)

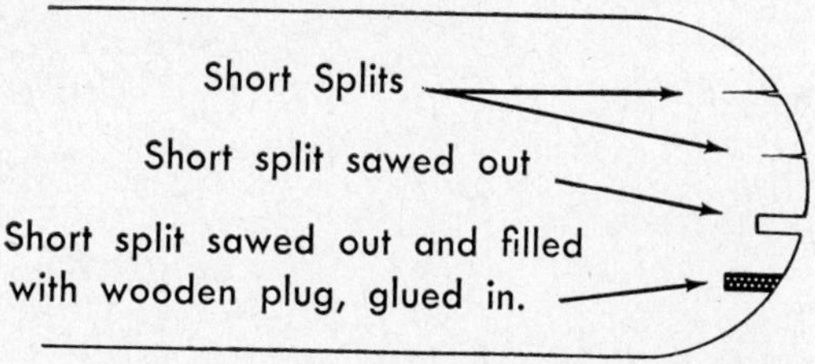

Short Splits

Short split sawed out

Short split sawed out and filled with wooden plug, glued in.

Fig. 6—Repairing short splits in a paddle.

SOME SPECIFIC CONTEMPORARY PADDLES

The paddles illustrated and described below (Figs. 7, 7A, 7B) are representative of types now in use in this country. All the single-blade paddles have leather chafing collars. (See pages 65, 72–74 for instructions on how to put these on.) Some have blades painted in club colors. Others have natural wood finish, varnished.

PRIMITIVE PADDLES

Since many canoeists have a great interest in styles of paddles, some made by primitive people are shown on pages 66, 67, and 68 (Figs. 8, 8A, 8B, 9, 9A).

MAKING A PADDLE

Making a paddle by homemade methods is tedious. It is more efficient to buy one. If, however, you are handy with tools, or if you would gain pleasure and recreation making a paddle, there is ample reason to believe that you can make a satisfactory one if you do not hurry. Buy the stock all cut out and planed to the measurements shown in Fig. 10, or similar measurements modified for a paddle of suitable size for you or the person you're making it for. The paddle shown in these illustrations is a hardwood paddle; the wood is ash. If you make a softwood paddle (probably of spruce) as you are likely to do, you may use the same measurements. Or for a measure of security it may be wise to increase the front to back measurement of the shaft, A, from $1\frac{1}{4}$ inches to $1\frac{3}{8}$ inches. If you do this, rest assured that the shaft will not break under vigorous paddling done with strong arms.

Glue the pieces together with a good waterproof glue. Mix the glue as the instructions on the container direct; guard against too watery a mixture. Be very careful that you arrange the pieces for gluing so that the shaft piece, A, has the edge grain (the narrow, straight lines of wood fiber) facing to the front and rear (see Fig. 10). The wing pieces, B and C, will fall into position without chance of error because of the difference between their width and thickness. You should have specified that these pieces be cut so that the flat grain (the wide, often curving, lines of wood fiber) is on the wide surface. You may improve the appearance of the blade and in

some cases increase its strength if you arrange the two wing pieces so that the direction of the flat-grain patterns on the wing pieces is symmetrical and when possible curved toward each other (see Fig. 10).

When you have applied the glue to the proper surfaces of B, C, and A, use C-clamps to hold them in place until the glue is dry. If you don't have 6-inch C-clamps, use rubber bands cut from a discarded tire tube (see Fig. 10). If you use the rubber bands, practice applying them with the dry pieces before proceeding with the glue because they have to be doubled to be tight enough, are a little awkward to handle, and the result may be glue all over your hands and clothes. (You will get glue on your hands anyway, but not necessarily on your clothes.) When B and C are in place, glue on the two small pieces, D and E. It is a good idea, before starting, to take the sharpness off the outside edges of the pieces B and C, using a plane or coarse sandpaper. Then you won't cut the rubber bands while forcing them into position.

FIG. 7—1. A single-blade spruce paddle with a spoon blade. This one was made by splicing a T-shaped grip onto the broken shaft of a set of double-blade paddles. Although not common, these paddles are found in use occasionally, in this country and abroad. They are believed to have a margin of superiority for straight-away paddling but are probably inferior for all-round use. This one has two emblems denoting the owner's canoe club and Olympic team affiliation. On its shaft is a turkshead knot for decoration.
2. An ash paddle of one-piece construction with a T grip shaped to please the owner, and a turkshead and emblem for decoration.
3. A custom-made paddle of one piece construction. Note the T grip and the unusual neck below it. The emblem has significance to the owner of the paddle.
4. A homemade three-piece spruce paddle for a five-year-old child. It is decorated to make it more of a treasure to the child—hence motivating him not only to use it for paddling but to take better care of it, thus starting the habit of carefulness with equipment and aiding the child's development of appreciation of useful things.
5. A child's paddle of one-piece construction, decorated for the same reasons cited for 4.

When the glue is dry, take off the C-clamps or rubber bands and trace in dark pencil the pattern of a favorite paddle on both sides (Fig. 10A). Your job will be more accurate if you make a cardboard pattern from your favorite paddle, rather than to trace around the latter onto the new paddle. All you'll need is a pattern for the area of the grip and another for the area of the upper part of the blade (Fig. 10A). The curve at the tip you can make with a compass. The width of the shaft and the width of the center portion of the blade were figured into the original cutting of stock. When the lines have been traced on both sides, cut off all wood outside these lines. If a band saw is available, this will be a simple job; otherwise, you must be patient, using draw knife, block plane, and wood rasp (at top of grip). (Fig. 10B.) Note: A modelmaker's small, convex-bottom plane is a good tool for getting the desired concavity at the throat area (see Fig. 10D).

FIG. 7A—6. An ash paddle of one-piece construction with a decorative turks-head on the shaft and a canoe club emblem on the blade. Its grip is a modified T often used in Maine.

7 and 8 are three-piece spruce paddles made specifically for canoe racing by a company specializing in the manufacture of racing oars and sculling oars for college crews and rowing clubs. The round tip paddle, 7, was often called the Samoset model, after a well-known canoe club of that name. 8 is a "square-tipped racing blade," or Riedel model after a famous canoeist by that name. The adhesive-tape chafing collar on 8 was often used on racing paddles instead of using leather collars because it did not materially increase weight. The tape was kept waxed with ordinary paraffin wax. 7 and 8 are each 68 inches long. 7 has a blade about 7 inches wide; 8, a blade $7\frac{1}{4}$ inches wide and a weight of 2 pounds, $2\frac{1}{2}$ ounces. 9 is a homemade paddle patterned after the two racing paddles, but with certain changes to satisfy the maker. The narrower blade is believed wide enough for most purposes and decreases weight. This paddle weighs 1 pound, 11 ounces. It is 68 inches long and has a blade 6 inches wide. 9 is made of five pieces merely for uniqueness; the light wood is spruce; the dark wood, mahogany. The paddle would be a little lighter if it were all spruce. Its shaft is $1\frac{1}{4}$ inches front to back, and $1\frac{1}{8}$ inches side to side. Front-to-back measurement for spruce should be about $1\frac{3}{8}$ inches rather than $1\frac{1}{4}$—unless the paddle is to be used only under controlled conditions.

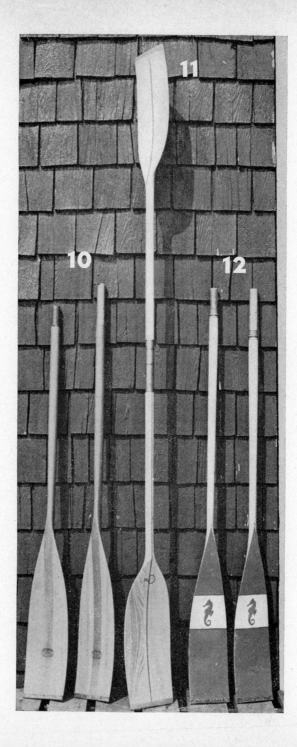

The next step is to draw center lines down the front, back, and sides of the shaft and grip, and around the edges of the blade (see Fig. 10B) as a guide for the remaining work.

Then using draw knife, jack plane, block plane, wood rasp, coarse and fine sandpaper, work the paddle down to a final shape similar to that of your favorite paddle, incorporating whatever refinements you might wish, such as an improved grip, or thinner blade. (Fig. 10C and Fig. 10D.)

A word of warning: Be careful with hand and power tools. If you have not used a draw knife before, you will almost certainly cut yourself unless you are careful at all times. A woodworker's vise and a workbench will make your work easier and safer.

PUTTING A LEATHER COLLAR ON A PADDLE SHAFT

A leather collar protects the paddle shaft and the outwale of the canoe when the two come in contact during the J stroke, especially when the latter is done in solo paddling. A good substitute is adhesive tape spiraled on the shaft with an overlapping spiral for double thickness. It is lighter than leather, hence often preferred on paddles used in racing. The

Fig. 7B—10. A set of racing-type double-bladed paddles with ferrules. Often the racing type are made as a single unit, without ferrules. These are 9 feet in over-all length. The blade is 6½ inches wide at the widest part and is 22½ inches long. Near the throat, the shaft from front to back measures 1⅜ inches and from side to side ⅞ inch. Near the ferrules, the shaft becomes cylindrical and has a diameter of 1⅜ inches. The weight of the set is 3 pounds.

11. A set of Olympic racing-kayak double blades. They are 7½ feet long; the blade, 7½ inches wide; the shaft has a diameter of 1⁷⁄₁₆ inches.

12. A set of cruising-type double blades similar to 10, except that the blades are a little narrower and have less perfect spoon shape.

It is of interest that the combined length of blades of 10 is equal to about 42 percent of the over-all length of 9 feet. This agrees with the relationship of the blades to over-all length in single-blade paddles, which ranges between 41 and 42 percent for most well-made paddles.

Fig. 8—Six models of canoe paddles made by American Indians for use with their birchbark canoes. The original of the decorated model at the left was about 66 inches long and its blade about 6½ inches wide. The original paddles from left to right were made by Indians of the following tribes: 1. Malecite Indian; 2. Slave Indian (Northwestern Canada); 3. Algonquin; 4. Passamaquoddy-Malecite; 5. Eastern Indian-Hybrid (north shore of Lake Huron, Canada); 6. Abnaki Indian. (Courtesy, E. T. Adney Collection, The Mariners' Museum, Newport News, Virginia)

Fig. 8A (left, opposite page)—Primitive paddles made by Indians of the Pacific Coast in southeastern Alaska. The designs are in red and black paint. The large paddle is 59¾ inches long; its blade is 6⅝ inches wide. The other paddle is 57 inches long and its blade is 5¼ inches wide. (Courtesy of Smithsonian Institution)

Fig. 8a

Fig. 8b

Fig. 8b (right)—*South Sea Island Paddles.* Paddles made by natives of islands in the Pacific. From left to right:

1. *Manihiki Island.* The paddle is 58 inches long. Its blade is 4 inches wide.
2. *New Zealand.* The paddle is 61 1/16 inches long. Its blade, 4 7/8 inches wide.
3. *Easter Island.* The paddle is 73 7/8 inches long. The lower blade is 8 1/16 inches wide; the upper blade, 8 7/8 inches wide; the spike, 8 1/2 inches long.
4. *New Zealand.* The paddle is 78 inches long; its blade, 6 1/8 inches wide.
5. *Buka Island, Solomon Islands.* The paddle is 79 3/4 inches long, with a blade 7 3/4 inches wide. (Courtesy of Peabody Museum of Salem, Mass.)

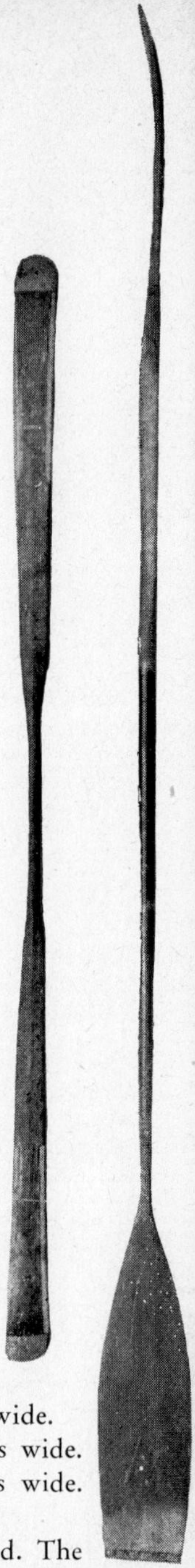

FIG. 9 (left)—*South Sea Island Paddles*. Paddles made by natives of islands in the Pacific. From left to right:

1. *Hawaii*. The paddle is 59 inches long; its blade, 10³⁄₁₆ inches wide.
2. *Cook Islands*. The paddle is 58⅝ inches long; its blade 8½ inches wide.
3. *Austral Islands*. The paddle is 47¼ inches long; blade, 13⅞ inches wide.
4. *Austral Islands*. The paddle is 49¹⁄₁₆ inches long; blade, 7¾ inches wide.
(Courtesy of Peabody Museum of Salem, Mass.)

FIG. 9A (right)—Primitive and modern double-blade paddles compared. The small one at the left was made by an Eskimo in Greenland about 1882. The other was in use at the Potomac Boat Club, Washington, at the time the photograph was taken in 1930. (Smithsonian Institution photograph)

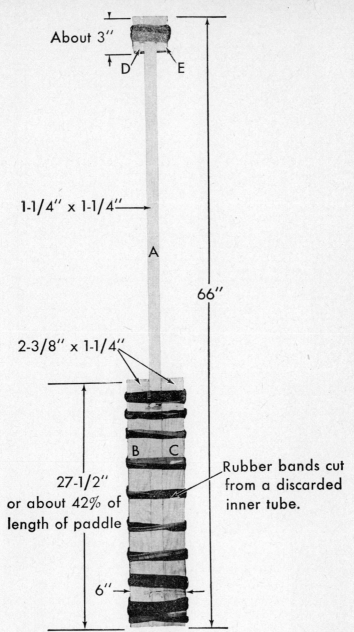

About 3"

D E

1-1/4" x 1-1/4"

A

66"

2-3/8" x 1-1/4"

B C

Rubber bands cut
from a discarded
inner tube.

27-1/2"
or about 42% of
length of paddle

6"

FIG. 10—First step in making a paddle.

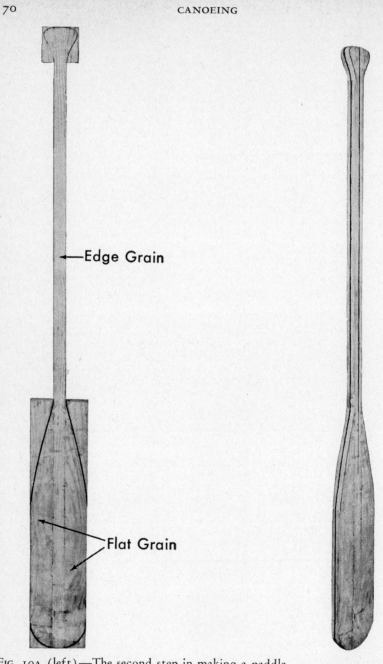

—Edge Grain

Flat Grain

Fig. 10A (left)—The second step in making a paddle.
Fig. 10B (right)—The third step in making a paddle.

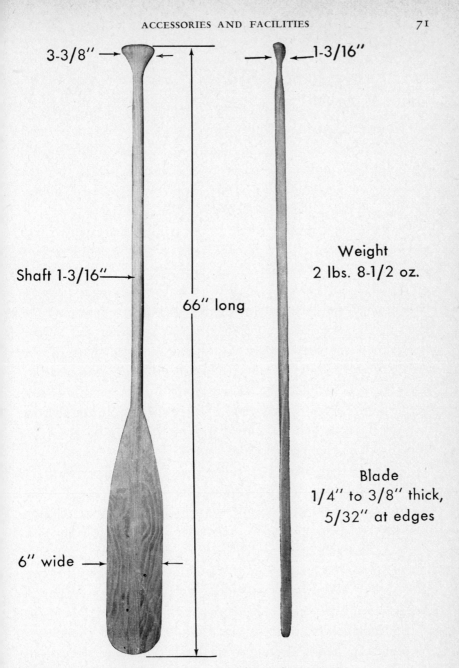

3-3/8"

1-3/16"

Shaft 1-3/16"

Weight
2 lbs. 8-1/2 oz.

66" long

Blade
1/4" to 3/8" thick,
5/32" at edges

6" wide

FIG. 10C (left)—Paddle ready for varnishing (front view).
FIG. 10D (right)—Finished paddle (side view).

latter should be kept waxed with paraffin. The area to be covered ranges from 8 to 12 inches, measured from the throat of the paddle up the shaft. To determine the exact area to be covered in the case of an individual paddle, mark the shaft of the paddle at the little-finger edge of where your lower hand grasps the shaft while you are paddling. Cover the shaft from this point on down the shaft to the throat of the paddle. Leather can be bought in hobby shops or shoe repair shops. Or you can use a discarded belt or similar material.

Measure the circumference of the paddle shaft where you marked it. Using that measure, make a diagonal cut at one end of the strip of leather (for example, from A to A′ in Fig. 11), cutting off a triangular piece of leather leaving a diagonal edge at that end. Wrap that diagonal edge squarely around the shaft at the place marked and continue spiraling the leather strip down the shaft. Mark it for cutting just short of the throat of the paddle. Remove the leather and cut the diagonal edge (B to B′ in Fig. 11). This diagonal cut should also equal the circumference of the shaft of the paddle. (If the leather is quite thick, it may be a little stiff for easy handling. If you find this to be so, soak it in water until it softens.)

Put the leather back on as follows: (1) Spiral about half the leather around the shaft, beginning at the point marked. Hold it firmly in place with a couple of turns of inexpensive friction tape (A and B of Fig. 11A). (2) Coat with plastic resin glue (mixed thick) the rest of the shaft to be leathered (C in Fig. 11A). Spiral the leather on this portion, wipe off the excess glue with a damp cloth, cover the leather with waxed paper, and then apply several double turns of friction tape to hold the leather in place (C to D in Fig. 11B). The waxed paper prevents the tape from sticking to the leather or being glued to it. (3) Remove the two friction-tape bindings at the unglued portion (A and B in Fig. 11A), unwrap the leather, put glue on the shaft, spiral the leather back on again, wipe off surplus glue, wrap it with wax paper, and apply friction-tape bindings to hold it firmly in place until the glue dries (A to B in Fig. 11B). (4) When the glue has dried, remove the tape and the wax paper. The job is done (Fig. 11C), except for rounding the edges of the leather at each end (A and B in Fig. 11C) by trim-

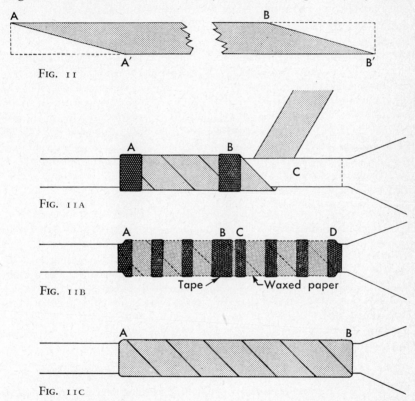

FIG. 11—Both ends of the leather strip must be cut diagonally. The length of the diagonal equals the circumference of the paddle shaft at the place where it will be applied.

FIG. 11A—A and B are tape bindings that hold the leather in place.

FIG. 11B—The leather has been spiraled on, covered with waxed paper, and held in place with tape bindings.

FIG. 11C—The finished job.

ming them carefully with a pocket knife and then smoothing
them with sandpaper.

PLACEMENT OF CANOE THWARTS

The typical stock model canoe is provided with seats for the
paddlers to sit upon; and the thwarts are located in relationship to the seats rather than to efficient paddling. Most canoe

FIG. 12—Location of thwarts in a canoe of 17 feet length or less. When solo
paddling under normal conditions or when heading into the wind, End A is
the bow. In normal weather the paddler locates himself at thwart 2 and uses
the cruising position for paddling. When paddling into the wind, he may
use the upright kneeling position or the high kneeling position, locating
himself somewhere between thwarts 1 and 2, closer to thwart 1 in a very
strong wind. When paddling downwind, End F may become the bow, with
the paddler using the cruising position at thwart 1 or some other type of
kneeling near thwart 1. In tandem paddling using cruising positions for
paddling, the bowman is located at thwart 1 with weight concentrated at
B; sternman is located at thwart 3 with concentration of weight at "S."
(See Chapter V for more information.)

FIG. 13—Application of formula for location of thwarts in a canoe 18 to 20
feet. In solo paddling under normal conditions, End A is the bow with the
paddler using thwart 3. When paddling before the wind, a solo paddler may
use End F as bow, positioning himself at thwart 2. For paddling into the
wind, End A could be the bow, with the paddler using either the upright
kneeling position or the high kneeling position between thwarts 2 and 3,
probably quite close to thwart 2. In a very severe headwind a paddler might
elect to use End F as the bow and position himself at thwart 3. In tandem
paddling, End F is normally the bow. "S" is the probable center of weight
the sternman brings to bear on the canoe as he takes the conventional cruising position, sitting on thwart 1, with both his knees on the canoe bottom.
"B" is the same in respect to the bowman at thwart 4. Note the distance of
"S" and "B" from their respective ends of the canoe. Since it is customary
for the heavier of the two to paddle in the stern position, the canoe will
trim well with this thwart arrangement. If it is necessary for the lighter man
to paddle in the stern position the canoe may be paddled with End A as the
bow, with the sternman using thwart 4 and the bowman using thwart 2.
This would also be a suitable arrangement in heavy weather when paddling
before the wind. For paddling into the wind, End F could be the bow, with
the sternman at thwart 2 and the bowman using the upright kneeling position somewhere between thwarts 3 and 4, to be determined by trial and
error in accordance with severity of conditions. (For more information see
Chapter V.)

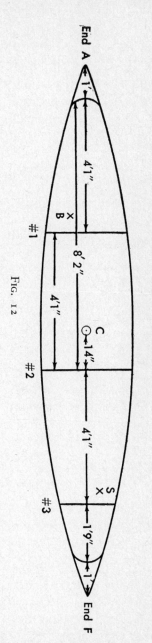

16 Foot Canoe

Fig. 12

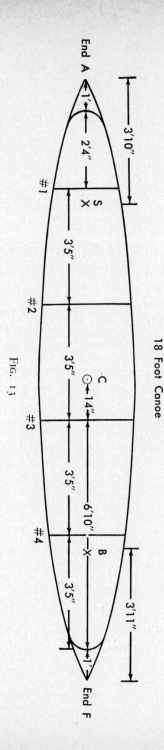

18 Foot Canoe

Fig. 13

manufacturers will omit the seats and locate the thwarts where the buyer wishes them. Likewise a canoe owner may take the seats out of his canoe if he wishes and relocate the thwarts where he wishes them to be. As indicated elsewhere many times in this book, the Red Cross Water Safety Service stresses the advisability of learning to paddle from positions that keep one or both knees in contact with the bottom of the canoe, as did the Indians and voyageurs. This not only increases the stability and safety of the craft, but improves paddling efficiency by enabling the paddler to effectively use the power of his trunk and thighs in conjunction with his arms. Another advantage coming from the ability to use any one of a number of types of paddling positions is the freedom with which the paddler can shift himself from place to place in the canoe in order to use the forces of wind or current to his advantage. Proper location of thwarts aids him greatly, and removal of the seats gives more room in the canoe. Here are two formulas for locating thwarts in a canoe. One applies to canoes of 15, 16, and 17 feet and would of course be suitable for canoes less than 15 feet; the other applies to canoes of 18 to 20 feet. Larger canoes require special planning.

Formula for thwart location in canoes of 15, 16, and 17 feet. Locate or relocate the amidships thwart 14 inches aft of the exact fore-and-aft center of the canoe. Measure from this thwart, at its new position, forward over the centerline of the canoe to the bow deck. Divide this figure by two and use the quotient as the measurement for determining the location of the bow thwart and the stern thwart. To do this, measure forward from the "offset" amidships thwart to determine the location for the bow thwart; measure aft from the "offset" amidships thwart to determine the location of the stern thwart (see Fig. 12). In practical application of this formula, it may be found that the forward crosspiece of the stern seat is about where the position for the new stern thwart is to be. If it is only a matter of a difference of 2 or 3 inches, it is common sense to use the bolt holes already in the gunwale, holding the forward crosspiece of the stern seat, to secure the new thwart in place after the seat has been removed. This same principle applies when replacing a bow seat with a bow thwart.

The thwarts may be of the type ordinarily used in canoes, held by one bolt at each end; or they may be of straight-edge type, 3 or more inches wide and held more securely to the gunwales with two bolts at each end. An improved job may be easily done with the wider thwart by cutting it to extend the full width of the canoe, planking to planking, notching it to fit between ribs, and thus having the bolt holes farther from the ends of the thwarts and therefore less likely to break out through the end grain. The bolts should be of brass or other rustproof metal and have large washers between the bolt nut and the underside of the thwart. The nuts should be tightened firmly and kept that way to lessen the danger of the gunwales breaking at a bolt hole. Holes left in the gunwales should be plugged and sealed. The plug may be set in water-resistant glue. Later the area should be varnished. If you plan to rig your canoe for sailing, make the stern thwart of material not less than 4 inches wide. Fig. 12 shows thwart locations according to the formula explained above for canoes of 17 feet or less. A canoe of 16 feet is shown and the measurements are actual measurements in a 16-foot canoe with decks 1 foot long.

Formula for thwart location in canoes of 18 to 20 feet. Locate, or relocate, the amidships thwart 14 inches forward of amidships (Fig. 13). Measure from the "offset" amidships thwart to the nearest deck. Halve this figure and use the quotient as follows: (1) From the "offset" amidships thwart, measure toward the nearest deck the amount of the quotient to determine the location of the bow thwart (No. 4 in Fig.

13). (2) Measure from the "offset" amidships thwart toward the farthest deck an amount twice the quotient to determine the location of the stern thwart (No. 1 in Fig. 13). (3) Measure in the direction of the farthest deck the amount of the quotient to determine the location of the fourth thwart, halfway between the stern thwart and the "offset" amidships thwart (No. 2 in Fig. 13). Fig. 13 shows the application of this formula to a canoe of 18 feet, assuming decks are 1 foot long and not taking into consideration any tumblehome at bow and stern.

In actual application it will usually be found that the amidships edge of the stern seat will be a little closer to the end of the canoe than the location for the stern thwart as determined by this formula. If this is so, it is a good plan to use the bolt holes at this point and locate the new thwart here rather than drilling more holes in the gunwales. In fact, in many instances it may be common sense not to remove the stern seat at all, but rather to leave it in place and readjust the other thwarts as necessary. In some instances it may not be necessary to move the thwart labeled No. 2 in Fig. 13. It may be within a few inches of the indicated position as originally located, which would be close enough.

KNEELING PADS

Kneeling positions on which safety and efficiency in paddling are primarily based are uncomfortable for most persons unless they use suitable kneeling pads or cushions. There are a variety of types; some are described below. (See Fig. 14.)

Inner tubing and sponge rubber (Fig. 14—No. 3). Two sponge rubber household kneeling pads are inserted in a section of inner tubing turned inside out. Ground rubber particles could be used in place of the sponge rubber. The edges of the tubing are vulcanized together at each end. Air trapped within may be let out by puncturing the tubing with a small nail and kneeling on the pad while the nail is in place. Sideward pressure with the nail will allow air to escape. When the nail is removed the hole will close tightly enough to make the tube covering waterproof.

Canvas covered (Fig. 14—Nos. 1 and 4). A canvas-covered

FIG. 14—Kneeling pads: (1) Heavy-gabardine sewed pad, filled with granulated cork. (2) Several (six) layers of household sponge rubber pads (regular size, cut in half) sewed together, and covered with ticking or denim. (3) Two household sponge rubber kneeling pads inserted in a section of a tire tube, after which the ends are vulcanized. (4) Sewed canvas pad, filled with ground particles of rubber from a tire retreading shop. (5) A hot water bottle filled with sawdust.

pad can be made of any size, as desired. The usual size for one knee is about 6 by 8 inches, by 2 or 3 inches thick. It may be filled with cork shavings, ground cork, or ground particles of rubber from a tire-retreading shop. It is easy to make. Fold a piece of canvas in the middle, sew up two sides, leaving one open. Put in the filler and then sew up the remaining side.

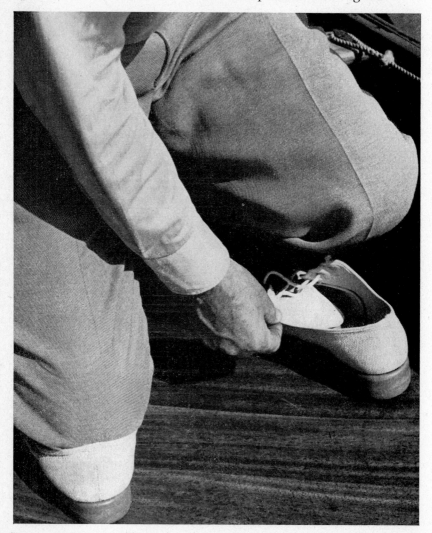

FIG. 14A—Sponge rubber soled shoes make a satisfactory substitute pad.

A rubber hot-water bottle (Fig. 14—No. 5) filled with sawdust or ground rubber makes a good kneeling cushion. When all the sawdust has been put in it, screw the stopper in tightly. Kneel heavily on the pad and unscrew the stopper just enough to let out the trapped air, then tighten the stopper again. This pad is large enough for only one knee. A pad under one knee is usually adequate since most of the body weight is on one knee, that of the paddling side, even when the paddler is kneeling on both knees. Two pads can be used if desired, but the use of a large, comfortable pad is encouraged if the smaller, more convenient sizes are uncomfortable.

Miscellaneous: A large plastic sponge for one knee; a bedding roll or soft pack to straddle; commercial strap-on pads (unpopular with canoeists); the inside of a shoe with sponge rubber sole (Fig. 14A); several layers of sponge rubber sewed together and covered with cloth (preferably denim) or ticking (Fig. 14—No. 2); any improvisation.

PADDLE RACKS

Paddles will last a long time if they are carefully used and properly stored. Often paddles are broken when left lying around on the ground, dock, or other unsuitable place. Maple paddles left in direct sunlight often warp.

Whether you have one or two paddles of your own, or many paddles for which you are responsible, you should carefully

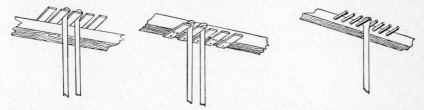

FIG. 15—Simple ways to utilize a beam in a boathouse, basement, locker, or other building to accommodate a couple of paddles. This could, of course, be extended for more paddles.

plan where to keep them. Hanging them up by their grips is probably the best plan. Figures 15 and 16 will suggest how to do this. Details and measurements are purposely omitted because improvising with available materials and space to accommodate paddles of varying size grips may be not only necessary but also more enjoyable than following precise specifications.

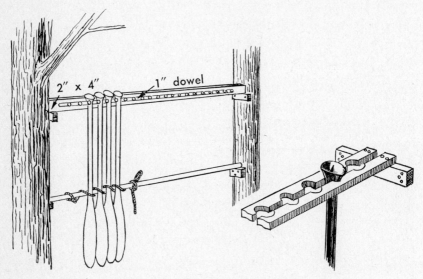

FIG. 16—Paddle rack set up between two trees. This type rack for several paddles could be put on the side of a building, or built into a locker. At the right is shown a rack made by drilling a series of 1-inch holes 2 inches apart (on center) in a board and then ripping the board down the center and nailing the two halves onto blocks so that they are about 1½ inches apart.

RIGGING CANOE WITH LINES

It is desirable that a canoe be rigged with a bowline (painter) and a stern line. There are occasions when it is feasible and necessary to tie up a canoe to the lee side or downstream side of a dock for brief periods. The painter (bowline) or stern line or both would be used. A line would be required when towing another canoe, swimming while towing the canoe, and in recovering a submerged drowning victim.

Suitable line for a painter or stern line is good quality cotton line or nylon, ⅛ to ¼ inch in diameter. Drill a quarter-inch hole in the bow deck and in the stern deck. Smooth the rim of each hole with a countersink and sandpaper. Lead the stern line through the hole in the stern deck and tie a figure-of-eight knot in its end so that it will not pull through (Fig. 17). Do the same with the bowline. Put a cleat on each end of the amidships thwart, near the gunwales (Fig. 17A). With plenty of

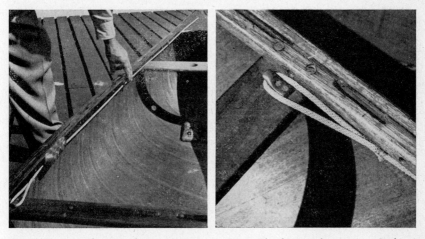

FIG. 17—Stern line in place.   FIG. 17A—Detail of stern-line eye and cleat.

slack in the lines, put an eye in the end of each (Fig. 17). Then place the eye of one on a cleat (Fig. 17A) and take up the slack at the other end, changing the location of the figure-of-eight knot correspondingly and cutting off the excess line, whipping the end if it is three-strand line. Do the same with the other line. Put a couple of cleats along the inside of the inwale to hold the line over against the gunwale and out of the way (Fig. 17). The cleats are hand-carved out of hardwood usually, but of course small brass cleats would be satisfactory. Synthetic resins, which can be worked like wood, make good cleats.

CANOE CHECKBOARD

If you have several canoes in use, a checkboard will assure that you always know what people are out and in which canoes (Fig. 18).

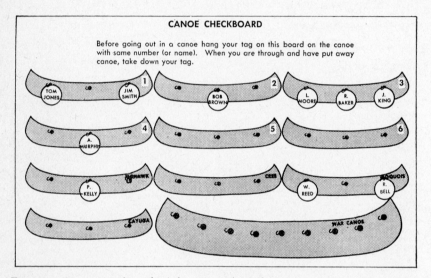

FIG. 18—A suggested method for control of the use of canoes at a summer camp. The tags are metal with adhesive tape stuck on them. The names are written on the tape. In this way the metal tags serve from year to year by merely replacing the adhesive tape.

CANOE RACKS

Ideally the canoe should be stored in a canoe house where it has protection from the elements. This involves an economic factor that cannot always be accepted. In this case, during off season, it may be kept inside any dry building: the dining hall at camp, or your garage or barn.

During the canoeing season, a canoe left out of doors should be kept out of the direct rays of the sun; keep it either under shade trees or under a specially constructed shelter.

Whenever possible, indoors or outdoors, place your canoe on a properly constructed rack. Study the following illustrations

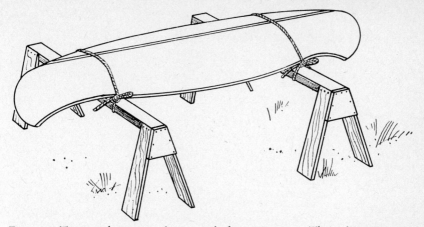

Fig. 19—Two sawhorses used as a rack for one canoe. Their distance apart is equal to one-half the length of the canoe. Ordinarily, tie the canoe to the horses as shown. If very heavy winds are expected or if the canoe is not to be used for a long time, it will be safer to secure it with staked-down lines.

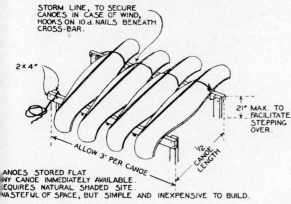

STORM LINE, TO SECURE CANOES IN CASE OF WIND, HOOKS ON 10 d. NAILS BENEATH CROSS-BAR.

2 × 4″

21″ MAX. TO FACILITATE STEPPING OVER.

ALLOW 3′ PER CANOE

½ CANOE LENGTH

CANOES STORED FLAT
ANY CANOE IMMEDIATELY AVAILABLE.
REQUIRES NATURAL SHADED SITE.
WASTEFUL OF SPACE, BUT SIMPLE AND INEXPENSIVE TO BUILD.

Fig. 19a—An inexpensive, easy-to-construct rack for several canoes. 2 by 4 stock is recommended. If made wide enough for more than four canoes, an extra supporting post may be needed at the center of each bar.

Fig. 19b—More economical manner of storing canoes on two-bar rack. First one is flat, others nested against each other. Provides adequate three-point support, but free selection of canoes is difficult. Do not nest steeper than 45° angle. Equip rack with storm lines unless site is completely protected.

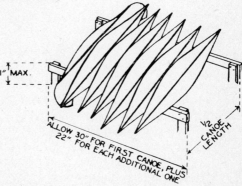

21″ MAX.

ALLOW 30″ FOR FIRST CANOE, PLUS 22″ FOR EACH ADDITIONAL ONE

½ CANOE LENGTH

and adapt them to your needs (Figs. 19, 19A, 19B, 19C, 19D, 19E, 19F, 19G).

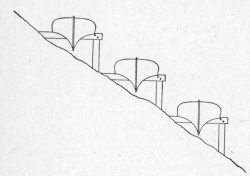

FIG. 19C—A head-on view of how to adapt the flat rack construction shown in Fig. 19A to the side of a hill.

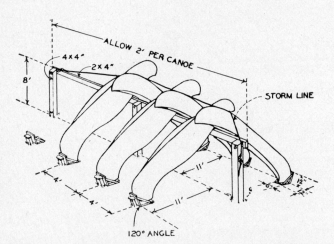

FIG. 19D—Single-bar rack, convenient for adult one-man handling but rarely used. Any canoe is immediately available. Requires natural shaded site and ample ground space. Layout is based on 18-foot guide canoes.

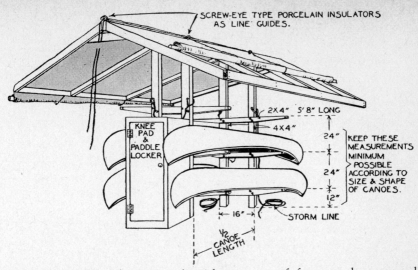

FIG. 19E—A vertical canoe rack with canvas roof for use where natural shade is not present. A simpler version would eliminate the roof and the locker. Canvas roof has furling rigging in case of wind-storm. Canoes lashed with storm lines. 18-foot canoes illustrated; with careful planning, a stack of eight 15-foot "Ojibway" canoes will fit in same over-all height (5 feet to top crossbar).

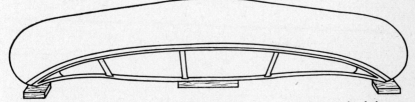

FIG. 19F—When racks are not available and your canoe must be left temporarily on the ground, turn it bottomside up and place a piece of flat board, a chip, or even a flat stone under each part touching the ground—namely the two ends and one gunwale where the latter touches the ground.

FIG. 19G—Where racks are not available, canoes are frequently slung to the overhead in a canoe house, garage, basement, or any building to be used. The rope used for the sling may be attached to eyescrews in the overhead as shown in the illustration, or by tying the rope around a beam. The other ends of the two lines required should have eyes tied or spliced into them. Hooks, as shown in the illustration, should be provided for these eyes.

CANOE DOCKS

The term "dock" as it is used in this book is a colloquialism referring to a pier constructed to facilitate launching and landing of canoes. Common usage makes the term preferred.

The illustrations (Figs. 20, 20A, 20B, 20C, 20D) show a variety of types of canoe docks. From among them you should be able to select one that will be suitable for your need. Details regard-

FIG. 20 (left)—An L dock—popular in summer camps that have only a few canoes.

FIG. 20A (right)—An alongshore dock used where the water is fairly deep (2 feet or more) close up to shore.

FIG. 20B (left)—A T dock very suitable in summer camps where a number of canoes are often being launched or landed at the same time.

FIG. 20C (right)—A finger dock, or I dock, suitable for private use for just a few canoes or only one.

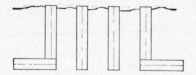

FIG. 20D—A combination of L docks and finger docks used where there are a large number of canoes to be launched and landed at the beginning and ending of activity or instructional periods. This arrangement is in lieu of lengthening the parts of a T dock or L dock where water drops off deep a few yards offshore. In this way all the dock structure, permitting the simplest methods of construction, remains in relatively shallow water.

ing size and materials are intentionally omitted, for the most part, because economy and personal satisfaction comes from doing the job yourself and using whatever materials you may have on hand, making the dock as long, or as short, as narrow, or as wide as you please.

The type of dock support you use will depend upon the nature of the bottom; but the heavy, expensive type such as

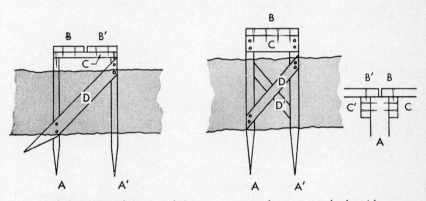

FIG. 21 (left)—Simple type of driven support for a two-plank-wide canoe dock. A and A' may be 2 by 4, 2 by 6, or 4 by 4 inches, or they may be round posts. C is a 2 by 4 or a 2 by 6 inches nailed on top of A and A'. B and B' are the planks. D is a 1-inch board, 4 or more inches wide, for diagonal bracing. As shown, the end may be pointed and driven into the bottom merely as a convenient way of holding it in place for nailing. This bracing prevents sideward movement. The planking, nailed to each support as shown, prevents longitudinal movement. When driving A, hold a piece of 2 by 4 on the end of it so that it will not split; the same for A'. A and A' will not remain exactly vertical while being driven, but can be forced into position when C is being nailed on. Use an iron bar (crowbar, wrecking bar or timber bar) to make a hole into which to start the post. Not only will this help keep the post straight while it is being driven, but it will enable you to avoid driving the post onto a rock.

FIG. 21A (right)—A driven support similar to the one in Fig. 21 except that C is nailed on both sides of A and A' rather than on top of them, and there are two diagonal braces (D and D'). Plank B is nailed flush with C; this would be done at the end of the dock, to have a strong and finished looking job. When a dock is to be extended more than one plank in length, ends of the planks are nailed as shown in the inset. Enough supports will be needed under a plank type of dock to eliminate excessive springiness.

that needed for larger craft or for a swimming dock should be unnecessary.[1] Ordinarily, driven supports are satisfactory for a canoe dock (Figs. 21 and 21A), but when the bottom is too hard for driving posts with an ordinary sledge hammer or maul, weighted supports will be needed (Fig. 21B). They may be preferred also for reasons of long-range economy, especially in regions where the water freezes in the winter, or where the docks are to be used for only a short time each year, thus making removing them at the season's end a wise procedure. Where there is a significant rise and fall of water level, a float will be needed, with a ramp connecting it to shore or to a higher solid dock (Fig. 21C).

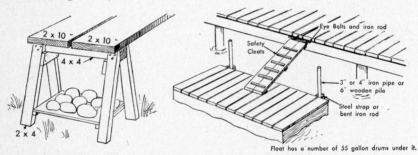

FIG. 21B (left)—A sawhorse type of weighted support for a canoe dock two planks wide. When you can't drive posts into the bottom, it will be necessary to use this or some other type of weighted support. At the season's end, this type can be removed—a desirable feature in regions where the ice forms heavy and hence lasts for a long time. Legs of this support should be made the right length for the depth of water. Where there is a normal slope to the bottom, each horse will be of different length than the others.

FIG. 21C (right)—Where there is deep water or where the rise and fall of the water level is too great for use of the solid support, a float will be better.

PORTABLE SLIDING SEAT AND OUTRIGGERS

A canoe makes an excellent rowing craft when equipped with detachable outriggers and sliding seat rowing equipment

[1]For more detail on the layout and construction of docks, the reader may consult A Camp Aquatic Program, by Richard H. Bearse and Sidney C. Hazelton (Hanover, N.H., S. C. Hazelton, 1952).

(Figs. 23 and 23A). It has more maneuverability and some of the carrying capacity of the typical rowboat and some of the speed of a racing shell. Rigging a canoe in this manner is a measure of economy in so far as it permits one craft to perform the function of two interchangeably.

The equipment under discussion was designed and built by Waldemar Van Brunt Claussen several years before his retirement from the position of Assistant Director of the Water Safety Service, American National Red Cross. The drawings (Fig. 22) of this equipment were done by him and he posed for and supervised the photographs used to illustrate its use. Mr. Claussen's article that appeared in the January–February 1947 issue of *The Reporter* (former publication of the First Aid and Water Safety Service) has been adapted here to explain how to make this equipment.

The drawing (Fig. 22) shows a sliding seat unit that can be readily placed in a canoe; outriggers that can be easily clipped into the slots of the open gunwale without the use of bolts, screws, or other permanent fastenings; and a pair of well-balanced, light oars that can be made from a pair of larger ones.

The seat frame (Fig. 23B), a rectangular affair 49 inches long, 9½ inches wide, and 4 inches high, can be made from the planking of a light packing case. If you wish to keep the outfit really light, cut the lightening holes indicated. Any of the modern plastic resin glues make for excellent assembly, although screws may be used if desired. Foot-plates, toe-straps, and heel board, are easy to devise. The seat, the foot-plates, usually called boots, and the tracks may be purchased from the manufacturers of racing shells, or obtained secondhand at some large rowing clubs having old shells that eventually have to be broken up. The equipment in the shell is usually saved when one is broken up. Toggles on the center partition (Fig. 23C) are to prevent longitudinal creeping of the seat frame

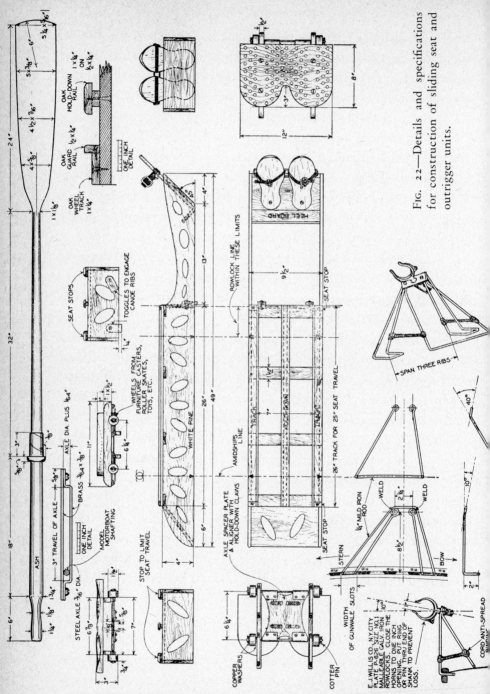

FIG. 22—Details and specifications for construction of sliding seat and outrigger units.

while in use. Yet the toggles can be turned up to permit transfer of the frame to a smooth-interior plywood canoe or skiff. Note also the turnbuckles (shown in Fig. 23A and 23C), which prevent lateral movement.

In ribless canoes a ⅛-inch galvanized or stainless-steel wire rope (cable) attached to each end of the sliding seat unit and to pad eyes on the inside stems at each end of the canoe will hold the unit securely in position. Each cable could have snap hooks at both ends or be permanently fastened to the seat and have a snap hook at the other end. There should be a turnbuckle in the middle of one of these cables in order to take up slack and make the cables taut while the unit is in use and to slack off in order to take the unit out of the canoe. The oak tracks, guard-rails, and hold-down rail present a little work in sawing and planing if no power tools are available, because these parts should be true and smooth. The commercial seat has the hold-down brackets ("fingers," or "claws") attached to the seat. They engage the outer edges of the tracks thus making the center hold-down bar unnecessary.

The sliding, or rolling, seat portion is interesting to make. The part you sit on may be flat, if a pad of some kind is used with it; but a more shipshape job calls for gouging this 12″ by 8″ by 1″ piece of softwood into a typical saddle-seat form. The gouging job can be done with an ordinary straight ¾-inch gouge chisel followed by rubbing with coarse and fine sandpaper on an oval-shaped cork rubbing block (or a wooden block faced with felt or foam rubber). Lightening holes again are drilled (Fig. 23B), and it might even facilitate the gouging to drill them first.

Wheels are obtained by dismantling the casters from some old article of furniture. Even the wheels from roller skates or some inexpensive toy may be adapted to the purpose.

Round iron rod may be used for the axle; but for a durable

FIG. 23—The designer and maker illustrates the "catch" position at the start of the rowing stroke or "pull." Note that the seat is at the starting end of the slides.

FIG. 23A—Position at the end of the rowing stroke, just before feathering the oars for recovery. Note that the seat is now at the other end of the slides. Note also that the amidships thwart has been temporarily removed for this activity.

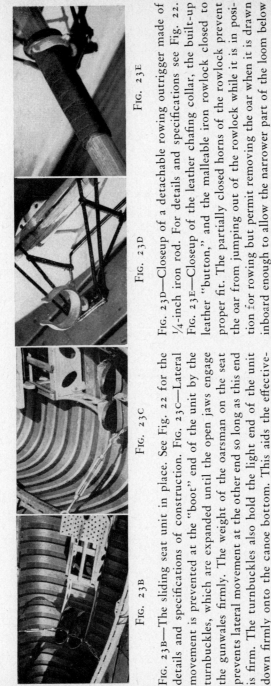

FIG. 23B   FIG. 23C

FIG. 23D

FIG. 23E

FIG. 23B—The sliding seat unit in place. See Fig. 22 for the details and specifications of construction. FIG. 23C—Lateral movement is prevented at the "boot" end of the unit by the turnbuckles, which are expanded until the open jaws engage the gunwales firmly. The weight of the oarsman on the seat prevents lateral movement at the other end so long as this end is firm. The turnbuckles also hold the light end of the unit down firmly onto the canoe bottom. This aids the effectiveness of the wooden toggles located on the center partition. They are there to prevent longitudinal creeping of the unit during rowing; their ends project down between the ribs.

FIG. 23D—Closeup of a detachable rowing outrigger made of ¼-inch iron rod. For details and specifications see Fig. 22. FIG. 23E—Closeup of the leather chafing collar, the built-up leather "button," and the malleable iron rowlock closed to proper fit. The partially closed horns of the rowlock prevent the oar from jumping out of the rowlock while it is in position for rowing but permit removing the oar when it is drawn inboard enough to allow the narrower part of the loom below the leather to be lifted out. The button, or collar, at the upper end of the leather prevents the oar from sliding out through the rowlock and thus keeps it in correct position.

rig for adult use, a mild steel axle is better. The axle may be bought in ³⁄₁₆-inch diameter stock and 12-inch lengths, at model shops where it is sold as shafting for model motorboat construction. Simplest manner of keeping the wheels on is to use washers and cotter pins after cutting the rod to proper length and carefully drilling the ends.

The axle-keepers and bearings are designed to provide 3-inch travel for the axle; these may be iron or brass. They may be attached with offset bends in the keeper, or the bends may be eliminated and washers or spacers slightly thicker than the diameter of the axle used.

The spacer plate, which keeps the axles in parallel alignment, should be about as thick as the diameter of the axle. The plate is held to the axle by light brass or tin clips bent around the axle and riveted to the plate.

The "fingers," or "claws," to engage the hold-down rail, and the rail itself are not strictly necessary for use of the equipment when rowing, but they are a worthwhile convenience because they keep the seat permanently attached when the frame is lifted into or out of the canoe. One or two pairs of claws may be used; these are readily bent and then riveted to the spacer plate. They should fit the hold-down rail snugly, without binding.

Each end of both tracks should be provided with "stops" to prevent the seat wheels from over-running. The two at one end may be permanently glued, but the other two should be held by screws, which will make it easy to remove the seat for repairs or refinishing.

Twenty feet of ¼-inch iron rod; one pair of size No. 1 malleable, galvanized iron, U-type rowlocks; and four ³⁄₁₆-inch flathead stove bolts, with nuts and washers, provide the equipment for the outriggers (Fig. 23D).

The upper member of each outrigger is planned to span

three ribs; to have rectangular claws that fit snugly into the gunwale slots; to have the pulling arm slightly longer than the thrust arm; and to have a 10° tilt at its outer end. An 8½-inch extension is suggested. This may be increased if oars longer than those illustrated are used. If the problem of bending neat, round eyes, as illustrated, is beyond the capacity of your equipment, then ordinary hairpin bends around the bolts will serve amply well. For rigidity sufficient to permit the application of full adult power when rowing, it is recommended that a spot weld be made to fasten each eye to the part of the rod that passes around outside it.

The lower, or down-thrust, member of each outrigger bears against the outside of the canoe about 5 inches below the gunwale (Fig. 23D); it may have a piece of rubber tubing slipped over it before final attachment. Assembly of the outrigger is completed by applying fishline bindings tightly (and varnishing them) over thin wood dowel spacers (Fig. 23D) having their ends notched to fit the round rods. The dowels could be replaced by iron rods of the same length and cut from the material used for the rest of the outrigger. The advantage of the iron rods is that they can be quickly and permanently welded in place.

Horns of the open rowlock should be pressed together in a vise until the inside diameter of the lock is a close, but not a tight, fit around the leathered part of the oar loom (Fig. 23E); this will eliminate annoying loose play and also will secure the loom against any possibility of jumping out; yet the oar can be removed by drawing it inboard until the thin part of the loom will pass the narrowed horns. The 10° cant of the rowlocks should be adjusted, if necessary, until the "button," or leather collar, bears evenly against the face of the lock when the oar is immersed at pulling depth. To prevent accidental loss of the rowlocks, insert a pin or ring in the eye at the end of the shank.

Oars for use with this outfit should be 6 feet 8 inches long overall for this specific canoe, with leather and button applied at location shown. ARC 1065–15, *Formula for Correctly Fitting Oars to a Boat* (see Fig. 24), contains information on location of leather and button that will contribute to more efficient rowing. You may wish to incorporate this information when preparing your oars and outriggers. Flat-blade oars of ash or spruce are not difficult to make by hand, even without a lathe, and it is even simpler to merely work a large heavy pair down to the dimensions shown. If spoon-blade oars (sculls) are available, or if your handicraft ability is equal to the task of producing them, you'll find that they are the finishing touch necessary to make this equipment one of the pleasantest thrills in your aquatic experience. You may purchase sculling oars from manufacturers who make racing shells and oars. They will measure 9½ feet and have their leathers and buttons located for sculling (rowing) with oarlocks 60 inches apart. If you purchase the sculls, you'll also have to purchase sculling oarlocks; no other type will be satisfactory. You will have to

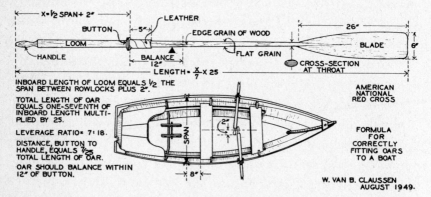

FIG. 24—This drawing was prepared after the drawing showing how to make the sliding seat and outrigger rowing equipment. Because its recommendations for locating the leather and button on an oar will contribute to more efficient rowing you may wish to incorporate them when preparing your oars and outriggers.

make the outriggers large enough to place the oarlocks 60 inches apart at their points of attachment to the outriggers.

RIGGING A CANOE FOR SAILING

ARC 1065–8, a drawing entitled *Cruising Lateen Rig for Ojibway Model Canoe* (Fig. 25) gives details and specifications for making an excellent canoe sailing rig. In some cases it will be wise to follow the plan precisely; in other cases modifications may be indicated for individual reasons. Experience with this plan, however, has shown that it may be used as an excellent point of departure for each specific detail.

Since this is a book on canoeing, a general discussion of sailing will not be included. Consult books on how to sail small boats to learn the principles of sailing before undertaking to sail a canoe or to make a sailing rig for a canoe. It is also wise to become a canoeist before becoming a canoe sailor unless you already are experienced at sailing small sailboats. Even in the latter case, it would be wise to undergo a period of orientation to the canoe in its typical role before undertaking to sail it, because it is far less stable than sailboats and could embarrass a good sailor who had not first become oriented to its unique characteristics.

However, some interpretive comments relating to the drawing and possible modification of the drawing add information that pertains specifically to sailing a canoe and hence is not found in texts on sailing boats.

1. All the fittings indicated should be brass ones preferably, but they may be of galvanized iron.

2. The 6-inch threaded rods, which hold the leeboards to the 4 x 4-inch endpieces of the leeboard thwart, could be $\frac{3}{8}$ inch thick instead of $\frac{5}{16}$ inch, especially if they are brass, to provide greater strength. An easy way to get such rods is to buy brass bolts and saw off the heads.

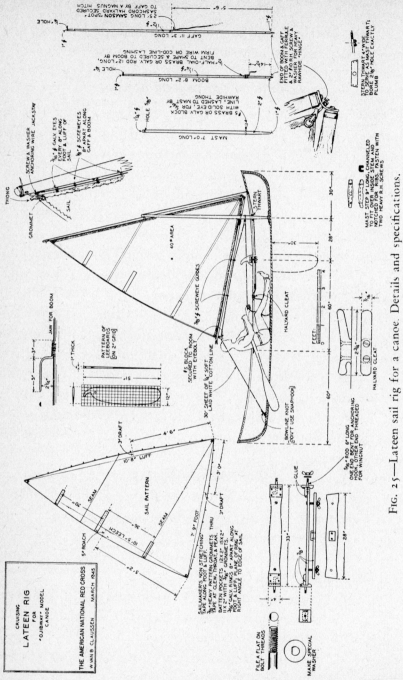

FIG. 25—Lateen sail rig for a canoe. Details and specifications.

3. If you plan to sail with only one leeboard, you will only have to rig the bolt at one end of the leeboard thwart.

4. A brass washer ⅛ inch thick and at least 2 inches in diameter has been found to be very suitable between the wing nut and the leeboard. It is customary to glue leather ⅟₁₆ to ⅛ inch thick to the face of the 4 x 4-inch endpieces. When doing this glue job, place wax paper over the leather during the application of pressure because the leather will be easily torn if dried glue sticks its outer surface to another object.

5. If you plan to sail with only one leeboard, you will be sailing quite like you would in a centerboard sailboat: the board will be down continuously except when you are running before the wind. Filing a flat on the bolt threads and making a special locking type hole in the washer will not be necessary. Experimentation has revealed that the relatively few times the board is changed from one position to the other makes tightening up on the wing nut no inconvenience.

6. An alternative to securing the end of the sheet to the pad eye on the inside stem is to lead it through a hole in the deck and tie a figure-of-eight knot. This will move the sheet back out of the way of the steering paddle when the latter is changed from side to side in tacking, but will theoretically decrease the stability of the craft slightly, because it's attached higher on the canoe.

7. It is wise to have your sail made by a sailmaker. Sailmakers advertise in yachting and boating magazines. There are also many who do not advertise but may be found in seaports along the coast. Homemade sails are rarely ever satisfactory. Show the drawing (Fig. 25) or a copy of it to the sailmaker. He will use it as his guide and make you a good sail.

8. Specify to the sailmaker whether you prefer to have a bolt rope along the foot and luff of your sail, instead of the jackstay-and-eyes arrangement shown in the drawing. You will

then, of course, have to proceed with the "hollow" spar construction rather than that shown in the drawing. For each spar (boom and gaff) start with two pieces of straight-grain spruce, ¾ inch by 1½ inches, of the required length. Cut out the ¼-inch x ⅜-inch slots (Fig. 25A) on a table saw either by using a dado head or by making several cuts of a cross-cut blade, starting at one end and stopping within 2 inches of the other end. Then plane off the 1/16 inch at the outer edge of each slot (Fig. 25A). Round and smooth these outer lips, and then glue the two pieces together. When the glue is dry, shape the spar with appropriate hand tools and sandpaper (Fig. 25B), but retain the same measurements from end to end rather than tapering as indicated for the solid spars. With a pocket knife, cut away the lips of the slot about 3 inches at the outhaul end of the spar and smooth the area with sandpaper (Fig. 25C). At the tack end of the spar, similarly cut away the lips of the slot at its very beginning, making a widened opening about 3 inches long to admit entrance of the bolt rope of the sail

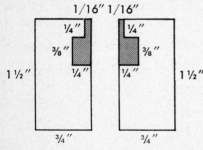

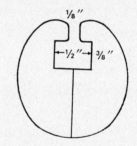

FIG. 25A—Cross section of two halves of hollow or slotted spar. Checkered portion is cut out from one end to within 2 inches of the other end. A bench saw should be used, with a dado head or several cuts of a crosscut blade to remove the ¼ by ⅜ inch portion. The 1/16 by ¼ inch portion may be easily taken off with a plane and sandpaper.

FIG. 25B—Cross section of two halves glued together. The lips of the slot are rounded and smoothed before the gluing is done. The slot should also be smoothed with sandpaper before the gluing. After the glue is dry, the spar is worked down with hand tools to the shape shown.

(Fig. 25C). The bolt rope and hollow spar arrangement will not permit lashing the jaw to the boom nor tying or hitching the halyard around the gaff. Fig. 25D shows an alternative

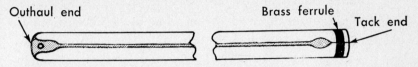

FIG. 25C—At the open end of the spar, the lips of the slot are cut away and smoothed for a distance of about 3 inches and a hole is drilled as shown for the outhaul thong. A brass ferrule is put on the closed end. At this end of the slot, the lips are also cut away and smoothed over for a distance of about 3 inches to permit entry of the bolt rope into the slot.

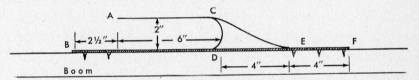

FIG. 25D—A jaw attached to a hollow or slotted boom. Its line of attachment is 90° from the line of the slot. The material is brass ⅛ inch thick and ½ inch wide. The U-shaped piece, AB, is the actual jaw. DF is brazed onto it at D. The curved piece CE is brazed to the unit at C and E. The unit is attached with ⅝-inch brass screws as shown.

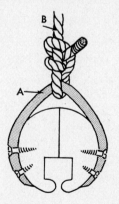

FIG. 25E—Alternative method of securing the halyard to the gaff when the hollow or slotted type of spar will not permit hitching around it. A is rawhide ⅛ inch thick by 1 inch wide where it lies on the spar. It is narrowed to about ½ inch where the halyard is secured. Four screws are used on each side. The upper ones are ⅝ inch long and the lower ones ½ inch. B is the halyard secured to A.

method of attaching a jaw to the boom. Fig. 25E shows an alternative method of securing the halyard to the gaff.

9. If the mast is worked down to 1¾ inches thickness rather than 2 inches, it will have adequate strength if it is a good, straight-grain piece of spruce. The smaller measurement will permit gluing a leather chafing collar on the mast where it goes through the hole in the thwart. A collar 2 or 3 inches long and 1/16 to 1/8 inch thick is typical. Often the canoeist will work a turkshead knot on the upper portion of this collar to dress it up.

10. After sailing the canoe a couple of times, the mast will be chafed by the jaw of the boom. This will indicate the place to put a chafing collar of leather to protect the mast from further chafing. A collar 4 or 5 inches long is typical. It is rather important to work a turkshead knot around the leather at each end, or to build up each end by gluing on a strip of leather ½ to ¾ inch wide and ¼ inch thick. This is done in order to keep the jaw on the leathered portion at all times.

If the rig is set up as indicated in Fig. 25, the canoe should sail well. To assure good relation between the center of effort on the sail and the location of the center of resistance of the hull and leeboard, sail the canoe close-hauled on a day when

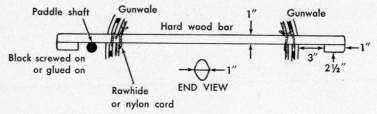

FIG. 25F—A wood bar tied across the gunwales about 2 inches aft of the thwart against which the sailor leans (Fig. 25) is a good aid to steering for the beginner and in fact adds to the ease and enjoyment of handling the sailing canoe for nearly anyone. The buoyancy of the paddle keeps its shaft pressing up against the bar. In steering, the shaft may press against the outwale or against the block on the end of the bar, as need be. This gives somewhat the feel and control of a rudder-and-tiller assembly.

the wind is brisk but with few waves. (Note that the paddle is on the leeward side. It is always on the leeward side, changing as the tack changes.) If her tendency is to gently round up into the wind when you make no effort to steer, you have the leeboard located correctly. If she rounds up into the wind sharply, move the leeboard slightly aft, repeating this adjustment if necessary until the desired moderate tendency to round up into the wind results. If on the other hand the tendency is to fall off before the wind, the leeboards must be moved forward step by step until the correct adjustment is made.

A canoe should be sailed without heeling, in so far as possible. The sailor can easily shift from the position shown in Fig. 25 to one in which he lies up along the gunwale to windward to keep her sailing flat.

Serving the shaft with a strong cord will help to keep it against the outwale while you are steering. Wetting it frequently decreases its tendency to slip. In the beginning you will have some trouble steering with a free paddle; it is somewhat more difficult than using the typical rudder and tiller unit on a sailboat. As an aid during the learning period and for increased ease and enjoyment of canoe sailing, you can tie a wood bar across the gunwales about 2 inches aft of the thwart against which you lean (Fig. 25). This bar helps keep the steering paddle in position and adds to the ease of steering (Fig. 25F). When your rig is well balanced, however, your paddle blade merely trails in the water like the rudder of a boat, with pressure applied inward on the grip as needed to keep the canoe from rounding up into the wind. That is why it is important to keep the paddle on the leeward side, and to have a mild weather helm as explained above.

THE CANOE AS A SHELTER

Canoeists doing canoe camping ordinarily use a suitable tent for overnight shelter, but under favorable conditions a canoe may be quickly rigged for sheltering its crew for the night. Figures 26, 26A, 26B, and 26C show some of the ways in which this may be done.

Fig. 26—Simple shelter afforded by turning the canoe over and placing a waterproof groundcloth under it and the sleeping bag on the groundcloth. The center thwart has been temporarily removed to give the sleeper more freedom of movement.

Fig. 26A—Adding a 5- by 7-foot tarpaulin (or any similar waterproof material, such as a poncho) will provide better protection from the weather and will extend the shelter area wide enough for two persons. The far side of the tarps is tied with cord to the inwales or thwarts.

Fig. 26B—By using your river pole or any similar stick for a ridgepole, you'll be able to place the length of the tarps at right angles to the canoe, thus making a shelter for two persons, who can sleep with their heads and shoulders under the canoe and legs extended outward.

Fig. 26C—Using an available log in this manner to support one end of the canoe provides more overhead space, which may be desirable under some circumstances.

CHAPTER IV

CARRYING, LAUNCHING, AND BOARDING

CARRYING

The inexperienced person may regard a canoe as awkward and difficult to carry. Actually, the contrary is true if effective methods are employed and canoes of suitable size are used.

Only in special situations and circumstances should canoes be pushed or dragged to the launching place, for normally this practice may be expected to damage the canoes. It is better to carry the canoe. There are several methods of carrying that can be used, depending on the number of people available, the weight of the canoe, and other factors.

Two-Man Carry.—Having one person at each end is a typical way to carry a canoe (Fig. 1). Note that the man at the front has inverted his hand for the carry. There are two ways of rotating the arm to a palm-out position. The proper way, and the easier of the two, turns the point of the elbow out away from the body. This inverted-hand method of carrying allows the arm to rest against the body, making carrying easier than if the arm encircles the end of the canoe. The man at the rear is on the same side of the canoe and uses the same arm for carrying. This prevents the canoe from falling sideward out of the front man's hand.

Two-Man Carry, Alternate Method.—It is easy for two persons to carry a canoe on their shoulders. First, two paddles are lashed between the amidships and stern thwarts as a carry yoke (Fig. 3). The canoe is then lifted to the overhead position and carried in such manner that the paddle blades rest on the shoulders of the person at the rear, and the bow deck on one shoulder of the person in front (Fig. 2). The person at the front is closer to the end of the canoe than is the person at the rear; therefore, there is relatively equal division of work even though the former uses only one shoulder. Shifting from shoulder to shoulder is easy in the front position, and is usually done if the carry is long.

Carry-Amidships.—Before launching the canoe, it is desirable to shift from the end-carrying positions to positions opposite each other amidships (Fig. 4). This is true for both of

Fig. 1—A two-man method of carrying a canoe.

Fig. 2—A tandem shoulder-carry.

Fig. 3—Paddles lashed in place to serve as a yoke at the rear position in the carry shown in Fig. 2. The narrow material holding the blades to the stern thwart is nylon parachute cord, but rawhide, rubber, or any similar strong material could be used. The material holding the shafts to the offset amidships thwart is rubber cut from a tire tube.

the two-man carrying methods described. The transfer may be done by setting the canoe down on the ground or dock. If the ground is not smooth, however, the bottom may be damaged. In this case the shift may be made without setting the canoe down, by having the carriers move toward each other along opposite gunwales—with equal timing so that the canoe remains in balance and an end doesn't bang on the ground. Frequently this carry-amidships is used as a method for mak-

FIG. 4—A carry amidships. It is used in the approach to a two-man launching.

ing fairly short carries when there are no obstructions, such as trees, or no narrow docks to traverse.

Four-Man Carry.—It is often advisable for several persons to carry a canoe: for example, when the people are small or the canoe is large and heavy. Carrying a heavy canoe without sufficient help is discouraging to the canoeist and ought to be avoided. A four-man carry is a typical one for carrying heavy canoes or for children (Fig. 5). On a portage, lightweight equipment may be left in the canoe.

When there are rocks, stumps, brush, or other forms of

rough terrain on a portage, the canoe may be carried bottom-up in order to protect it from damage (Fig. 6).

On long carries, it may be advisable for the four-man carry to be done on the shoulders. The carry is easier this way and obstructions are more easily avoided.

Three-Man Carry.—This is a good compromise between the two-man carries and the four-man carries, and is especially good when one person is larger and stronger than the other two—as in the case of a man and two girls (Fig. 7) or a counselor and two campers. If the smaller two are relatively very

FIG. 5—A simple four-man carry especially recommended for children.

FIG. 6—Four-man carry with the canoe turned bottom-up to protect it from obstructions.

small, they should carry near the end of the canoe; the nearer they each approach the size and strength of the larger person, the farther they should be from the end, thus assuming a larger portion of the total weight. This carry may also be done with the canoe bottom-up to clear obstructions, or at shoulder level for greater ease on longer carries (Fig. 8). In the latter case, the two at the front rest the canoe gunwales on their shoulders and the one person at the rear places the deck on his shoulder. A folded item of clothing will pad a shoulder for greater comfort.

Chain Carry.—A number of canoes may be carried by the same number of persons plus one when the chain carry is used

Fig. 7—Carry-by-three   Fig. 8—Shoulder carry-by-three.

Fig. 9—Chain carry.

(Fig. 9). The canoes are lined up end to end, and the carriers take their places. The carrier at the front of the column and the one at the rear each have only one canoe end to lift and carry; the other carriers each have two ends to lift and carry. The latter carriers should consequently be stronger than the former. The carriers of each canoe are on the same side of that canoe. This enables the encircling arm of the man at the rear of each to hold the canoe from rolling away from the arm of

FIG. 10—Second step: the canoe turned over and lifted to shoulder height.

FIG. 11—Third step: placing the canoe on the roof rack.

the forward carrier, who uses the preferred inverted-hand grip.

Two Persons Lifting a Canoe on and off a Car.—Canoeing activity today very often involves use of an automobile for transportation to and from the water. Roof racks are almost standard equipment for canoeists. Lifting the canoe on and off is made easier and more efficient if the two lifters proceed as follows, thereby avoiding the risk of dropping the canoe: Carrying the canoe by its ends, bring it alongside parallel to the car and three or four feet away. Face each other, and be sure that your hands are in corresponding positions on the canoe ends; the hand away from the car should be at the bottom of the end of the canoe and the other hand at the point of the end. Carefully turn the canoe over to the bottom-up position and lift it to shoulder height (Fig. 10). Then sidestep (military fashion) toward the car until you can place the canoe on the roof rack (Fig. 11). To take the canoe off, reverse the procedure. It is important to remember the position of the hands when taking the canoe off. Dropping the canoe is almost always caused by incorrect placement of hands.

Details of tying the canoe on can be found on pages 122–125.

One-Man Carry on Hip.—The easiest way for one person to

FIG. 12—One-man carry on hip; used for short distances.

FIG. 13—One-man shoulder carry; for short carries with a light canoe.

carry a canoe a short distance is to grasp it by the near gunwale with both hands at a place of balance amidships. The canoe is thus lifted and rested against the hip during the carry (Fig. 12). This is also the method one man uses for handling the canoe just before launching it, regardless of the method he used for carrying.

One-Man Single-Shoulder Carry.—One-man carries should be employed only by mature males and with lightweight canoes. Experienced canoeists may undertake these lifts with heavier canoes. The shoulder lift (Fig. 13) is practical for carries of moderate distance. A pad on the shoulder will make the carry more comfortable. In this and all one-man carries, one must guard against and make allowance for wind. If the wind is strong, one-man carries are inadvisable, except for the experienced canoeist.

One-Man Overhead-Shoulder Carry.—This carry, used on portages, is probably the most efficient and practical of all one-man carries. The paddles are lashed between thwarts (Fig. 16). Note that the blades of the paddles are slipped under rawhide thongs permanently in place on the offset 'midships thwart. The shafts are secured to the bow thwart with rawhide. These permanent fittings are carefully placed so that the blades will rest comfortably on the shoulders and so that the shafts will be far enough apart to allow the head to pass easily between them. This is done by trial and error, using temporary

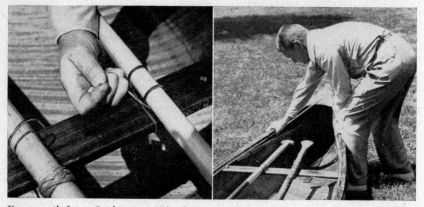

Fig. 14 (left)—Lashing paddle shafts to thwart. The rawhide is knotted at one end and passed up through a small hole in the thwart and down through another hole about 1¼″ away, leaving a loop through which to pass the grip and shaft of the paddle. This is shown at the left. The loop is drawn down tightly onto the shaft. The rawhide is then brought up around one edge of the thwart and once more looped around the shaft as shown at the right. It is then given one full turn around the thwart, a full turn around the base of both loops, and is then jammed tightly between the shaft and the thwart as shown.

Fig. 15 (right)—Grasping gunwales near bow to start the lift.

lashings. Light line would serve as well as rawhide; sometimes strips of rubber have been used to provide permanent fastenings for both shaft and blade. The rubber strips have the advantage of not needing to be tied and untied in use. First, secure the paddle shafts in place (Fig. 14). Grasp the gunwales near the bow (Fig. 15) and start the lift. With one end still on the ground, lift the canoe to a rest position on your thigh. Then lift it to shoulder height and turn it over as you lift it above your head (Fig. 16). Then move backward until you can lower the canoe on your shoulders (Fig. 17). With a little

FIG. 16 (left)—Lift at shoulder height.

FIG. 17 (right)—Lift completed, canoe balanced and being carried. Canoeists sometimes pad the blades for greater carrying comfort. Items of clothing or kneeling pads are useful.

minor adjustment for balance and with hands holding or resting on the inwales as shown, or on the paddle shafts, you are ready for a long carry. If your canoeing activity involves a lot of portaging, you may prefer to use a ready-made *yoke* available from some canoe manufacturers (Figs. 18 and 19). A headstrap, called a *tumpline*, is sometimes attached to the yoke so that the carrier's head and shoulders share the work (Figs. 20 and 21).

Amidships Lift for Straight-Arm Overhead Carry.—Carrying a canoe overhead with arms straight is useful for placing a

FIG. 18 (left)—A ready-made yoke in place for carrying the canoe. It is attached to the gunwales a couple of inches forward of the center of the canoe so that the canoe will come into balance when the carrier holds onto the gunwales in front of him.

FIG. 19 (right)—A yoke in use.

canoe on a high rack, on the top of a car, or for carrying a canoe a short distance when other types of one-man carries would be awkward because of obstructions. To start the lift for the straight-arm overhead carry, grasp the near gunwale amidships with both hands, shoulder-width apart, and lift the canoe a little off the ground. Make minor adjustments of hand positions if necessary to get the canoe in balance (Fig. 22). Roll the canoe sharply on your thighs, flipping the far gunwale upward and catching it with one hand (Fig. 23). (If the 'midships thwart is missing, don't use this method: it may damage the canoe unless the canoe is otherwise well constructed.) Then, change the grip on the near gunwale so that the thumb is on the inside (Fig. 23). Finally, swing the canoe up overhead, aiding with a lift of one knee if necessary, to the position

FIG. 20—A homemade headstrap, or tumpline, attached to a yoke. The strap is woven fabric, 1 inch wide. A piece of an old belt, about 2 inches wide, was slotted and slipped onto the strap for wider bearing surface on the head and for consequent greater comfort. The buckle permits adjustment for proper fit.

shown in Fig. 24. Only physically mature males should use this carry. Lock your elbows and keep your arms vertical to take some strain off muscles.

Modified Overhead Carries.—Lowering one gunwale to shoulder level is a restful modification of the straight-arm overhead carry. It is sometimes used in place of the latter. It is used often to avoid limbs of trees or other obstructions (Fig. 25). This position is also the first step in lowering the canoe from the straight-arm overhead carry position to the ground. Lowering the canoe still more so that it rests in the crook of the arm (Fig. 26) is a modification having the same advantages

Fig. 21—Carrying a canoe, using a yoke fitted with a tumpline. Women should carry only lightweight canoes, and should have help in getting them into carrying position.

Fig. 22 (left)—Start of lift for straight-arm overhead carry; lift at balance point, keep back straight, press canoe against thighs.

Fig. 23 (right)—Second step: flip canoe up so that you can grasp the far gunwale. Keep your back straight at all times throughout the lift.

Fig. 24—Canoe in balanced overhead position.

and more. For example, the carry is especially valuable when you're dodging low limbs of trees.

One-Man Carry with Canoe in Upright Position.—This carry (Fig. 27) should be used only by experienced adults. If used by others, it might result in strained muscles or a damaged canoe. Its advantages to the canoeist are that small items of gear may be left lying in the canoe during the carry and that the canoe may be shifted from shoulder to shoulder merely by ducking the head under it. When a canoeist is experienced enough to use this carry, he will not need to be told how to get it to his shoulder. For this reason, no explanation of the details is given.

One-Man Placement of a Canoe on a Car.—Placing a canoe on the roof rack of a car is easy from the straight-arm overhead carry position. Stand close to the car midway between the two carry bars. Lean toward the car until you can rest the back of your forearm on the car roof (Fig. 28). This will give you the leverage you need to lower the canoe the remaining distance till the gunwale rests on both bars. Then grasp the other gunwale with both hands (Fig. 29) and slide the canoe into its proper position. If the bars are not covered with a soft

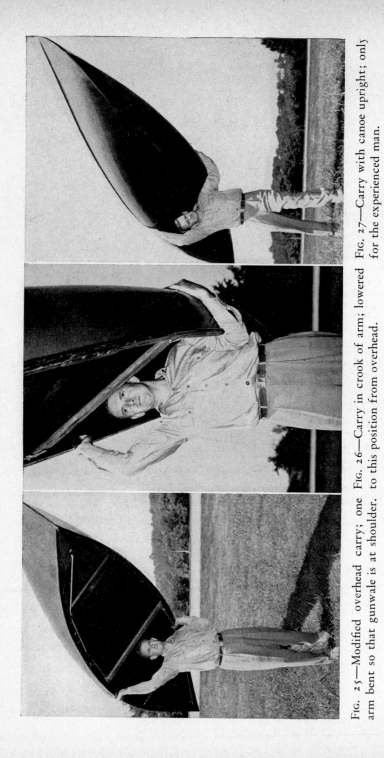

FIG. 25—Modified overhead carry; one FIG. 26—Carry in crook of arm; lowered FIG. 27—Carry with canoe upright; only
arm bent so that gunwale is at shoulder. to this position from overhead. for the experienced man.

FIG. 28—Lowering canoe onto roof rack from the straight-arm overhead carry.

FIG. 29—Moving the canoe over to the centered position on the roof rack.

material, sliding the canoe into place will scrape the varnish off the gunwales of non-metal canoes. In this case, it is better to lift the gunwale off one rack and set it over a few inches and then do the same at the other rack, repeating this alternate procedure until the canoe is in place. You can do this without changing the position of your hands on the near gunwale.

Note: Be sure paddles and other gear are secure in your canoe before putting it on your car (Fig. 30).

Fig. 30—This is an efficient way to arrange paddles and river pole for a trip by car. The lashings or thongs used for positioning paddles as shoulder rests for portaging are used, except that the shafts must be under the thwarts rather than on top of them. The blades may be either under or on top. Kneeling pads may be jammed into the ends of the canoe.

Tying a Canoe on a Roof Rack.—The primary consideration in tying a canoe on a roof rack is that it be secure enough so that it will not be blown off when the car is under way on the highway. Minor considerations are to have (1) a rig that does not take an unnecessarily long time to secure or untie; (2) is not way out of proportion in excess of what is needed to safely transport the canoe; (3) is neat and shipshape. There are many commercial rigs on sale in hardware stores, department stores, and other places. Nearly all of them are quite adequate. It is not intended here to recommend a specific way to carry and tie on a canoe, but rather to show an example of some of the things to consider if you have not already acquired experience and a way of your own.

FIG. 31—Carrying a canoe on an automobile. Note the turnbuckle rig to hold the rack to the roof. The line is secured to the rack with a running bowline.

Commercial roof racks in many cases are secured to the roof with a strap and hook arrangement that is adequate. A good substitute of greater reliability is a turnbuckle rig (Fig. 31). Most commercial racks have straps and buckles for tying on the canoe. If rope is used, it may be secured to the rack on one side with a running bowline (Fig. 31) and tied to the other side with one or two round turns and two half hitches (Fig. 32).

Rubber products are sometimes used in place of straps or rope for securing the canoe to the roof rack (Fig. 33). For

FIG. 32 (left)—A round turn, or two, and two half hitches are used to tie the line to the rack to hold the canoe in place.

FIG. 33 (right)—Securing a canoe to the roof rack using a device made of rubber shock cord, a short piece of manila line, and an S hook. It is secured the same on the other side.

added security, especially on long trips when wind may be encountered, you may wish to tie down the canoe fore and aft as a secondary measure (Figs. 34 and 35).

By lengthening the carry bars with temporary, improvised attachments, two canoes may be carried side by side on a car roof.

Canoe Trailers.—The American Red Cross has available for limited distribution a W. Van B. Claussen drawing entitled *Suggestions for Home-Made Trailer for Six Canoes and Duffle,*

FIG. 34 (left)—Securing the front end of the canoe to the bumper using a rig made of shock cord, S hooks, and an eyebolt (at the deck). Line could be used in the same manner; manila, three-strand cotton line, or sash cord are typical; nylon could be used.

FIG. 35 (right)—The end of the canoe at the rear of the car is secured using inner-tubing rubber bands and manila with an S hook at the lower end and an eyebolt at the canoe deck.

ARC 1065–12. During recent years lightweight metals and small wheels have become popular. These features of trailer building could be incorporated with suggestions of the drawing if desired, otherwise the specifications could remain as they are. The drawing is presented on the following page in three parts (Figs. 36A, 36B, and 36C). The measurements given are for a specific canoe as indicated. They could be altered to conform to the length, width, and curvature of other types of canoes. The maximum height of 7 feet 3 inches is established to permit the loaded trailer to pass through the average garage

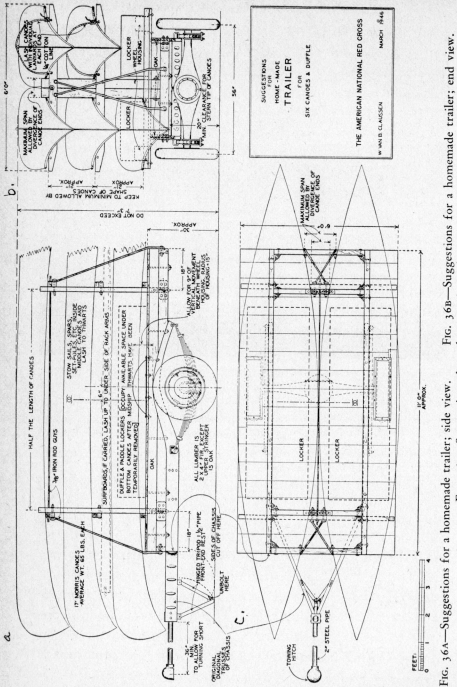

FIG. 36A—Suggestions for a homemade trailer; side view.   FIG. 36B—Suggestions for a homemade trailer; end view.

FIG. 36c—Suggestions for a homemade trailer; top view.

door and to maintain a low center of gravity. At the same time, it allows the indicated minimum road-clearance of 20 inches, which is sufficient to keep the tail ends of the two bottom canoes from scraping when you negotiate dips and rises in country roads or woodland trails.

This design contemplates use of any standard, popular-priced passenger car chassis. It can also be built on a special set of wheels-and-axle designed for trailer use. A wide choice of woods and construction materials is possible, including the use of pipe for uprights and crossarms.

LAUNCHING

Putting the canoe in the water and taking it out should be done carefully and smoothly and without damage to the canoe. Ordinarily, the canoe should not be pushed, pulled, or slid into or out of the water over beach, banking, or dock. When launching, it is best to let the canoe right down onto the water from a lift position. It should be lifted with the same care when being taken out of the water.

FIG. 37—Launching at a bank.

Two-Man Launching.—The canoe is launched hand-over-hand, end-first, onto the water (Figs. 37 and 38). When it is entirely clear of the dock or bank, the canoe is let down on the water full-length, and by hand manipulation brought around parallel and alongside. To lift the canoe out, the steps are re-

Fig. 38—Launching at a dock.

Fig. 39—Launching at a beach.

versed. If launching at a shallow beach (Fig. 39), the canoe is launched at right angles to the beach and held with its end just touching bottom at the water's edge.

Tandem Cross-Corner Launching.—When two dock sections are at right angles to one another, often it is convenient and easy for two persons to launch the canoe across the corner (Fig. 40) and likewise to lift the canoe out across the corner.

One-Man Launching, End First.—From a simple lift position, the canoe is fed end-first onto the water (Fig. 41). When the whole canoe is clear of the dock or bank, it is let down on the water and by hand manipulation is brought around to a parallel position alongside. To lift the canoe out, the steps are reversed.

FIG. 40—Cross-corner launching or lifting out.

FIG. 41—A one-man launching, end first.

Parallel Launching.—An experienced canoeist frequently employs the parallel method of launching. It is practical especially with a lightweight canoe. The canoeist's toes are even with the edge of the dock or extended slightly over (Fig. 42). The canoe is allowed to slide down over the knees onto the water (Fig. 43), the ends of the toes preventing it from scraping against the dock. Two canoeists may employ the same method with greater ease (Fig. 44).

FIG. 42—Start of parallel launching.

Fig. 43—Parallel launching being completed.

Fig. 44—Two men using the parallel method of launching. The bend of the knees helps to extend the canoe out over the water.

BOARDING

Since a canoe afloat is not a solid immovable base, the beginning canoeist must acquire agility and a sense of balance before being able to board the canoe with smooth, flowing movements characteristic of the experienced canoeist. The best way to acquire this agility and balance is to slow down the boarding process so that it becomes a series of deliberate, controlled movements. When mastered, these movements may be blended gradually to achieve the desired smoothness.

Stand or kneel on one knee, near the edge of the dock, facing the bow of the canoe (Fig. 45). Place the other foot in the canoe, directly over the keel. Keep your body weight on the foot or knee on the dock. Then transfer your weight from the

Fig. 45 (left)—Boarding a canoe at a dock, first step; body weight on foot on dock, other foot placed on centerline of canoe.

Fig. 46 (right)—Second step: weight transferred to foot in the canoe in a downward direction while hands grasp the gunwales.

Fig. 47—Third step: foot on dock has been placed beside the one in the canoe.

dock directly downward onto your foot in the canoe and at the same time grasp both gunwales with your hands (Fig. 46). Remove your foot from the dock and place it beside your other foot in the bottom of the canoe (Fig. 47). You are now aboard and may take your position for paddling. For debarking, get up to this latter position from your paddling position and reverse the procedure for boarding. Boarding and debarking at a bank involve the same principles.

When two people board a canoe from a dock or bank, the bowman usually boards first because the bow position is a little closer to amidships than the stern position and the canoe will consequently remain in better trim than it would if the sternman entered first. Sometimes, however, when the canoeists are large and the canoe not commensurately large, it may be better to have the sternman board first, but not at the stern position. He should board just aft of the amidships thwart, kneel on both knees, and hold onto both gunwales. Then the bowman should board and take his normal paddling position, after which the sternman moves back to his normal position. Boarding in this way follows the principle of keeping the canoe on even trim during the procedure. When there is a passenger, he should board first. It makes little difference whether bowman or sternman boards next, for in either case the canoe will remain on fairly even trim fore and aft. To debark from the canoe, reverse the procedure.

To board a canoe at a beach or shallow-water shore, one man adjusts the canoe so that its end is just barely touching bottom at the water's edge, and braces the canoe between his knees and with his hands. The other steps around him and into the canoe, walking down the centerline (Fig. 48), holding onto the gunwales, to his position at the far end. The man on shore then moves the canoe out about a foot farther away from shore and steps in (Fig. 49) and, with the same procedure,

FIG. 48—Boarding a canoe at a beach or shallow-water shore; one man holds the end while the other boards.

FIG. 49—Boarding a canoe at a beach or shallow-water shore; second man boarding while first aboard controls the canoe with his paddle. This canoe has been launched stern first.

moves to or beyond amidships until the canoe is afloat and free of the beach. The first man in then moves the canoe out away from the beach (Fig. 50) and the other moves to his paddling position.

When canoeists paddle ashore for a temporary stop, they often carry the canoe a short way up from the water, where they leave it for the short stop. When it is time to launch the

FIG. 50—First man aboard moves the canoe out away from shore. In this case the canoe is headed bow out.

FIG. 51—Boarding a canoe by stepping in from shallow water. The canoe is completely waterborne and parallel to the shore.

canoe, it is therefore launched stern-first. When a canoe is carried by two persons from one body of water to another, it quite naturally is launched bow-first, heading in the direction of travel.

When boarding a canoe at a beach or wherever the water is shallow or when there is a current, the canoeist often places the canoe parallel to the beach rather than at right angles to it. He moves it out into water of several inches depth and steps in (Fig. 51), using the same principle of boarding as applies to boarding from a dock or bank—namely, stepping into the center and grasping both gunwales. Canoeists using this procedure should either be barefoot or wear canvas shoes.

For boarding one canoe from another, follow the procedure for boarding from a dock (Figs. 52 and 53).

FIG. 52—Boarding one canoe from another; keeping your weight on the centerline and your hands on the gunwales, place one foot into the canoe to be boarded.

FIG. 53—Second step: transfer your weight downward to the foot in the canoe and at the same time transfer both hands to its gunwales. All that remains is to place your other foot in the boarded canoe and take a kneeling position.

CHAPTER V

POSITIONS IN THE CANOE

The art of paddling can best be developed by following the example of skillful canoeists: paddling from a kneeling position. Furthermore, safety is enhanced—or at least embarrassment and inconvenience are avoided. Kneeling positions provide firm contact with the hull below the water level. The paddler thus becomes in a sense an integral part of the canoe, better able to make it respond accurately to his strokes. The risk of capsizing or falling overboard is practically eliminated because the "cargo," or controlling parts of it, bring pressure to bear "down in the hold."

Sitting on the seats without having at least one knee in contact with the bottom of the canoe not only makes skilled paddling more difficult, and efficient paddling impossible, but also constitutes loading the "cargo" on the "main deck," thus greatly increasing the likelihood of the paddler's falling overboard or capsizing the canoe.

The principle may be illustrated by imagining a large ball rolling. It has an axis—an imaginary line about which it revolves. It would be an act of sensitive balancing to sit on top of that ball and not roll off, because the force of your weight would be above the axis of the ball. If on the other hand you were to get inside the ball you could lie down, sit, kneel, or even stand; and the ball would not roll, because the force of your weight would be below the axis of the ball.

The canoe has an axis, an imaginary line running fore and aft a few inches above the keel, about which it revolves when it rocks from side to side. If you sit on the seat without having at least one knee exerting controlling pressure on the bottom, the force of your weight is above the axis and can cause you to fall overboard or capsize if it gets only a little off center.

A practical way to test this is to lie down in the bottom of the canoe and roll from side to side. You will find it impossible to capsize or swamp the canoe unless you roll up onto a gunwale and bring your weight to bear on it. This latter maneuver is difficult, so for all practical purposes it is considered impossible to capsize a canoe while lying in the bottom. If you sit in the bottom and rock the canoe from side to side—even pressing down hard on each gunwale in turn—you will find that, though you can force the gunwale down enough to ship a little water, the canoe will not tip over.

In the kneeling position on both knees, you can rock the canoe from side to side and find it is impossible to capsize it. In this case, however, you can lose your balance and fall overboard, perhaps swamping or capsizing the canoe in the process. In ordinary canoeing activity, this is unlikely if you are careful. And once you develop at homeness in the canoe, it almost never happens.

The high kneeling position and even the standing position are in themselves stable because they exert the force of all the body weight onto the bottom of the canoe. The canoeist must, however, have good personal balance and agility when using these positions so that he will not fall out.

It is important to have a good kneeling pad to make kneeling more comfortable. There is a description of pads, with illustrations, in Chapter III.

ONE-MAN (SOLO) POSITIONS

There are several positions for one-man paddling. These will be considered in respect to the forms of kneeling and to locations in the canoe.

The Cruising Position.—This position is that of kneeling on both knees on the bottom of the canoe while at the same time sitting on a thwart or on the forward part of a seat. For solo paddling this should be done as near to amidships as thwart-placement will permit, except that ordinarily an amidships thwart is not used unless it is offset. (See Chapter III for information on efficient thwart placement.) The most efficient all-round solo paddling position uses an amidships thwart that has been specially located about 14 inches aft of amidships (Fig. 1). A comfortable modification of the cruising position on

Fig. 1 (left)—Solo-paddling position using offset amidships thwart, both knees on bottom.   Fig. 2 (right)—Straddling a bedroll or similar gear is a comfortable modification of the cruising position.

both knees is to straddle a bedroll or similar gear (Fig. 2). This permits adjusting your location in the canoe with less regard to location of thwarts. It has been found good for children who cannot sit on a thwart and at the same time kneel on the bottom because the distance between the thwart and the canoe bottom is too great. When a canoe has its amidships thwart located at the exact center of the canoe, the normal location for the paddler is at a quarter thwart (Fig. 3A), not at the stern thwart.

The One-Knee Cruising Position.—This is often called the *relief position* because it is frequently alternated with the normal cruising position. The paddler sits on the thwart while kneeling on one knee and extends the other leg forward. He should brace the forward foot against the edge of a rib or in some other manner. He always kneels on the knee that is on the paddling side (Fig. 3).

FIG. 3 (left)—The one-knee location of paddler, often called the relief position.

FIG. 3A (right)—Normal cruising position, when a canoe has its amidships thwart located exactly at the center of the canoe.

Upright Kneeling Position (Fig. 4).—This position not only is a good relief from other positions, but also has some very distinct advantages. It allows the paddler to change his location in the canoe irrespective of thwart location because it does not involve touching a thwart. In this respect, it is like the high kneeling, or racing, style of kneeling; but it is easier to learn, less tiring, and more stable. It is a fine style of kneeling for paddling in the wind; it allows good power application, stability, and precise adjustability in respect to utilizing the force of the wind to the paddler's advantage. The paddler kneels on both knees, with thighs and trunk erect, and faces slightly toward his paddling side. He should kneel close enough to the side to be able to paddle most efficiently. His knees normally will be a comfortable distance apart, wider apart in rough water conditions.

Fig. 4 (left)—The upright kneeling position; on both knees, thighs and trunk erect, facing slightly toward paddling side. (*Note:* The high position of the paddle is due to shallow water and is not typical of this style of paddling.)

Fig. 5 (right)—High kneeling position, showing body facing slightly toward paddling side.

The High Kneeling, or Racing, Position.—This form of kneeling is used exclusively by all participants in the organized sport of canoe racing and by many other experienced canoeists for covering distance in the shortest time and with the least effort. It requires much practice and the conditioning of special muscles. The position is essentially on one knee and the opposite foot, with the body erect and facing slightly toward the paddling side rather than directly forward (Fig. 5).

There are a number of important factors in this form of kneeling. A firm kneeling pad is placed in the bottom of the canoe at the paddling position (Fig. 6). Assuming, as illustrated, that the paddler is going to paddle on the left side, he kneels on the pad with his left knee. His thigh and trunk are erect above his knee (Fig. 7). This almost straight line from knee through hip through shoulder is not vertical, but nearly so, usually slanting forward about 10 degrees. His left leg, below the knee, extends diagonally across the canoe with the bottom surfaces of his toes, or the bottom of the toe of his

Knee slightly bent.

Toe turned in diagonally across centerline

Firm kneeling cushion placed a little to the left of centerline in this narrow canoe, closer to the side in a wide canoe.

In a narrow canoe sometimes the ankle may be braced under a thwart.

Toe of shoe grips bottom. Leg extends diagonally across canoe.

Fig. 6 (left)—High kneeling position, showing kneeling position and position of forward foot.

Fig. 7 (right)—High kneeling position, side view.

soft-soled shoe, gripping the bottom of the canoe between two ribs (Fig. 7).

The right leg is extended forward with only a slight bend at the knee (Fig. 6). The foot is placed firmly on the ribs of the canoe and the toes are pointed diagonally toward the left—not straight ahead. The foot is placed comfortably more to the right in the canoe than is the left knee. This gives a firm triangular base consisting of the left knee, the left toes, and the right foot. Pointing the toes of the right foot diagonally across the canoe rotates the right leg, partially locking the right knee, and thus reducing to a minimum any hinge action at the knee. This lessens undesirable body motion and promotes smoother paddling.

The position of the right foot is of additional importance. Generally its location will be approximately over the keel. Pressure will be exerted by heel and toe, with the emphasis on one or the other as need be, to control and stabilize the position.

Canoes of the type shown in the accompanying illustrations have straight keel lines. They have little or no rocker to the bottom, thus biting down into the water relatively from stem to stern. This means that the canoe holds a straight course nicely and therefore does not turn easily or move sideward easily if it has a conventional keel.

Bends in a river are therefore negotiated by heeling the canoe to the side opposite the direction of the bend. This is done, without stopping paddling or changing the position of the knee, simply by moving the forward foot from its normal position to a position nearer the side of the canoe.

There is sometimes a question as to whether the paddler should kneel close to the side of the canoe or close to the centerline. If you are comfortably close to the side, paddling is easier. On the other hand, the canoe goes faster if it is riding on its normal lines rather than being heeled over very much. Obviously, a compromise position will enable the paddler to be near enough to the side to paddle efficiently and yet keep the canoe nearly on its best lines. This will result in only a little heeling in a narrow canoe and somewhat more in a wider one.

Standing Position.—Although not recommended for novices, the standing position of paddling is useful and reasonably efficient under some circumstances. It is a good relief form on long cruises, may be used for the purpose of looking farther

FIG. 8—The standing position for paddling.

ahead when approaching shallow rapid water, or simply for the fun of adding to the stock of canoeing skills.

Note in Fig. 8 that both feet are on the keel line—probably so that the *arch* of the forward foot is directly over the keel, while the *heel* of the other is directly over the keel. The back leg presses against the thwart. Under some conditions the forward leg would press against a thwart instead, depending upon the desired trim and such factors as amount and position of duffel or the position of another person, either passenger or paddling partner.

TWO-MAN (TANDEM) POSITIONS FOR PADDLING

When two people paddle together in a canoe, they are spoken of as a tandem crew, or as paddling in tandem. The forms of kneeling are the same as those used for solo paddling, but the locations of the paddlers are different.

FIG. 9—Tandem cruising position.

The typical and conventional tandem cruising position is that in which the sternman is located at the stern thwart and the bowman at the bow thwart (Fig. 9). A less common but excellent position, especially for rough water, is the so-called *heavy-weather position* (Fig. 10). In this position, the paddlers turn the canoe around using the stern as the bow so that they can position themselves closer together by having the bowman use the amidships thwart and the sternman the bow thwart.

This arrangement requires the offset amidships thwart. With both paddlers nearer the middle of the canoe, its ends rise more easily when encountering waves, thus lessening to a great degree the risk of shipping too much water when paddling in rough weather.

FIG. 10—Tandem heavy-weather position.

FIG. 11—Father and son. This is the same arrangement as the heavy-weather position. It places the teacher and pupil close together for instruction and safety. The boy wears the lifejacket until his swimming ability is adequate to permit him to discard it. Meanwhile he learns to paddle the canoe.

The heavy-weather positioning of a tandem crew is also excellent when an experienced adult wishes to teach a child how to paddle (Fig. 11). It places the adult and the child close together, which is good from the standpoint of safety and for coaching. It also provides best trim of the craft. If the child is deficient in swimming ability, he should wear a lifejacket until he has learned to swim well enough to be at home in the water.

When a canoe does not have the offset amidships thwart arrangement, the *upright kneeling position* (Fig. 12) is good

FIG. 12—A tandem crew using the upright kneeling position. This method of paddling is easier to learn than the high kneeling position, allows easy fore-and-aft adjustment of locations in the canoe without much consideration to thwart location and allows greater power application than the normal cruising positions. It is excellent for paddling into a strong headwind.

for tandem paddling in heavy weather because it does not involve the use of a thwart. This is true also of the *high kneeling position* (Fig. 13).

In tandem, the high kneeling (racing) position is fundamentally the same as for solo paddling (Figs. 5, 6, 7). The added factor is to position yourself in the canoe with consideration for your partner. Since the two paddlers will counterbalance each other, each may kneel closer to the side of the canoe. The difference in weights will determine how close each may kneel to the side and still maintain even trim to the craft from side to side. It is customary for the two to kneel closer together in the canoe when using this position. The experience of racing crews has indicated the superiority of this.

FIG. 13—A tandem crew using the high kneeling, or racing, position.

The position of both should also be such that the canoe trims even fore and aft. This can be achieved by slight adjustments after the approximate positions have been taken. It will be necessary to have a third person, on the pier or shore, to accurately estimate trim. If this is not possible or practicable, one may tell how the trim is by the feel of the craft under way at a little more than moderate speed. If too heavy in the bow, usually the canoe will steer with some difficulty and will plow water, pushing out a bow wave. If the craft is too heavy astern, the bow will rise noticeably more than it should when speed is attained, and there will be an actual "feel" of the stern dragging too deep in the water.

POSITIONS WITH PASSENGER

A typical passenger-paddler combination is that of the fisherman and his paddler. When the fisherman is trolling (Fig. 14), he should sit in the bottom of the canoe using the forward thwart for a backrest, with a cushion under him and another

FIG. 14—Position of paddler and fisherman when trolling.

at his back if he desires. His paddler has both knees on the canoe bottom. Since this arrangement is stable, there is no danger of capsizing during the excitement of catching a fish. When the fisherman is casting (Fig. 15), it is customary and safer for him to face forward and take a kneeling position. In quiet water areas he may at times sit on the seat or thwart for greater comfort. The novice should not do this, however, without keeping in mind the risk of falling overboard or capsizing. If he catches a fish, the fisherman should drop back to a kneeling position for greater stability.

FIG. 15—Position of paddler and fisherman when casting.

FIG. 16—A typical paddler-passenger arrangement, when the paddler is not greatly heavier than the passenger.

FIG. 17—Passenger-paddler locations that give reasonably good trim to the canoe when there is a great difference between their weights.

FIG. 18—Passenger-paddler arrangement achieving good trim and keeping the occupants close together.

When fishing is not involved, the passenger always sits in the bottom. Usually the passenger uses the bow thwart for a backrest, using cushions if desired. The paddler is located at the stern thwart (Fig. 16).

A way to arrange the positions of paddler and passenger when there is a great difference between their weights is shown in Fig. 17. The paddler uses the stern end as the bow so that he may kneel on the amidships side of the bow thwart and so that the passenger may sit forward of the offset amidships thwart. This keeps the canoe on reasonably good trim fore and aft in spite of the extreme difference between weights.

When the weight difference is not so great, or when an adult has two children for passengers (Fig. 18), the paddler may use the bow thwart and have the passenger(s) sit facing him at the amidships side of the offset amidships thwart. Reasonably good trim results, and the occupants are able to remain close together.

In general the principle is to arrange paddler and passenger so that the canoe trims well. Since there is not space to illustrate all possible arrangements, follow the principle for best results. For example, some canoes with a center thwart located dead center have two quarter thwarts equidistant from the center thwart. The arrangement indicated in such a case would be to have the paddler use one of these thwarts, facing amidships. The passenger would sit in the bottom facing amidships, using the other quarter thwart for a backrest.

When There Are Three in a Canoe.—The placing of the occupants when there are three people in a canoe follows the same principle of maintaining good trim of the canoe. If the third person is a passenger, he should sit in the bottom near amidships (Fig. 19). A cushion to sit on and one for a backrest is customary.

Under some conditions, such as when the wind makes paddling difficult and there is a long way to go, it may be wise for all three to paddle (Fig. 20). The bowman and the man in the center both paddle on the same side, the sternman on the opposite side. The canoe may be trimmed well and paddled efficiently in this way.

FIG. 19—Tandem crew with passenger properly located.

FIG. 20—Three-man crew. It is often advisable for all three to paddle rather than for one to be a passenger.

EXCHANGING POSITIONS IN THE CANOE

Exchanging positions in a canoe while afloat is not dangerous if safe methods are used. Exchange of positions is often desired to give paddling experience in both positions and to provide relief.

The change is done in the following manner: The bowman

FIG. 21—Exchanging positions in canoe, the sternman moves forward to the bow position.

stows his paddle in the bow, or places it amidships if it is a favorite paddle and he wishes to use it when he has changed to the stern position. The sternman keeps his paddle in the water for control and stability. The bowman then places his hands on the gunwales and rises to a crouched position, feet close together over the keel, and then steps backward over the bow thwart to take a seated position in the bottom amidships, with hands on the gunwales. The seated position should be slightly toward one side to leave room for the sternman to step by him. He should also be prepared to drop one hand off the gunwale when the sternman steps by him. When the bowman has reached this position, the sternman stows his paddle or places it in the canoe amidships if he is to use it in the bow. In the latter case the bowman should relay it along to the bow. The sternman then places both hands on the gunwales, rises to a crouched position, and walks forward on the median line of the canoe, keeping his hands on the gunwales at all times. When he reaches the seated bowman, he steps around him (Fig. 21) and continues on to the bow position where he takes the correct kneeling position, mans his paddle, and gets it promptly into the water for control and stability. When this has been accomplished, the person sitting in the bottom rises and steps backward while keeping contact with the gunwales to take a new position at the stern. When the paddle is manned, the exchange is complete.

Straddling the seated person, rather than stepping around him (Fig. 22) also works well.

SPECIAL CONSIDERATIONS WHEN THE WIND IS BLOWING

Paddling on quiet smooth water is restful, peaceful, and charming in a way all its own; but it is confining because such water can be found only in certain places or at certain times. If one does much canoeing, he will have to encounter and cope with the force of the wind from time to time. It is harder work, but there is a satisfaction in store for the paddler who uses the force of the wind to his advantage and has success rather than disappointment.

When you are paddling solo and the wind is blowing hard enough to make paddling difficult with the canoe trimmed in the normal manner, you will have to change its trim so that

FIG. 22—The sternman may pass the seated bowman by straddling him just as easily as stepping by him, in some instances. The methods are interchangeable.

FIG. 23—Paddling into the wind, solo. Note that bow is down.

FIG. 24—Paddling downwind, solo. Note that stern is down.

the wind will help you. How you do this will depend upon the direction from which the wind is blowing. When paddling into the wind, have the canoe trimmed heavy at the bow (Fig. 23). When paddling downwind, have the canoe trimmed heavy at the stern (Fig. 24). In other words, the end that is pointing into the wind should be deeper in the water than the other end. The light end as a result is blown downwind, thus keeping the canoe on a straight course. The normal cruising position on both knees (Fig. 24) or on one knee (Fig. 3) is adequate when you're going downwind; but either the high kneeling position (Figs. 5, 6, and 7) or the upright kneeling position (Fig. 4) will be better going into the wind because you can paddle with greater power. When paddling across the wind, locate yourself in the canoe so that it trims in such a way that as the wind blows the light end, the bow turns toward your paddling side. If you do this you will not have to steer, in the usual sense of the term; in other words, the wind will be helping you keep the canoe on a straight course. For example, if you are paddling across the wind and wish to paddle on the downwind side, which is usually the best thing to do, you should move farther aft, thus trimming the canoe so that it is light in the bow (Fig. 25). If, on the other hand, you wish to paddle on the windward side of the canoe when going across

FIG. 25—Going across the wind, solo, paddling on the downwind (leeward) side. Note that bow is high.

the wind, you should move forward of amidships, thus trimming the canoe so that the stern is light (Fig. 26).

If when traveling across the wind, paddling directly amidships, the canoe trimmed even fore and aft, your canoe tends to turn into the wind, it is because the wind has more effect on the stern (riding away from water) than on the bow (knifing into water). This is more noticeable in a canoe that has a relatively straight keel than in canoes with the typical rocker-bottom lines.

FIG. 26—Going across the wind, solo, paddling on the windward side. Note that the stern is high.

The foregoing facts about trimming the craft in the wind are not merely theoretic advantages. They are so functional that they make reasonably comfortable paddling possible in wind conditions that are ordinarily regarded as prohibitively severe. A paddler will discover, however, that as his skill develops he will be able to cope with moderate wind conditions while located at the normal solo paddling position amidships regardless of his heading.

Tandem crew members encountering strong wind should move to positions closer together and hence nearer the amidships portion of the canoe (Fig. 10). In a three-thwart canoe with offset amidships thwart, this means that the sternman turns around and uses the side of the amidships thwart nearest him, while the bowman merely steps back over his thwart, turns around, and uses the other side of it (compare Figs. 9 and 10). The upright kneeling position (Fig. 12) permits making the necessary adjustment without respect to thwart location; so, too, would the utilization of a pack or bedroll (Fig. 2). The high kneeling position (Fig. 13) is superior for those persons experienced in using it, but the position will tire others quickly because it employs normally little-used muscle groups. With the weight of the crew located closer to amidships in this manner, the bow and stern are lightened so that they may rise and fall more easily with the waves, thus avoiding taking on water. Since a tandem crew does not have the same problem of steering that a solo paddler has, their prime concern is lightening up the ends of the craft. It is true that the principles of using the wind to help steer would apply in tandem paddling as well as in solo paddling, but the advantage gained in that respect might be overcome by the risk of shipping water. For example, if the bow of a canoe with tandem crew were made heavy to help steer when paddling into the wind, it would not rise on big waves but would bury in and ship water. Likewise, when going downwind, if the stern is made heavy to help with the steering, there is risk that following waves will put water in over the stern of the canoe. For these reasons it is best that tandem crew members stay close together and in severe wind and wave conditions lighten the bow slightly when heading into the wind and lighten the stern when going downwind. If you're shipping water when heading directly into the waves, set a course at a slight angle to them. At the same time, try to keep the gunwale on the windward side a little higher than the other gunwale. You can tack (zigzag) up to windward in this manner, and downwind also—although the latter is more difficult in most severe conditions. If conditions get very bad, it is best to sit in the bottom and concentrate on keeping the canoe from swamping until the storm blows over or until you have been blown in to shore or within reaching distance of protection from the wind, such as the lee of an island or projecting land. If the canoe should swamp, follow the rescue measures indicated in Chapter VII. They work in the most severe of circumstances.

CHAPTER VI

PADDLING

Handling a canoe with precision is more quickly learned if the art of paddling is broken down into specific components called strokes. Once these strokes are learned, they may be combined and blended as desired or required for smooth and skillful paddling.

THE BOW STROKE

The bow stroke is used to move the canoe ahead. It is the stroke used by the bowman or, in fact, by all paddlers except the sternman, in any size canoe with any number of crewmen when the canoe is being moved directly ahead. The bow stroke is regarded as the foundation stroke upon which all others are built and will therefore be explained in more detail than the others.

One hand grasps the grip of the paddle and the other hand grasps the shaft several inches above the blade. The hands thus placed should not be more than a few inches farther apart than the width of the paddler's shoulders.[1] The bottom arm is extended forward full length, but in a relaxed, not strained, position. The upper arm is bent at the elbow so that the fist is in front of the shoulder, at shoulder height, and the elbow is at shoulder height or lower, as desired. This is the starting position of the stroke (Fig. 1). The blade bites the water as the bottom arm pulls directly backward and the upper arm drives forward from the shoulder. If the elbow of the upper arm is

---

[1]*For some experienced paddlers, the position of the lower hand on the shaft is where the fingers lie when the grip is placed well up into the armpit and the arm allowed to lie straight along the shaft.*

Upper arm bent.

Hands a little more than shoulder width apart.

Lower arm straight.

FIG. 1—Start of the bow stroke.

Upper arm pushes forward and across the front of the body.

Lower arm pulls

Start

Midpoint

FIG. 2—Midpoint of the bow stroke.

not at approximately shoulder height initially, it must be raised
as soon as the stroke begins in order to get the maximum
power with that arm. The upper arm is expected to do fully
as much work as the bottom arm; and for a long time, until
the muscles involved are built up, the paddler will think it is
doing more. The movement of the upper arm must be so
directed that it will not only exert steady power but will permit paddling close to the side of the canoe. Its drive is therefore diagonally forward (Fig. 2), ending when the arm is fully
extended and out over the water (Fig. 3). The bottom arm
pulls backward until the hand is at, but not beyond, the hip
or thigh (Fig. 3). The effective-power interval of the stroke
is from the forward position to a little beyond the vertical
position of the blade. This is the reason for stopping the stroke
when the bottom hand is at the hip. There is no need to be
precise about this, for the stopping point comes naturally to
most persons. Carrying the stroke farther aft is more unnatu-
ral, but sometimes deliberately done with the belief that it
improves the stroke. It must be remembered that in paddling,
the paddle is not pulled through the water. Rather, the paddle
bites the water as it is inserted into it—almost as though the
water were a solid—and the canoe is moved to the place where
the paddle grips the water. It can be seen, then, that if power
is exerted when the blade is much beyond the vertical, the
canoe will be drawn down into the water, producing a drag
and putting unnecessary movement, or bobbing, into the craft.

At the end of the stroke, both arms are relaxed completely,
the top arm dropping as though into the canoe. This action,
aided by the buoyancy of the paddle, will cause the blade to rise
promptly but gently to the surface. The recovery is made by
feathering the blade in a wide sweep above the surface of
the water to the starting position. The blade is not exactly flat
during the recovery. Rather, its leading edge is elevated slightly

Upper arm fully extended with hand over water.

Bottom hand stops at hip.

FIG. 3—End of the bow stroke.

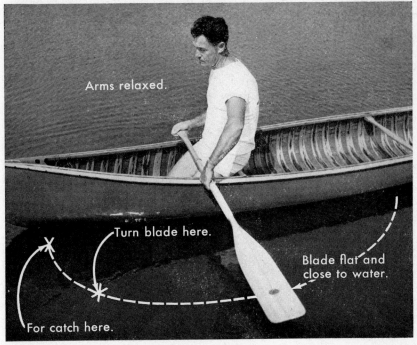

Arms relaxed.

Turn blade here.

Blade flat and close to water.

For catch here.

FIG. 4—Bow stroke recovery.

so that if the blade hits the tip of a wave it will be deflected instead of burying into the water. Furthermore, the recovery should be made close to the water and relatively quickly, with as much relaxation of arm muscles as possible—all essential to smooth, graceful, and sustained paddling (Fig. 4).

No appreciable body motion is necessary with the bent-upper-arm method of paddling described above. Only a slight rotation of trunk and shoulders accompanies the arm action. In paddling, elimination of unnecessary body motion contributes to the desired grace, smoothness, and efficiency.

THE BACKWATER STROKE

The backwater stroke is used to stop headway and to make the canoe go backward. In the first sense it is usually called "holding." The movements involved are in general the reverse of those used in the bow stroke. The backwater stroke starts where the bow stroke finishes. The bottom arm pushes forward while the upper arm pulls backward (Figs. 5 and 6). The recovery

Pull with upper arm.

Push with lower arm.

Fig. 5—Start of backwater stroke.

Fig. 6—Middle portion of backwater stroke.

Fig. 7—End of backwater stroke.

Leading edge up a little.

Blade flat and close to water.

FIG. 8—Recovery of backwater stroke.

is from forward to aft with the blade feathered or not, as the paddler pleases (Figs. 7 and 8). If there is much headway on the canoe, the backwater stroke will be initially merely *holding*. It will not be possible to follow through completely until the canoe has stopped. Once stopped, the canoe will make way astern with repeated backwater strokes. Fig. 9 illustrates how a tandem crew applies backwater strokes for holding or going astern. The curved path of movement for the stroke in the case of both the bowman and the sternman is to keep the canoe pointed straight ahead as it stops or moves astern. This will be clearer after you have read the discussion on the J stroke and on the reverse J stroke. At the start of the backwater stroke, the blade should be held in the water squarely as power is applied. As skill is acquired, however, the paddler will learn

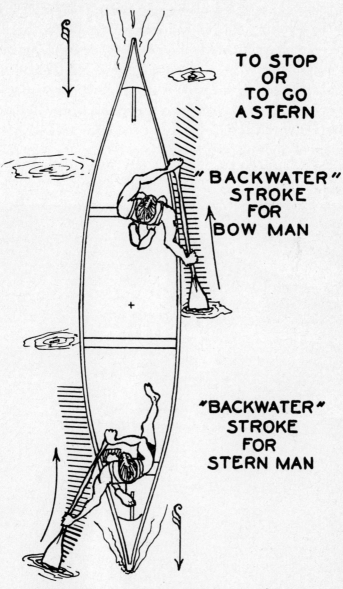

TO STOP
OR
TO GO
ASTERN

"BACKWATER"
STROKE
FOR
BOW MAN

"BACKWATER"
STROKE
FOR
STERN MAN

FIG. 9—Backwater strokes done by a tandem crew.

to modify the stroke by pitching the blade a desired degree in order to check sideward movement as the canoe is brought to a stop by *holding* or is moved astern by repeated backwater strokes. An alternate method of *holding*, or stopping the forward movement, when the canoe is moving relatively slowly, is to slice the paddle into the water slightly forward of your position in the canoe. Then, hold the paddle firmly in the vertical position with the flat surface of the blade faced against the direction of motion. The shaft of the paddle may be held firmly against the gunwale of the canoe to increase the effectiveness of this method of *holding*.

FIG. 10—Start of draw stroke.

THE DRAW STROKE

The primary purpose of the draw stroke is to move the canoe sideward. Its mechanics are fundamentally the same as those of the bow stroke except that it starts abeam rather than ahead and moves at right angles to the canoe rather than parallel to it. The start of the draw stroke is directly abeam of the paddler's position in the canoe (Fig. 10). The draw is directly in toward the paddler, ending about 6 inches away from the side of the canoe (Fig. 11) so that the resulting sideward movement of the canoe will not override the paddle

FIG. 11—End of draw stroke.

blade and jam it under the side of the canoe. Recovery is usually made over the water, as in the bow stroke. Care is given to dropping the upper arm toward the bow at the end of the stroke. This causes the blade to slice smoothly up to the surface of the water. Both arms are relaxed and the blade is feathered, keeping it close to the surface. If desired, however, recovery may be made through the water by turning the blade 90 degrees in either direction and slicing it through the water to the starting position (Fig. 12).

FIG. 12—Draw stroke recovery through water. This is more frequently done over water as in the bow stroke.

The draw stroke may be modified to a diagonal draw of any desired degree. You may wish to move the canoe slightly ahead or astern while moving it sideward. In these cases you would start the draw stroke from forward or aft of the true lateral position. It should, however, normally finish at the paddler's hip as does the regular draw stroke. In moving the canoe diagonally sideward in this manner, reach toward your objective with your paddle. This is a good general rule for determining the starting point of a diagonal draw. The same principle is involved if you are attempting to move the canoe sideward with the draw stroke and a headwind is causing a compromise result—namely a movement that, although sideward, is also diagonally to the rear. You can correct the condition by using a diagonal draw, which starts forward of the starting position of the regular draw stroke. If the wind were blowing from astern, you would make similar adjustments in the opposite direction.

Fig. 13—Doing a pivot turn with draw strokes.

If the wind is from abeam and one end of the canoe swings
while you are moving it sideward with the draw stroke, you
can correct the condition by starting the draw directly abeam
as usual but finishing it forward or aft of your position as
necessary in accordance with whichever end is swinging.

In addition to its function of moving the canoe sideward for
a lone paddler, the draw stroke may be used in tandem paddling by both bowman and sternman to turn the canoe about
(Fig. 13). It may also be used in coordination with the pushover stroke to enable a tandem crew to move the canoe sideward (Fig. 16).

FIG. 14—Pushover stroke; starting position.

PUSHOVER STROKE

The pushover stroke is the opposite of the draw stroke in the same way that the backwater stroke is the opposite of the bow stroke. Its purpose is to move the canoe sideward in the direction opposite the paddler's side. The stroke starts with the paddle blade near or somewhat under the side of the canoe, and the upper arm out over the water (Fig. 14). The push, directly abeam, is exerted with the bottom arm, while the

FIG. 15—Pushover stroke recovery by turning blade and slicing back to starting position. It also can be done over water.

upper arm is pulled in toward the paddler. The bottom-arm action is more powerful if started with the elbow close to the hip bone, and the wrist and forearm lined up straight behind the heel of the hand (Fig. 14). The recovery may be made over water. If so, the blade should be sliced into position from the direction of the stern rather than being dropped vertically into position. Usually it is more efficient to turn the blade 90 de-

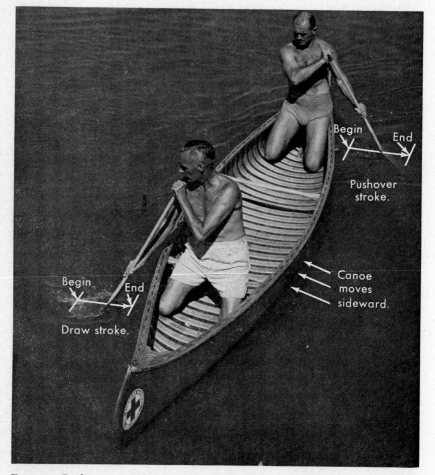

FIG. 16—Pushover and draw strokes coordinated to move canoe sideward; bowman does the draw and the sternman does the pushover. The canoe moves toward the bowman's side, broadside.

grees at the end of the stroke and slice it back through the water to the starting position (Fig. 15). The pushover stroke is often used in tandem handling in coordination with the draw stroke to move the canoe sideward (Fig. 16). A variation of the pushover stroke is done by using the gunwale of the canoe as a fulcrum rather than pushing outward with the bottom arm; it is rougher but effective. As in the case of the draw stroke, the pushover stroke may be modified to a diagonal pushover by pushing out in a direction, or angle, forward or aft of abeam. This may be necessary at times because of conditions of wind or current or when it is desired to move the canoe ahead or astern, while at the same time moving it sideward.

SWEEP STROKES AND REVERSE SWEEPS

Sweep strokes, as the name implies, are wide sweeps of the paddle to swing the canoe for pivot turns or partial turns, to maneuver among obstacles, to follow along the bends of streams or rivers, to effect sudden changes of direction in formation paddling, to aid in holding a straight course in crosswinds, and for general incorporation with other strokes as may be necessary for precise control of the canoe. Reverse sweeps are the opposite of the sweeps and have many of the functions indicated for the sweeps.

Full Sweep.—A full sweep covers an arc of about 180 degrees, from approximately directly ahead to directly astern. It is used by one man paddling from a position at or near amidships. The solo paddler may use the whole full sweep or any portion of it, according to how much he wishes to turn the canoe. When efficiently done, the stroke has a path of movement that is a true arc of a circle beginning at the bow and ending at the stern. The basic arm movements are the same as those used in the bow stroke except that the upper arm pushes out from near the waist rather than from near the shoulder, and the bottom arm swings wide over the water in a broad sweep away from the side of the canoe (Fig. 17). The first 90 degrees of the sweep, from directly ahead to broad on the beam, pushes or swings the bow of the canoe in the direction opposite the paddling side. The second 90 degrees, from broad on the beam to astern, draws or swings the stern toward the paddling side. If the canoe has no forward movement at the outset, it can be turned completely about with several of these strokes without being moved out of its general location on the water; in other words, it will do a pivot turn. In actual practice, this pivot turn may be aided by slacking off on power application during the midpoint of the stroke and emphasizing the first 60 degrees and the last 60 degrees of the arc. This is because the middle 60 degrees will have a slight tend-

Fig. 17—Full sweep and full reverse sweep.

ency to move the canoe ahead as well as swing it. Recovery of
this stroke is the same as the recovery of the bow stroke,
stressing relaxation of arms, blade feathered, and close to the
water, except that the hand on the paddle grip remains at waist
level rather than returning to shoulder level (Fig. 18).

The Reverse Sweep in Solo Paddling.—The reverse sweep
may be done by starting astern and ending ahead for a full
180-degree arc and the direct opposite of the full sweep. The
arm action is similar to that of the backwater stroke except for
the low position of the upper arm and the wide sweep away
from the side of the canoe (Fig. 17). When this type of reverse
sweep is done, recovery is similar to the recovery of the backwater stroke except for the low position of the upper arm

Keep blade flat - leading edge elevated slightly.

FIG. 18—Recovery for full sweep and full reverse sweep.

Fig. 19—Start of inside pivot turn.

Fig. 20—Inside pivot turn continued; turn blade over when it is abeam and complete the reverse sweep.

FIG. 21—Recovery to starting position, for inside pivot turn.

Start on "off" side.

Start

Stop

Jump canoe

FIG. 22—Start of outside pivot turn sequence.

(Fig. 18). If the canoe is turned this way for only a slight number of degrees, the paddler does not need to use all 180 degrees of the arc. He may use only about 90 or less. If his intention is to turn 180 degrees—or for special reasons more than that—he will be doing a pivot turn with his paddle on the inside of the circle. This is often called an *inside pivot turn.* There is a more efficient way to do this inside pivot turn. This is accomplished by doing a succession of reverse sweeps with underwater recovery. The reverse sweep starts near the stern (Fig. 19) and goes to a position approximately abeam. Then the paddle blade is turned over and the reverse sweep completed (Fig. 20). On the recovery, the paddle blade is sliced

FIG. 23—Finish outside pivot turn with full sweep on normal paddling side.

quickly through the water parallel to the canoe back to the
starting position. Smoothness of recovery is enhanced if the
paddle is lifted enough so that none of the shaft is in the water
as the blade is sliced through the water (Fig. 21). The opposite
of the inside pivot turn is an *outside pivot turn*. The paddler
does a cross-bow draw (pp. 200, 202). He does this without
changing the position of his hands on the paddle (Fig. 22). As
part of the same motion, he jumps the paddle blade over the
bow and does a full sweep on his normal paddling side (Figs. 22
and 23). The recovery is done as one continuous movement.
As a substitute for the cross-bow draw, some paddlers like to
use a reverse sweep done by bracing the paddle grip behind the
back (Fig. 24).

FIG. 24—Alternate method of doing the reverse sweep portion.

Sweeps and Reverse Sweeps of 90 Degrees and Less.—In

tandem paddling, sweep strokes and reverse sweeps are done through an arc of 90 degrees or less. The bowman executes a sweep stroke from directly ahead to directly abeam of his own position in the canoe, thus swinging the bow away from his paddling side. He does a reverse sweep from directly abeam of his position to directly ahead—or just opposite, as the name indicates. Fig. 25 shows the bowman doing both strokes. Since the bowman is located forward of the pivotal point of the canoe, any sweep or reverse sweep paddling done outside the quadrant indicated in Fig. 25 will tend to neutralize the stroke by working in the wrong direction. For example, if the bow paddler carries his sweep stroke much beyond the point shown

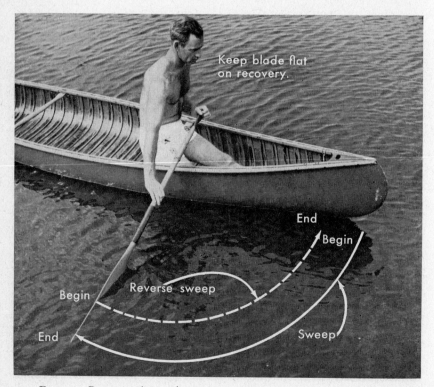

FIG. 25—Bowman doing the sweep stroke and reverse sweep stroke.

in Fig. 25, it will be directed in toward the canoe, thus tending to pull the bow back toward the paddling side.

The sternman's sweep starts abeam of his own position and goes 90 degrees to astern, pulling the stern over to his paddling side. Any sweep starting forward of this will have the negative effect described in relation to the bow sweep stroke, above. The reverse sweep for the sternman starts astern and goes 90 degrees to abeam of the paddler (Fig. 26).

The recovery for these strokes is low, with flat or feathered blade as mentioned for the strokes discussed above.

In tandem paddling, the bowman often uses a sweep of 45 degrees or less as needed to swing the bow slightly or to help keep the canoe on course in a crosswind. This sweep of small degree is usually done at the forward part of the bowman's

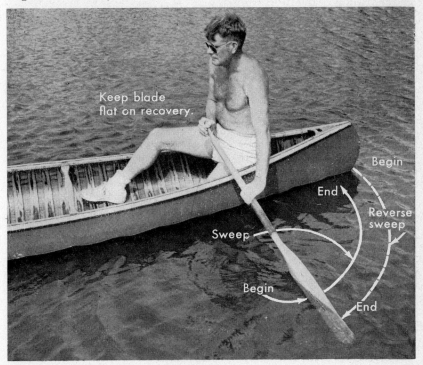

FIG. 26—Sternman doing sweep and reverse sweep strokes.

90-degree quadrant. Sometimes, however, the bowman will not use a sweep in a crosswind, but will resort to what is called "paddling wide." This is merely doing the regular bow stroke out about a foot or more away from the side of the canoe. Usually, there is just a shade of the sweep stroke at the very beginning of it. There is more forward propulsion to this method of holding the canoe on course than using a regular sweep stroke. When under way on a straight course, the sternman also resists crosswind by "paddling wide." When necessary, he adds a sweep of small degree at the very end of the stroke.

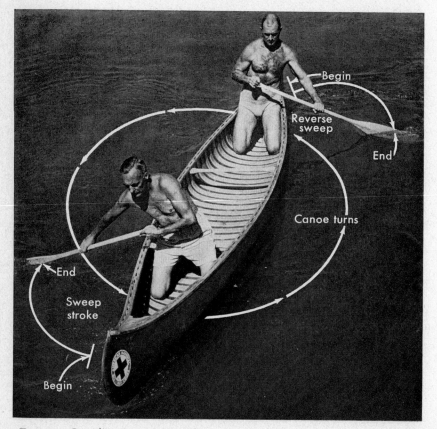

Fig. 27—Coordinating sweep and reverse sweep strokes to do a pivot turn.

When sharper turns are done, the bowman and sternman coordinate sweep strokes and reverse sweep strokes, each using the full 90-degree arc (Fig. 27).

THE J STROKE

The J stroke is used to keep the canoe on a straight course. It is used almost continuously in solo paddling, when going straight ahead, and by the sternman of a crew whenever needed.

The J Stroke in Solo Paddling.—Since it is impossible to paddle directly under the keel of a canoe, a paddling stroke tends to throw the canoe off course in the direction opposite the paddling side under normal conditions of little or no wind or current. It is therefore necessary to do something to offset this and keep the canoe on a straight course. Most beginners solve the problem by paddling first on one side and then on the other or by trailing the paddle astern at the end of each stroke, using it as a rudder. Both of these practices are rela-

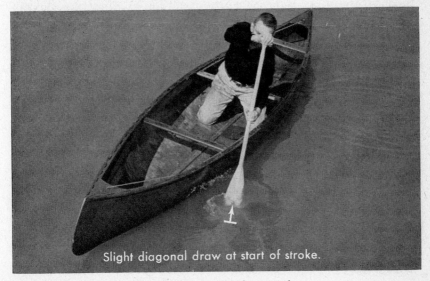

Slight diagonal draw at start of stroke.

FIG. 28—Start of solo J stroke.

tively inefficient. The steering stroke, called the J stroke, is used by experienced canoeists. Doubtless it has been so named because in its unrefined form it actually forms a J when done on the left side of the canoe, and a reflected J when done on the right side of the canoe. Not all skilled paddlers do the J stroke alike in detail; therefore, an effort is made here to acknowledge shades of variation. In general the J stroke may be regarded as a modified bow stroke. In solo paddling the stroke usually starts slightly away from the side of the canoe and proceeds as a diagonal draw of slight degree (Fig. 28). This holds the bow over toward the paddling side. The emphasis on this diagonal draw will depend upon conditions of wind or current; sometimes none will be needed. After the diagonal draw, the stroke is the same as the bow stroke during the forward pulling portion, except that an effort is made to paddle as much under the side of the canoe as is possible (Figs. 29 and 30). A little more than halfway through the stroke, the inside edge of the blade is turned gradually toward the rear to a final angle of about 45 degrees (Fig. 30). This is done by flexing both wrists. Some paddlers start to turn the blade a little before the halfway point of the stroke, others at the halfway point, and some a little more than halfway. Pulling the paddle through the water with the blade at an angle in this manner forces the stern of the canoe to move away from the paddling side, thus helping the initial diagonal draw to hold the canoe on a straight course. Toward the end of the stroke, the shaft of the paddle slides along the gunwale (outwale portion) for a distance of 6 to 10 inches to take the strain of steering off the muscles of the lower arm. When first learning the J stroke, it may be necessary to do a prying action against the gunwale at the very end of the stroke, thus actually doing a J on the left side or a reflected J if on the right side. As skill comes, however, this prying action will gradually lessen and finally be

FIG. 29—Midpoint of J stroke.

FIG. 30—J stroke pattern and recovery.

eliminated if desired. It must be mentioned, though, that some very excellent paddlers do use a prying action of a refined sort when doing the J stroke. Rather than turning the inside edge of the blade toward the rear about halfway and continuing to pull straight back, they wait longer before turning the blade and then turn it more quickly, though smoothly, just before touching the gunwale with the shaft. When the shaft touches the gunwale, the blade is directed diagonally to the rear at about the same degree as the initial diagonal draw at the start of the stroke. A rare number of paddlers have with much perseverance acquired the ability to paddle solo for sustained periods without touching the gunwales. They use the diagonal draw at the beginning, paddle well under the side of the canoe as in the above methods, but at the end of the stroke substitute for the foregoing methods a quick 90-degree flip of the blade, which accomplishes the same results without the need of using the gunwale. Any skilled paddler can employ this method for a limited period, but it tires the lower arm. Whether or not this method is worth the training necessary to enable a paddler to employ it untiringly for long periods is debatable.

At the end of the stroke, both hands and arms are relaxed, the upper hand dropping in over the canoe. The blade is rotated back to its normal position so that as it floats up to the surface of the water it lies on it flat. Recovery is made close to the surface of the water, blade nearly flat, the leading edge elevated just a little (Fig. 30) so that if a wave is hit during the recovery the blade will be deflected from it rather than bury into it.

The J Stroke in Tandem Handling.—In tandem paddling, the sternman uses the J stroke as often as necessary to keep the canoe on course. Because he is aft of the pivotal point (center) of the canoe, he does not employ the diagonal draw at the

FIG. 31—Start of J stroke at stern.

FIG. 32—End portion of J stroke.

start of his stroke; but, as in the bow stroke, he makes his catch close to the side of the canoe and exerts pressure directly aft, parallel to the canoe (Fig. 31). From halfway through the stroke to its completion, however, it is done the same as in solo paddling (Fig. 32) with the same possibilities of variation. The recovery likewise is the same relaxed movement described for bow stroke, sweep strokes, and solo J stroke. Similarly, the blade should be kept flat and close to the water during the recovery, with its leading edge elevated slightly (Fig. 33). In view of the fact that the canoe is narrow at the regular stern-man's position, he usually does not need to touch the gunwale when doing the J stroke. This is because his stroke comes closer to the keel line (under the centerline of the canoe) than

Leading edge angled up a little.

Blade flat and close to water.

FIG. 33—J stroke recovery at stern.

in solo paddling and hence is more effective with a minimum of steering movement. Also, when in the normal cruising position on both knees or one knee, his hip is close against the gunwale at this location and he can use pressure against his hip rather than the gunwale when extra steering pressure is needed.

The J Stroke in Crews of More Than Two.—Generally the J stroke for crews of more than two is done with little difference. The customary multiple crews are fours (often called "quads"), nine-man war canoe crews, fifteen-man war canoe crews, and in fact war canoe crews of a variety of numbers. The significant difference in the J stroke done by the sternman of these crews is the frequency with which it is necessary. That of course may depend upon the several factors of trim of craft, teamwork of the paddlers, direction and force of wind and current, and depth of water. Allowing for variables in the other factors, teamwork is probably the most important. The paddler next to the sternman, paddling on the opposite side, helps him steer a straight course. They share the responsibility, often without the exchange of a word. If the canoe starts to "run" (go off course in the direction opposite the sternman's paddling side), the last man on the other side swings it back and holds it on course. He does this by merely "paddling wide," that is, paddling farther away from the canoe than normal, or in more extreme cases by use of a sweep stroke. The sternman during this time would do a normal J stroke, easing off with it until the canoe could be kept on a straight course with little or no steering pressure to the J stroke, or with the actual substitution of the simple crew stroke (bow stroke). In severe cases on the other hand, when the canoe suddenly "runs" badly and the paddler on the other side cannot hold it on course or bring it back on course, the sternman may have to do very vigorous J strokes. He may even have to do a reverse quarter sweep and hold it at about 30 degrees from the stern, thus doing a stern rudder stroke (see page 202) until the canoe comes back on course. In very severe cases, the paddler on the other side could do a stationary draw (see page 203) to help bring the canoe back on course. These latter considerations are merely theoretic, for ordinarily a well-balanced crew paddles a canoe straight with not much difficulty. However, there is no good reason why the sternman's "helper" should not do a J stroke when the canoe is running severely off course in the opposite direction. In fact, the functions and methods of the two could be interchangeable, as situations demand, especially in war canoes.

BOW RUDDER

The bow rudder moves the bow of the canoe sharply in the direction of the bowman's paddling side. The canoe must be under way with at least moderate speed in still water and faster than the current in moving water, otherwise the reverse sweep, the draw stroke, or the sculling stroke (see page 208) should be employed. The bow rudder is done by placing the paddle blade in the water at an acute angle with the bow, an angle of 20 to 30 degrees initially, perhaps dropped back to an angle that can be held, depending upon the combination of speed at which the canoe is moving and the strength of the paddler (Fig. 34). The blade is in the vertical plane. The lower forearm of the paddler may be braced against the gunwale (Fig. 34), or the shaft and heel of the hand may be braced against the gunwale (Fig. 35), or the bow rudder may be done without contact with the gunwale of the canoe, depending rather upon efficient positioning and strength of arms (Fig. 36). When the bow rudder executed by the bowman is coordinated with a sternman's reverse quarter sweep, maintained at a position of stern rudder (page 202), the canoe moves diagonally sideward (Fig. 34). When it is co-

FIG. 34—The bow rudder, bracing against gunwale with forearm and paddle shaft. Combined with the reverse quarter sweep and stern rudder, it moves canoe diagonally sideward. The bowman's fingers should all encircle the shaft.

ordinated with a sternman's stationary draw (page 203), the canoe does a sharp turn in the direction of the bowman's paddling side.

The bow rudder is sometimes done in solo paddling; when done, it is most efficient in the manner shown in Fig. 37.

Bow turns

FIG. 35—Bow rudder, bracing with heel of hand. Combined with the sternman's stationary draw, it causes the canoe to turn in the direction of the bowman's paddling side. The sternman might in some cases use a series of sweep strokes, or he might use the sculling stroke to turn his end of the canoe.

Bow moves

FIG. 36—The bow rudder done without contact with the gunwales. The bracing is done with the arms and body. For most paddlers, the blade should be closer to the bow of the canoe.

Bow turns

FIG. 37—The bow rudder stroke done in solo paddling is usually done without contact with the gunwales.

THE CROSS-BOW RUDDER

This stroke is the opposite of the bow rudder and likewise depends upon sufficient headway. It moves the bow of the canoe sharply in the direction opposite the bowman's normal paddling side. It is done by swinging the paddle over to the opposite side of the bow and placing the blade in the water in the same manner as for the bow rudder (see above). Hand positions are not changed. The lower forearm may be braced

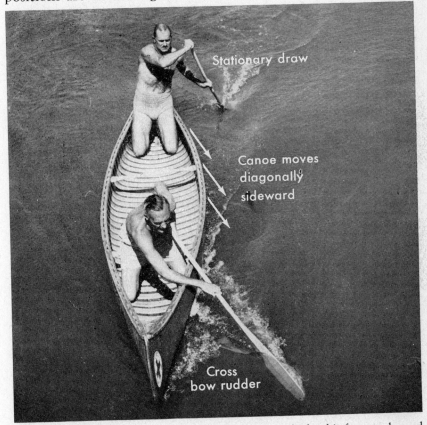

FIG. 38—A cross-bow rudder done by the bowman, who has his forearm braced against the gunwale. The shaft of the paddle is also pressing against the gunwale. Note that because the sternman does a stationary draw stroke in coordination with the cross-bow rudder, the canoe moves diagonally sideward.

against the gunwale (Fig. 38), or the heel of the hand may be braced against the gunwale (Fig. 39), or the stroke may be done without contact with the gunwales (Fig. 40). The upper hand should be at the side of the body above the hip, not in front of the body. In solo paddling also, a cross-bow rudder may be used to swing the canoe sharply in the direction opposite the normal paddling side (Fig. 41).

THE CROSS-BOW DRAW

When the canoe is going ahead slowly or heading downstream at about the same speed as the current, a cross-bow rudder is not very effective. A good substitute is the cross-bow draw, which starts almost the same as the cross-bow rudder by swinging the paddle over to the "off" side without changing hand positions on the paddle—except to slide the bottom hand

FIG. 39—The cross-bow rudder done with the bowman bracing the heel of his hand against the gunwale.

Bow turns

FIG. 40—The cross-bow rudder done without contact with the gunwales.

Bow turns

FIG. 41—The cross-bow rudder done by a solo paddler to turn the canoe sharply in the direction opposite his normal paddling side.

up the shaft a little farther than normal. From this position on the "off" side, a draw stroke or a series of them is done. Often only one is necessary, followed by a quick return to the normal paddling side (Fig. 42). Note that the paddle is not vertical as in a normal draw stroke, but has the blade angled forward so that the paddler's upper hand is below the level of the shoulder and his lower hand is well forward of his body. This gives desirable freedom of movement.

FIG. 42—Bowman doing a cross-bow draw.

THE STERN RUDDER

First of all, the stern rudder is the elementary method of steering a canoe on a straight course. It is done by merely trailing the paddle astern at the end of a stroke, without the turn of the blade characteristic of the J stroke, and by applying the necessary pressure of blade out away from the stern to keep the canoe on course. It is inefficient as a normal method of steering and is hence used only in special situations. For example, it is good to use in a shallow, weedy place, where the normal J stroke would result in weeds getting twisted around the paddle blade. It is also good in shallow, rocky places, where the twisting action of the J stroke might result in a split paddle blade if the blade should catch between two rocks. It is also an accepted method of moving the stern of the canoe sharply in the direction opposite the paddling side to help set it diagonally sideward when the bowman does a bow rudder or stationary draw (Fig. 34) or to help turn it abruptly if the bowman does a cross-bow rudder or stationary pushover. The stern rudder in these cases normally comes at the end of a reverse quarter sweep (Fig. 34).

THE STATIONARY DRAW

The stationary draw is used in solo paddling to move a canoe sideward toward the paddling side while under way without changing its heading. Sideslipping a canoe in this way is particularly advantageous when an obstruction such as a rock, log, or stump is seen too late to alter the canoe's course and steer around it. It is done by holding the paddle, blade in water, vertically about 2 feet away from the canoe more or less and somewhat aft of the paddler's position in the canoe. The forward edge of the blade is turned outward, away from the canoe about 45 degrees, and held there firmly (Fig. 43). Both arms are, of course, held rigidly in place so that the paddle acts as a rudder moving the canoe diagonally sideward. This means the lower arm must exert pressure toward the canoe while the upper arm exerts pressure away from the canoe. The exact location in which to hold the paddle cannot be stated. When it is in the right position, the canoe will move sideward without changing heading. Corrections are easy to make; if the bow moves over faster than the stern, move the paddle a little farther aft until the canoe moves sideward evenly. Rotating the trunk a little more toward the paddling side is an easy way to do this. If the stern is moving over faster than the bow, a correction may be made by moving the paddle forward a little way.

The stationary draw may be done on the "offside" also (Fig. 44). Considerable trunk rotation is necessary in order to get the paddle in the water far enough aft to assure that the canoe will move sideward squarely. The cruising position on both knees gives the most flexibility in this respect.

In tandem paddling, either bowman or sternman may use the

FIG. 43—Stationary draw stroke moves the canoe diagonally sideward to avoid objects directly ahead or for other maneuvering purposes. Theoretically, the paddle should be more vertical than shown here, but this is more typical.

stationary draw to move his end of the canoe diagonally sideward while the canoe is under way. For example, in Fig. 38 the
sternman does a stationary draw in coordination with the bowman's cross-bow rudder to move the canoe diagonally sideward. In Fig. 45 the bowman does a stationary draw in coordination with the sternman's stationary pushover to move the
canoe diagonally sideward. Obviously, the stationary draw is a
good substitute for the bow rudder. The effectiveness of the
stationary draw in any form quickly declines as forward movement slows. If additional sideward movement is needed, the
followup strokes to use are the draw and sculling strokes.

Canoe moves diagonally sideward.

FIG. 44—"Offside" stationary draw. The stationary draw may be done on the
side opposite the paddler's normal paddling side without changing positions
of the hands on the paddle. In this picture, the paddler's normal paddling side
is the left, but he is doing a stationary draw on the right. This stroke is a good
substitute for the stationary pushover in solo paddling.

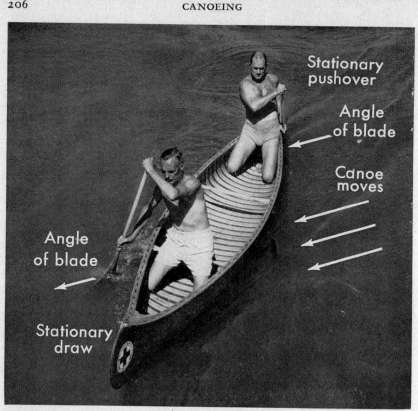

FIG. 45—Coordination of stationary draw and stationary pushover to move the canoe diagonally.

STATIONARY PUSHOVER

The stationary pushover is the opposite of the stationary draw. It moves the canoe diagonally sideward in the direction opposite the paddler's paddling side when the canoe has moderate to considerable headway. When a solo paddler sights an obstruction directly ahead and so close that he cannot safely pass it by altering his course and steering around it, he can sideslip it by using the stationary pushover. Other obstructions sighted farther ahead may influence his decision to use it, since the stationary draw would be normally selected because of its greater adaptability and ease of execution. There are, of course,

Canoe moves

Angle of blade

Fig. 46—The stationary pushover used to move the canoe diagonally sideward.

other maneuvering situations in which a paddler might wish to use the stationary pushover: for example, to move diagonally in alongside a pier.

To perform the stationary pushover, the paddle blade is "cut in" to a vertical position in the water, close to the side of the canoe as for the beginning of the regular pushover stroke. The forward edge of the blade is angled about 45 degrees toward the canoe. The shaft is held firmly against the gunwale (Fig. 46). Both arms are braced rigidly. The paddle in this position acts as a side rudder to move the canoe diagonally sideward in the direction opposite the paddling side. The paddler must brace himself well when doing this stroke, or he may fall overboard or lose his paddle. If the stern moves over faster than the bow, slide the shaft a few inches forward along the gunwale until the condition is corrected.

In tandem paddling, the stationary pushover instead of the cross-bow rudder may be used by the bowman. The sternman may use it instead of the stern rudder as used in Fig. 34. It may also be used in coordination with the stationary draw as shown in Fig. 45.

SCULLING STROKE

The sculling stroke moves the canoe sideward like the draw stroke. It is more efficient than the latter, however, since there is practically no negative phase or recovery interval. To do it, place the paddle blade in the water vertically a comfortable

Press outward with upper arm   Press forward with lower arm

Canoe moves sideward   End   Begin

Fig. 47—The sculling stroke; forward-pressure portion.

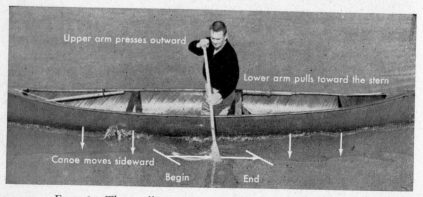

Upper arm presses outward   Lower arm pulls toward the stern

Canoe moves sideward   Begin   End

Fig. 48—The sculling stroke; backward-pressure portion.

distance from the canoe. Move it fore and aft in a path parallel to the canoe. This path should be 2 or 3 feet long. The leading edge of the paddle blade is turned away from the canoe at an angle of from 20 to 45 degrees to the path of the stroke. In detail, as the blade is pressed forward, its forward edge is turned away (Fig. 47), producing a diagonal pressure that moves the canoe sideward in somewhat the same manner that a revolving propeller moves a ship ahead as it screws its way into the water. At the end of the forward pressure, the blade is turned sharply so that the other edge is turned away. Then the paddle is moved toward the stern (Fig. 48) with the same effect of moving the canoe sideward.

If one end of the canoe starts to swing around when you are sculling in solo paddling, do the sculling a little more toward the other end of the canoe to correct the condition. If the wind is causing the canoe to move ahead while it is going sideward, increase the angle of the blade on the forward pressures and the forward movement will be checked. If the canoe is being blown backward while it is being sculled sideward, increase the angle of the blade on the backward pressures to check this condition.

In tandem paddling, the sculling stroke is used by either the bowman or sternman in place of the draw stroke and in place of sweep and reverse sweep combinations in pivot turns (Fig. 49). It is also used in coordination with a reverse sculling stroke to move the canoe sideward (Fig. 50).

Direction
of turn

FIG. 49—Sculling stroke in tandem to do a pivot turn.

FIG. 50—Sculling and reverse sculling strokes coordinated to move canoe sideward.

THE REVERSE SCULLING STROKE

This stroke has the same function as the pushover stroke: that of moving the canoe sideward in the direction opposite the paddling side. The position of the paddle in the water and the path of movement are the same as for the sculling stroke (page 208) with two exceptions: first, the path of movement

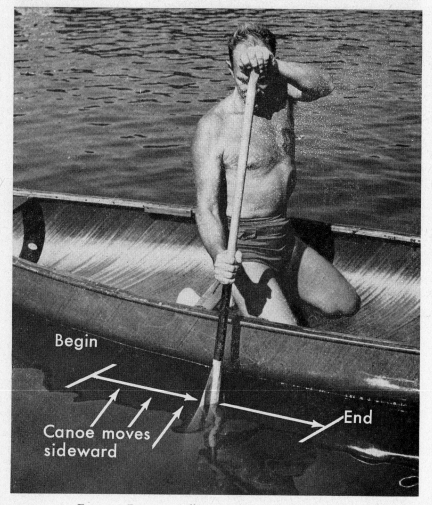

FIG. 51—Reverse sculling stroke, pressing forward.

is closer to the canoe (Figs. 51 and 52); second, the angle of the blade, though the same in degrees, is turned toward the canoe rather than away from it. Power application is opposite to that in the sculling stroke. Modifications to meet or counter-act the force of wind or current follow the same principles applied to these elements when doing the sculling stroke.

FIG. 52—Reverse sculling stroke, pressing to the rear.

REVERSE J STROKE

This stroke is used in solo paddling to keep the canoe on a straight course while paddling it backward. It does not have common use, for canoes are not paddled backward very often. There are times, however, when it is advantageous to do so. For example, if you paddle from open water up a cove or brook for some purpose and find it too narrow to permit turning your canoe around, you can easily back out if you are adept at doing a reverse J stroke. Canoeing instructors sometimes use it when teaching a canoeing class so they can go backward or forward interchangeably and still keep their eyes on the class activity.

To do this stroke, place the paddle blade on the water about as you would for the start of a backwater stroke; usually, it will be necessary to start the stroke out a little farther from the canoe than you would start the backwater stroke. This gives a little diagonal pull at the beginning of the stroke to hold the stern of the canoe in place (Fig. 53). After this initial diagonal phase, continue the stroke as you would a backwater stroke except for an effort to paddle somewhat more under the canoe. About halfway through the stroke, start turning the inside edge of the paddle blade forward by extending both hands at the wrists. This, you will note, is just opposite to what you learned for the J stroke, in which you turned the inside edge of the paddle blade to the rear by flexing both hands at the wrists. Allow the shaft of the paddle to contact the gunwale toward the end of the stroke to provide leverage if necessary (Fig. 54).

There seems to be less use for this stroke in tandem paddling; but when it is used, the bowman does it, leaving off the initial diagonal draw. The sternman would do an ordinary backwater stroke, sometimes combined with an initial diagonal draw or a

FIG. 53—Start of the reverse J stroke.

FIG. 54—Endpoint of the reverse J stroke.

modified reverse sweep, depending upon which was needed. The former would be necessary if the stern were running off course in the direction opposite the sternman's paddling side. Some degree of reverse sweep would be needed if the canoe were running off course toward the sternman's paddling side.

To stop and go ahead, do the obvious; stop the reverse J stroke and start doing the J stroke. If you should need to slip sideward while going backward you can do a stationary draw in reverse (Fig. 55). If you wish to turn sharply, you can hold the paddle firmly in a position of stern rudder in reverse or by

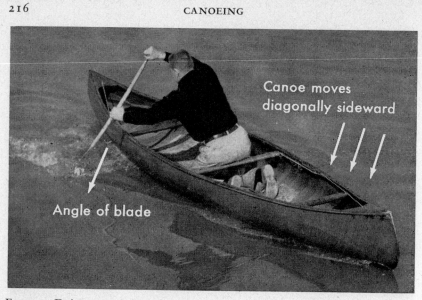

Canoe moves
diagonally sideward

Angle of blade

FIG. 55—Doing a stationary draw in reverse to sideslip while going backward.

Stern turns

FIG. 56—Turning the canoe while going backward.

starting a sweep stroke while the canoe is going to the rear (Fig. 56).

If you are in the high kneeling position, you can back the canoe by rotating your trunk as far in the direction of your paddling side as possible, exchanging hand positions on the paddle, and doing a regular J stroke (Fig. 57).

FIG. 57—Backing the canoe by rotating trunk to side and rear, exchanging hand positions on paddle, and doing a regular J stroke. This is practical only from the high kneeling position.

SILENT PADDLING

Silent paddling is a method of paddling in which the paddle blade remains in the water at all times. It is not an efficient way to paddle except in the case of the sculling stroke and the reverse sculling stroke, which have no significant recovery interval, and of the pushover stroke, where the over-water recovery is more cumbersome than recovery through the water. In other strokes, recovery through the water produces resistance to movement of the canoe through the water and also slows up the recovery. In its refined form, this method of paddling, however, is excellent for silent movement of the canoe through the water, which is sometimes desired by a hunter, photographer, or watcher of wildlife. The greatest degree of quietness in this method of paddling may be assured by remembering three essential things: first, be cautious and go relatively slow; second, keep all of the blade beneath the surface of the water while paddling to eliminate a gurgling noise that may result if part of the blade is above the surface; third, during the recovery movements, be sure that as you lead carefully with the edge of the paddle blade, the shaft is entirely above the surface of the water (reason: the shaft is wider than the narrow edge and may cause just a little noise, especially if the recovery movement is made rather quickly). For holding a straight course, you can use the J stroke by allowing the paddle to rotate in your hands at the end of each stroke to facilitate easy recovery, or you can use the stern-rudder type of steering.

DOUBLE-BLADE PADDLING

Double-blade paddling is superior to single-blade paddling for speed and for control of the canoe on open water, especially when wind and waves are high or the current is strong. The blades are set at right angles to each other so that when one blade is pulling, the other will cut through the wind rather than butt it (Fig. 62). The blades are kept in this position by setscrew-and-notch arrangements at the ferrules that join the two ends of the set of double blades (Fig. 58). The shaft between the two blades should be grasped in both hands, with hands a little more than shoulder-width apart and equidistant from the two blades. One hand is the control hand; that is, its grip is constant with no rotation of the shaft in it. The grip of the other hand is loose, permitting the shaft to make 90-degree rotations in it. If the blades are spoon type, it is necessary that they face in the proper direction in addition to being at right angles to each other. To set them correctly, therefore, partially engage the two halves at the ferrules, face the blade on the control-hand side toward the rear, rotate the other half so that its blade faces upward, then complete the engagement of

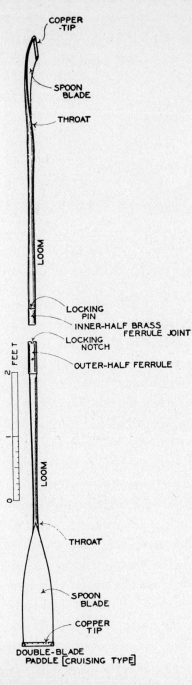

COPPER
-TIP

SPOON
BLADE

THROAT

LOOM

LOCKING
PIN
INNER-HALF BRASS
FERRULE JOINT
LOCKING
NOTCH
OUTER-HALF FERRULE

2 FEET

1

0

LOOM

THROAT

SPOON
BLADE

COPPER
TIP

DOUBLE-BLADE
PADDLE [CRUISING TYPE]

FIG. 58—Ferrules of a set of double-blade paddles, showing the setscrews and notches arranged so that the blades may be set at right angles to each other and in position for either right- or left-handed control.

Fig. 59—Setting a pair of double blades for right-hand control. Note that the right blade faces to the rear, while left blade faces up as the setscrew and notch are engaged.

the two halves locking the setscrew into the notch (Fig. 59). If you have not used double-blade paddles before, assume that your right hand is your control hand for the beginning. If you are not satisfied with the results, experiment with both sides to decide which is easier. The partial rotations, back and forth, mentioned above are necessary to place each blade in turn in position for a square catch. They are done by raising and lowering the control hand at the wrist (Figs. 60 and 61). The strokes are somewhat like sweep strokes rather than being done close to the side of the canoe like most single-blade paddling strokes. At the start of the stroke, the bottom arm is extended full length and the top arm is bent at the elbow so that the fist is in front of the shoulder (Fig. 62). The stroke is done by pushing with the top arm and at the same time pulling with the bottom arm (Fig. 63). When the stroke is complete, the bottom hand will be at the hip and the top arm will be fully extended. The hand at the hip is then simply raised to the position in front of the shoulder and the other arm lowered to the forward extended position for the beginning of the

Fig. 60—Left-hand control; left hand raised sharply on wrist. Right wrist is straight in position for catch.

FIG. 61—Left-hand control paddling: Left hand in position for catch, wrist fairly straight. The right wrist is also straight because shaft rotates in right hand.

FIG. 62—Start of stroke on right side.

FIG. 63—The pull of stroke on right side.

FIG. 64—Ready to catch for stroke on left side.

stroke on the other side (Fig. 64). Power application and rhythm is aided by a slight trunk rotation from side to side and a slight rolling of each shoulder in turn.

In double-blade paddling, spoon blades are regarded as superior to straight blades and, since there is a blade on each side of the canoe, there is less need for a variety of strokes than there is in single-blade paddling. Backwater strokes are neces-

FIG. 65—Backing with double blades.

sary and the draw stroke and sculling strokes may be used at times. A straight course is maintained by pulling equally on both sides under normal conditions. If the canoe is running off course because of adverse weather conditions, strokes on one side may be made stronger than on the other, or the shaft may be extended farther on that side to supply favorable leverage. Turns are made by backing on one side and pulling on the other. Backing is done with the convex surface of the blade (Fig. 65).

The sitting style of double-blade paddling shown in the illustrations in this section is the most efficient method. It re-

FIG. 66—Double-blade paddling, kneeling position.

quires a satisfactory seat (Fig. 67) and some method of bracing the feet, for good leverage depends upon firm foot bracing. One type of foot bracing shows up well in Figs. 62 and 63. Another is included with the seat in Fig 67. On the other hand, adequate double-blade paddling may be done from the normal paddling position (Fig. 66). In this case, it is not necessary to carry along a seat, though it is no trouble if made light. Of course, on a canoe trip, duffel could be used for a seat. When not in use, the two halves of the double-blade set can be tied up in the bow of the canoe (Fig. 68).

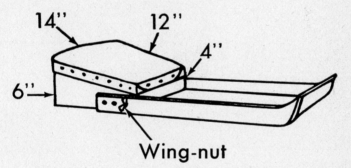

FIG. 67—Double-blade paddling seat. This is an example of a typical home-made one. Canvas is stretched over the frame, doubled under at the edges and nailed as shown. Or it may be more firmly attached with wooden strips screwed on over the doubled canvas in place of the nailing shown. The foot brace, if made detachable, can be used or not, as needed. Note that it has more than one hole so that it may be adjusted according to leg length in the event that it is to be used by more than one person from time to time. The overall length of the brace should be about 36 inches.

Fig. 68—Double-blade paddles secured in the bow; kneeling pad jammed in also. These two halves are tied with rubber bands (rawhide or cord are also used) as shown. The rubber does not loosen as the rawhide and cord will, but deteriorates more quickly.

CHAPTER VII

SELF-RESCUE METHODS

Self-rescue methods should be practiced until they are so well mastered that falling overboard, swamping, or capsizing cease to be emergencies and become instead mere incidents. These methods are, after all, nothing more than ways to handle a canoe and yourself in special situations. All of them are used in one or another novelty event indicating that, although requiring practice, they are not difficult, but actually fun.

SELF-RESCUE IF YOU FALL OVERBOARD

Capsizing and swamping are generally believed to be the only common situations from which the inexperienced canoeist must rescue himself. The truth is that often the canoeist loses his balance and falls overboard without swamping or capsizing the canoe. This is rare among trained canoeists who paddle from kneeling positions, but rather common among the untrained who sit on the seats with their knees elevated.

If you fall overboard, grasp the near gunwale with one hand as you go over the side. Do not allow your body weight to fall upon the gunwale, for doing so will nearly always swamp or capsize the canoe. Your grasp should be firm enough to maintain contact with the canoe; otherwise, it may be blown away by the wind faster than you can swim to recover it. If you lose your grasp on the gunwale when falling overboard, come to the surface, immediately swim to the canoe, and hold onto it for restful support and so that the canoe will not blow away. (If the canoe gets away from you and is being blown away faster than you can swim, swim to shore instead of trying to catch it. Swim slowly and rest frequently to conserve your strength.) If the shore is near, you may use the canoe for support while swimming with one arm and your legs, towing or pushing the canoe to shore (Fig. 1) where you may get back aboard.

Fig. 1—After falling overboard hold onto the canoe for support and so that it will not blow away. If near shore, swim it to shallow water and get back aboard.

If not near shore when you fall overboard, you will have to board the canoe from deep water. At a position where you can reach across the canoe, and yet as near to amidships as possible, grasp the far gunwale with one hand and the near gunwale with the other hand. Get your feet up near the surface of the water and keep them there with a flutter kick (Fig. 2).

With your arms, pull the canoe in under you. Help your arms with a continuous, vigorous flutter kick—or a sharp scissors kick followed by vigorous flutter kicks. Exert pressure downward on the far gunwale by elevating the elbow on that side as soon as possible. Continue to draw the canoe in under you until you reach a position of balance (Fig. 3). Then do a quarter turn or roll backward, and sit in the canoe (Fig. 4).

If the canoe is too wide for you to reach across as described

FIG. 2—Boarding a canoe from deep water, first step; hands in position, flutter kick near surface of the water.

FIG. 3—Boarding a canoe from deep water, second step; in position of balance on the gunwales.

FIG. 4—Boarding a canoe from deep water, third step; do a quarter turn and sit in.

FIG. 5 (left)—Boarding: Grasp the thwart with one hand more than halfway across the canoe, and the other hand on the near gunwale. With flutter kick and pull of arms, pull up to a position where you feel that most of your weight is on the thwart.

FIG. 6 (right)—Move the hand that is on the near gunwale over to the far gunwale.

in Fig. 2, it will be easier to board the canoe with the aid
of a thwart. To do this, grasp the thwart with one hand just
beyond amidships (more than halfway across the canoe) and
hold the near gunwale with the other hand. Do a flutter kick
and pull with both arms, pulling the canoe in under you until
you feel that your weight is supported mostly on the thwart
(Fig. 5). Move the hand that is on the near gunwale over to
the far gunwale (Fig. 6). Then move the hand on the thwart
down to the near gunwale and, with the strength of both arms

FIG. 7 (left)—Boarding: The hand that was on the thwart has been moved
down to the near gunwale and with leg kick and arm pull a position of balance is achieved.

FIG. 8 (right)—Do a quarter turn and sit in.

and a vigorous flutter kick, move up into a position of balance
on the gunwales (Fig. 7). Now do a quarter turn and sit in
(Fig. 8).

Another alternate method of boarding a canoe is a quick-
lunge method done at amidships. Grasp the near gunwale with
both hands, shoulder-width apart. Keep arms straight and
maintain your body at the surface by employing a flutter kick
(Fig. 9). Pull sharply with your arms and at the same time do
a vigorous scissors kick. With one arm, reach for the far gunwale, grasp it, and elevate that elbow immediately. Follow the

FIG. 9—Boarding with quick-lunge method; arms straight, body and legs up at the surface of the water.

FIG. 10—With pull of arms and vigorous scissors kick, lunge up over the canoe to position of balance.

scissors kick with rapid flutter kicks if necessary to reach the balanced position (Fig. 10). Then do a quarter turn and sit into the bottom of the canoe.

Still another method, one to try if you have difficulty with the others, is done as follows: Place your hands in the bilge (Fig. 11), press on them, and do a continuous flutter kick until you have pressed the canoe in under you (Fig. 12). Keep your head low, and when it is over near or against the far side, depending on your size, roll over to a sitting position (Fig. 13).

In tandem paddling, if both persons should fall overboard, boarding would be fundamentally the same except that one person could stabilize the canoe from the opposite side while

FIG. 11—Boarding: Place your hands in the bilge area of the canoe.

the other climbed aboard (Fig. 14). The person aboard could then sit in the bottom and stabilize the canoe while the other boarded in the same manner as shown in Chapter VIII in "Rescue of a Tired Swimmer."

GOING OVERBOARD

Going overboard from the canoe into deep water is a skill needed to practice getting back into a canoe from deep water. Knowing how to go overboard may be needed also by a canoeist who desires to go swimming. Sometimes the nature of the shore

FIG. 12—Boarding: Press on your hands and kick your legs until the canoe is under you.

is not suitable for making a landing, or the bottom near shore is unsuitable for swimming activity. In these cases, a canoeist often elects to swim farther out. When he does this, he loops the bow painter around his shoulder after he is in the water, towing the canoe while swimming, thus keeping his "life preserver," or "buddy," with him for instant use.

The first step in going overboard is to stand in the canoe with feet close together over the keel or centerline of the

FIG. 13—Boarding: Roll over to a sitting position.

canoe, grasping the gunwales (Fig. 15). With your weight supported by your arms, lift your legs over the side and separate them like a pair of scissors as they clear the side and start downward into the water (Fig. 16). When you enter the water, close the widely separated legs with a vigorous scissors kick to check momentum. The hand that was on the far gunwale transfers to the near gunwale (Fig. 17). The other hand and arm slap down on the surface of the water laterally and begin sculling to help the legs check the downward rush of the

Fig. 14—When two persons fall overboard, one helps stabilize the canoe while the other climbs aboard.

FIG. 15—First step in vaulting overboard into deep water; taking position.

body into the water. Entry into water has been made without losing contact with the canoe or submerging your head (Fig. 18). That is why vaulting overboard is preferred to diving overboard. If diving overboard is done, contact with the canoe is lost. In a breeze this would be dangerous because the canoe might be blown away faster than the canoeist could swim to recover it. Diving out is therefore discouraged as a general practice. If it is done with forethought, the dive should be made to leeward. If it is desired to go overboard quietly, simply reverse the steps followed when boarding.

FIG. 16—Start of the vault overboard into deep water.

FIG. 17—Checking downward momentum with vigorous scissors kick.

FIG. 18—Going overboard is accomplished without losing contact with the canoe.

HAND-PADDLING A CANOE

If you lose your paddle overboard and haven't a spare aboard, sit or kneel low on the bottom and use one hand and forearm as a paddle. In this manner, you will be able to maneuver your canoe slowly but surely into position to pick up your lost paddle, or to get back to shore if the paddle cannot be recovered or is broken in such a way as to be useless (Fig. 19). Be sure to use all your forearm as well as your hand to get added power. Positioning yourself properly to make maximum use of the wind is also important.

FIG. 19—Hand-paddling a canoe; use forearm as well as hand.

SELF-RESCUE IN THE EVENT OF CAPSIZING

When a canoe capsizes, stay with it. Use its buoyancy for support. If you're near shore, push or tow the canoe to shore by swimming with one hand and your legs. Rest as often as necessary. If shore is rather far away, roll the canoe over, get in it, and hand-paddle it to shore. If you are a skilled swimmer, it will be easy for you to learn how to empty the canoe with the shakeout technique; then you can board it, pick up floating gear, and continue your trip. If you are far from shore and help is coming, just hold on gently to the canoe until help arrives or roll it over and sit in it, which will be more restful.

The above represents a variety of ways in which self-rescue may be carried out in the event of a canoe's capsizing. They will be described in more detail below.

Swimming a Capsized Canoe to Shore.—When a capsizing takes place rather near to shore, the simplest method of self-rescue is to hold onto the bottom of the canoe with one hand and swim with your other hand and legs (Figs. 20 and 21). Take your time; rest as often as necessary. It is important not to climb on the canoe but to use it as a life preserver aiding your body's normal buoyancy. Keep your body down in the water, with just your head and one arm above the surface (Fig. 20). When there are two of you, hold onto the canoe from opposite sides (Fig. 21).

Fig. 20—Self-rescue with a capsized canoe near shore. Hold on and swim the canoe to shallow water or shore.

FIG. 21—Tandem crew using capsized canoe for self-rescue.

Boarding and Hand-Paddling or Paddling a Swamped Canoe.—When a canoe is capsized or swamped far from shore, the safest and least tiring procedure when help is not near is to get in it and paddle or hand-paddle it to shore. If it is capsized

FIG. 22—First step in boarding a swamped canoe; hands over centerline, legs kicking.

(bottom-up) take a position near amidships, reach across and grasp the far gunwale and slowly roll the canoe over to the swamped position. To board it, place both your hands inside on the bottom over the keel (centerline) (Fig. 22). Raise your legs to a position near the surface of the water and keep them there with a flutter kick. Press on your hands, kick with your feet, and half draw and half swim your way in over the canoe until your chin is over the far gunwale (Fig. 23). Keep as much of your body as possible in the water. Roll over on the back of your neck, spreading your arms along one gunwale and resting your legs in an extended position over the opposite

FIG. 23—Press and kick your way in over the canoe.

gunwale, producing an outrigger type of balance (Fig. 24).
This checks any tendency of the canoe to roll. Sit down in the
bottom and pivot around to a position where both legs are
under the amidships thwart, with the thighs (just above the
knees) pressing firmly up against the thwart near each gunwale (Fig. 25). The arms and hands may be extended sideways
and sculling done as necessary to maintain stability until you

FIG. 24—Roll over, with arms and back of neck on one gunwale, legs on the
other.

are adjusted to a comfortable position. You may then hand-paddle the canoe to shore (Fig. 25), or paddle to shore using the canoe paddle.

If the water is rough and large waves are pounding the shore, get out of the canoe as you get to shallow water or near shore, and hold onto the offshore end so that the canoe will be carried in ahead of you and not be thrown hard against you—which may cause you to be injured by rocks, gravel, or other under-water hazards. Although a metal canoe does not float due to in-herent buoyancy (as is the case with wooden canoes and wood-

Fig. 25—Pivot to sitting position and hand-paddle to shallow water or shore.

and-canvas canoes), it nevertheless *does* float (Fig. 26) because it has buoyancy chambers built into it. These in some cases are airtight compartments located at the ends of the canoe. In other cases, these compartments are not airtight but contain buoyant material, usually of plastic foam. The latter, of course, is more reliable because with it buoyancy of the canoe depends upon the buoyancy of this special material rather than upon the watertight integrity of air tanks.

Fig. 26—Self-rescue with a swamped metal canoe.

It will help your understanding of this particular self-rescue skill to bear in mind that the canoe remains afloat at the surface of the water—even when filled with water—because of its buoyancy, whether natural or artificial. Occasionally, the casual observer will think that because a canoe is upright and filled with water, it should consequently sink even though it has remained afloat when in the bottom-up position (capsized). This is because he has failed to realize that the canoe (wooden canoe) floats because the bulk of the materials of which it is made floats just as a log of wood or any material made of normal types of wood will float. The shape or form of the wooden object does not affect its floating qualities.

Another important consideration in understanding self-rescue in these situations is that the human body is also buoyant. It is supported by the water to the extent that the average person can remain motionless at the surface of the water simply by extending his head backward as far as possible to keep his face clear of the water. This is known as a vertical float. A canoe, even though swamped, has only to hold up the parts of

FIG. 27—Swamped canvas-covered canoe supporting three large men.

the body above the surface of the water, not the entire weight of the person using the canoe for self-rescue. This is why it is possible for it to support as many people as can comfortably get into a swamped canoe (Fig. 27).

EMPTYING A SWAMPED CANOE IN DEEP WATER

An advanced method of self-rescue is to empty the swamped canoe while in deep water. The simplest way to do this is to lie low in the canoe with only your face above water. Do a vigorous flutter kick, splashing the water out of the canoe until the freeboard gradually increases enough to allow you to sit without submerging the gunwales. The remainder of the water you may dispose of by bailing with your cupped hands, your shoe, or hat.

The Shakeout.—This is the most efficient method of emptying a swamped canoe. It is primarily a swimming skill rather than a canoeing skill. It should be deemphasized until other skills are mastered, because it is rarely needed.

After rolling the canoe to the rightside-up position, move to one end and face the length of the canoe. Force the end down into the water so that it is completely but shallowly under water. A vigorous thrust forward, arm's length, will cause about one third to one half of the water to come out

Fig. 28—The end thrust; first step in the shakeout method of emptying a canoe in deep water.

over the submerged end (see Fig. 28). Keep a firm grip on the end and raise it abruptly at the moment the water ceases to run out over the end; otherwise, much of it will be taken back in again. If the canoe is large and heavy, it may be necessary to stroke with one arm and the legs to accomplish the thrust. One or two more thrusts may be used if necessary. Hold the end firmly until the surge created by the thrust has quieted, then move to midships and grasp the gunwale with both hands, shoulder-width apart, with thumbs on the outside. Now begins the shakeout. Lower the near gunwale close to the water, leaving an inch or less of freeboard. Thrust directly forward from your shoulders to start the water surging from side to side.

Coordinate your leg kicks with your arm thrusts so that you do not hang onto the canoe. Do not pull the near gunwale under water. The scissors kick is most effective unless you happen to have an unusually strong breast-stroke kick. Time your thrusts with the surge of the water toward you so that the water will come out over the gunwale rather than hitting the freeboard and bouncing back into the canoe. The near gunwale will rise 2 or 3 inches between thrusts, but be sure that the far gunwale is always higher, so that there will be less depression of the near gunwale necessary before the thrust. This will help your timing. Constantly watch the surging water in order to establish the best timing.

It will be necessary to regulate your breathing so that exhalation takes place as the oncoming water clears the gunwale into your face. Timing rather than strength is the key factor in the whole operation. Many skilled persons can do the shakeout easily with one hand if the canoe is not too large. Your final

FIG. 29—The side thrust; the actual shakeout.

thrusts will have to be more vigorous to get out the last bit of water and make a thorough job of it (see Fig. 29).

When the canoe has been emptied, board it as described earlier in this chapter. Floating paddles and other gear may then be picked up. Hand-paddling may be resorted to in the event all paddles are adrift.

Though not necessary to know, the shakeout may eliminate long or harmful exposure if a capsizing occurs when the water is very cold.

The metal canoe will present the problem of modifying some of the procedures outlined in this chapter. The owner of a metal canoe should follow the recommendations of this chapter and find out where modifications are necessary.

EMPTYING A CANOE AT SHORE OR DOCK

Emptying a canoe at shore or dock may be difficult and may also damage the canoe unless you use suitable methods, some of which are described and illustrated in this section. Situations encountered that differ from these may be handled by applying ingenuity to the principles set forth here.

Emptying a Canoe in Shallow Water.—This should be done by lifting the canoe by its ends (Fig. 30). If it is bottom-up, it should be rolled sideward as the lift begins. This breaks the suction and makes the lift easier. If the canoe is in the swamped position initially, it should be rolled sideward before beginning the lift so that the canoe is lifted out of the water without lifting any of the water. When it is empty, it can be set down on the water or carried ashore as desired.

To empty the canoe in shallow water by yourself, move it in parallel to shore in about 18 inches of water. Stand on the offshore side and roll the inshore gunwale toward you, gently lifting the canoe out of the water. Continue to lift, with one shoulder under the gunwale if necessary, leaning backward so

FIG. 30—Two men emptying a canoe in shallow water.

that the strain on your back muscles will be less, until the canoe is entirely free of the water. Then rest the lower gunwale on one knee and set the canoe back on the water (Fig. 31).

One person may also empty a canoe in shallow water by getting in under it in water of about thigh-depth and lifting it clear of the water with back and shoulders and then turning it over and upright onto the water.

FIG. 31—After emptying the canoe alone, rest the lower gunwale on one knee and place the canoe upright onto the water.

Another method of emptying a canoe alone at shore is to
float the swamped canoe in to shore until one end touches bottom at the water's edge. If the end in deeper water is depressed
a little, the other end will go farther up onto the beach. Grasp
the deepwater end and slowly, without any lift, roll the canoe
over on its side. Then lift the canoe slowly so that the water
will run out. Or more accurately: lift the canoe out of the
water without lifting any water, so that only the end of the

FIG. 32—Emptying a canoe by lifting the deepwater end clear of the water
while the other end is on the beach or in very shallow water.

canoe is touching on shore (Fig. 32). When all the water has
drained out, roll the canoe upright and set it down on the
water.

Emptying a Canoe at a Dock.—If a canoe is to be emptied
at a dock, it may be done by following the principles of
emptying it over another canoe (see Chapter VIII). With the
canoe in the rightside-up position, lift one end slowly and
gently so that the canoe will slide out of the water without
lifting any water (Fig. 33). Bring the end in over the dock,
at which point a partner can help (Fig. 34). When the end is
in over the dock not more than 3 or 4 feet, roll the canoe over

FIG. 33—Emptying canoe at a dock. Lift slowly and gently.

FIG. 34—Lift the end in over the dock a few feet.

(Fig. 35) and continue hauling in until the canoe is in the balanced position (Fig. 36). It can then be turned upright and carried away or carried in its present position to a place where it can be set down on the dock or on a rack. Or it can be launched.

FIG. 35—Roll the canoe over and continue hauling it in, keeping it from bumping the dock at any time.

FIG. 36—Haul the canoe in until it is in a balanced position.

FIG. 37—Grasp the far gunwale and roll the canoe toward you.

Another good way to empty a canoe at a dock is to grasp the far gunwale near amidships as the swamped canoe lies alongside the dock and gently roll it toward you (Fig. 37). Then stand up and lift the canoe just enough to let the end of the bow and the end of the stern overlap the edge of the dock (Fig. 38). Finally, resume rolling the canoe toward you until it is out of the water and up on the dock (Fig. 39). Continue the roll until the canoe rests on the near gunwale and its ends, and the job is done.

FIG. 38—Ends of the canoe overlapping the dock.

FIG. 39—Rolling the canoe up onto the dock.

Aluminum canoes with buoyancy chambers in their ends may be easily emptied at a dock by lifting one end of the canoe (Fig. 40), gradually rolling it bottom-up so that it is empty and supported on the water by the buoyancy chamber in its other end (Fig. 41). By keeping the near end high, the canoe may be rolled upright without taking in any water.

FIG. 40—Emptying an aluminum canoe at a dock.

FIG. 41—Emptying an aluminum canoe at a dock. The buoyancy chamber in the end of the canoe supports it in this position.

CHAPTER VIII

RESCUE OF OTHERS

A canoe is not essentially a rescue craft. Except in the hands of a skilled canoeist, it is somewhat sensitive and unstable for general rescue purposes. A boat is the proper craft for rescue in most instances. In some cases, however, a drowning person far from shore may be reached more quickly by a canoe manned by a skillful paddler. Of course, when a canoe is the only craft on hand in an emergency, the rescue should be undertaken by anyone sufficiently skilled to protect himself. As the canoeist's skill in paddling and self-rescue develops, he should gradually develop his competence to help or rescue others. Through experience have come ways of doing these things that are efficient, adaptable, and not difficult to learn.

A TIRED SWIMMER

Keep your eyes on a swimmer who is too far from shore. If he gets tired, go alongside and offer help. It is better to turn broadside to him and extend your paddle (Fig. 1), rather than to come all the way in head-on and let the tired swimmer hold onto the bow—where he will be out of your reach. Then you have him at the widest part of the canoe, where you can control him and the canoe (Fig. 2). Note that in Fig. 1 and Fig. 2 the canoeist remains on his knees while extending the paddle to the tired swimmer and while talking to him as he holds onto the gunwale for rest. The canoeist is relying heavily on the use of the paddle to stabilize the canoe. It may be wiser for most paddlers to sit down in the bottom of the canoe before making contact with the tired swimmer so that they would be ready to brace against any unexpected attempt of an excited tired

swimmer to climb aboard before being told to do so (Fig. 4).
Placing a hand on the victim's shoulder will keep him from
boarding before he is instructed to do so.

In many instances it is only necessary to allow the tired
swimmer to hold onto the gunwale for a brief period of rest
and then accompany him while he swims to shore. In some
cases it may be wise to give him a tow; that is, paddle the canoe

FIG. 1—Extending the paddle to a tired swimmer.

to shore while the tired swimmer holds onto the gunwale (Fig. 3). This would be the best course when shore is reasonably close and also when the tired swimmer is too heavy to take aboard safely.

FIG. 2—Steadying the canoe while the tired swimmer holds onto the gunwale for a rest.

When the victim is very tired, far from shore, and not too heavy, he may be allowed to climb aboard (Fig. 4). He should climb in near amidships, where the canoe is widest. The rescuer may help with one hand while stabilizing the canoe with the other. Once aboard, the rescued person should sit in the bottom amidships while being paddled to shore.

A HELPLESS VICTIM

A very tired swimmer who cannot help in his own rescue will have to be lifted into the canoe—or if too heavy for that, tied or held to the canoe while being towed to shore. This is true also for unconscious but breathing victims and for those who have become asphyxiated.

If the rescuer has unusual "at homeness" in a canoe, he may

Fig. 3—Towing the tired swimmer to shore while he holds onto the gunwale. The canoe steers better if he holds onto the gunwale on the paddling side and far enough forward to give paddling room.

lift the victim in over the gunwale if the victim is not too heavy. This skill should be practiced sufficiently to give reasonable assurance that when used in a real situation it will not result in swamping or capsizing the canoe. The first step is to grasp the victim by his arms, near the armpits, and lift his trunk in over the gunwale (Fig. 5) until, by jackknifing, it is let down into the canoe. The legs are then lifted in and the

FIG. 4—Stabilizing the canoe while the tired swimmer climbs in. Note the counterbalancing pressure on the far gunwale, and the bracing of the right knee and the left foot against opposite sides.

FIG. 5—Lifting in a helpless victim, first step. Get his trunk up as high as possible and jackknifed into the canoe.

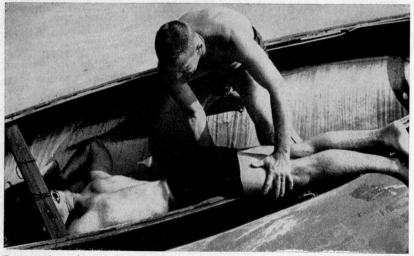

FIG. 6—Completing the lift-in; getting the legs in and positioning the victim in the bottom.

body positioned as comfortably as possible in the bottom (Fig. 6). If the victim is merely very tired, or unconscious but breathing sufficiently, the canoeist should paddle him to shore where further help will be available if needed. A tandem crew could lift the victim into the canoe more easily than could one man. The principles would be the same except that with one of them lifting on each side, the job would be easy enough for them to work from kneeling rather than standing positions.

If the victim is too heavy to lift, you may lash his wrists together under a thwart and tow him to shore (Fig. 7). Be sure his face is kept clear of the water at all times. A tandem crew would make the rescue simpler; one could hold the victim's

Fig. 7—When a victim is too heavy to be lifted in, his wrists may be crossed and lashed together under a thwart, using the end of the bowline (painter), the rescuer's belt, or other material. Thus secured with his face clear of the water he may be towed to shore and help.

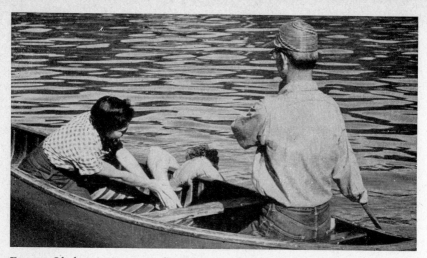

Fig. 8—If the victim is too heavy to be lifted in, even by two persons, one may hold his arms in over the gunwale, while the other paddles the canoe to shore and help.

Fig. 9—Loop made at the eye of the bow painter and placed around the ankle, before going overboard for a submerged victim.

forearms in over the gunwale (Fig. 8) while the other paddled
the canoe to shore and help.

Recovering a Submerged Victim.—In rare instances it has
been necessary for canoeists to go overboard to recover a submerged victim. A method should be employed that permits
the canoe to remain under control; for if the latter blows
away or is carried away by a current while the rescue of the
submerged victim is being undertaken, the rescuer and the
victim will be in danger. A tandem crew will not have trouble
in this respect; one canoeist can dive overboard for the sub-

FIG. 10—Hold the recovered victim to the gunwale while you proceed to
board the canoe, preferably with the quick-lunge method.

merged victim, while the other keeps the canoe under control nearby. A solo paddler should make a loop at the eye of his bow painter and place it around his ankle, making sure that the painter is not led under a thwart (Fig. 9). Or better still, if he has a long length of line in the canoe, he can loop it around one shoulder and under the opposite armpit. With either of these rigs he may then go overboard, recover the victim, bring him to the side of the canoe, fling both of his forearms in over the gunwale (Fig. 10), cast loose the line from ankle or shoulders, and board the canoe, with the quick-lunge method preferably (Fig. 11), being sure to hold the victim to the gunwale during all these latter steps. Once aboard, he will lift the victim in, if possible, or lash the victim's wrists under a thwart for towing to shore as discussed above.

Fig. 11—Completing the boarding of the canoe while holding the victim to the gunwale of the canoe.

Giving Artificial Respiration.—If the victim hauled into the canoe is not breathing, artificial respiration should be started at once. The back pressure-arm lift method is adaptable in this situation (Figs. 12, 13, and 14). Lay the victim out flat on his stomach. Bend both arms at the elbows and place one hand upon the other. Turn the victim's face slightly to one side with the upper part of the cheek resting on the hands. Be sure that his mouth and nostrils are clear of any water that might be in the bottom of the canoe. Follow the standard procedure for artificial respiration. The fact that the victim is in a canoe rather than on the floor of a classroom or on the ground does not change the procedure except in minor, nonimportant details, such as the crowding that the thwart locations may produce. If you have a partner, he should paddle the canoe to shore and help. Your attention should be devoted only to the artificial respiration.

RESCUE WITH CAPSIZED AND SWAMPED CANOE

If a tandem crew capsizes and for some reason one person is unable to care for himself, his more capable partner can hold his

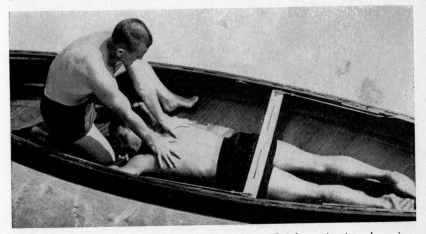

FIG. 12—Back pressure-arm lift method of artificial respiration done in a canoe; *place hands.*

Fig. 13—Pressure being applied.

Fig. 14—Arm-lift portion of resuscitation.

wrists over the bottom of the capsized canoe (Fig. 15) until
help comes or until quiet reassuring talk can enlist cooperation
of the weaker person so that both may enter the canoe and
hand-paddle it to shore.

If a canoe is capsized or swamped while a tired swimmer is
climbing aboard, it will be annoying but not serious. Under
the canoeist's guidance, both he and the tired swimmer board
the swamped canoe and hand-paddle it to shore.

If a canoe is capsized while you are hauling in a helpless victim, you may still proceed with the rescue. First get the victim's arms across the canoe bottom (Fig. 15). Let go of one
wrist so that you have one hand free and are holding the
victim with your left hand grasping his left wrist, or your
right hand grasping his right wrist, whichever is more natural
for you (Fig. 16). With your free hand, reach over the canoe,
grasp the far gunwale (Fig. 17), and roll the canoe slowly to

FIG. 15—One person helping or rescuing another by holding his wrists across
the bottom of the canoe.

FIG. 16—Hold the victim across the canoe with one hand to free the other to roll the canoe over under him.

FIG. 17—With the free hand, grasp the far gunwale and roll the canoe over under the victim.

FIG. 18—Transfer your hand from the victim's wrist to his chin and pull him over onto his back into the canoe.

the upright position. As the canoe rolls to the upright position, transfer your hand from the victim's wrist to his chin and pull him over onto his back and into the canoe (Fig. 18). Without letting go of the victim, quickly get into the swamped canoe, placing yourself behind and somewhat under the victim. Keep his head resting on your chest so that his face is out of the water and begin hand-paddling the canoe to shore (Fig. 19), provided, of course, that the victim is breathing.

It is conceivable that if a canoe does not have a painter or line of any sort, deliberately swamping it might be necessary so that it would not blow away during the recovery of a submerged victim. After the recovery, the procedure described above would be followed.

FIG. 19—Board the canoe, placing yourself behind and under the victim, keeping his head on your chest and his face out of the water at all times. Hand-paddle the canoe to shore if the victim is still breathing.

FIG. 20—Adapted type of artificial respiration; apply regular rhythmic pressures to the abdominal wall, lifting upward with both hands.

Modified Artificial Respiration in a Swamped Canoe.—If

the victim has stopped breathing, concern about getting to
shore becomes secondary to the immediate application of an
adapted form of artificial respiration; otherwise, the victim
may die. A good way to give artificial respiration under these
difficult circumstances is to apply regular rhythmic lifting
pressures against the victim's abdominal wall with both your
hands (Fig. 20). This will produce some exchange of air in the
victim's lungs, possibly enough to keep him alive until help
comes and better measures are possible. In some cases, if begun
soon enough after the onset of asphyxia, these pressures may
bring about early resumption of natural breathing. Lifting the
arms will be possible in most cases and will improve the resus-

FIG. 21—When possible, alternate lifting the arms with the abdominal pressures to get an increased volume of air exchange.

citation (Fig. 21). Lifting of the arms should be alternated with the abdominal wall pressure. Artificial respiration should be continued unremittingly until revival or unquestioned surety of death. If help is not seen coming, it will usually be wise to alternate quick hand-paddling movements with the artificial respiration, thus moving the canoe gradually closer to shore where help may be obtained and the resuscitation method improved.

CANOE-OVER-CANOE RESCUE

If you see a canoe capsize, your first concern should be for the upset canoeists. Rescue of their canoe and equipment is secondary, though nearly always the operation may be carried on as a whole. First, call to the distressed, directing them to remain with their canoe and to hold onto it for support. Approach the capsized canoe quickly but calmly, coming alongside parallel to it. Either side will be satisfactory unless there is a strong wind or current, in which case the downwind side or the upstream side is best. (The wind moves an empty canoe easily because it is afloat "on top" of the water; the wind has relatively little effect upon capsized or swamped canoes, because they are down deeper in the water and held in place by it. If the rescue canoe were to windward, it would be blown hard against the capsized or swamped canoe, making the rescue procedure difficult, hence the downwind side is advised. When current rather than wind is the prevailing force, the capsized or swamped canoe being down in the water will be moved along at approximately the speed of the current. This is true also of the empty canoe, but the latter is gripped only lightly by the current and can be paddled against it and maneuvered in it. Keeping to the upstream side of the distressed craft will therefore make it easier to do the rescue because it will avoid the risk of having the swamped or capsized canoe jammed under the rescue canoe by the force of the current.) Direct the victims, assuming there are two, to hold onto the ends of your canoe, one at each end. Hold the capsized canoe alongside with your paddle blade. When you are satisfied that the victims are safe and will remain in their places until given further instructions, proceed to rescue their canoe. Grasp the keel of the latter, or if it has no keel, place your hands on its bottom, and roll it slowly toward you. When the far gunwale is within reach, grasp it with your other hand (Fig. 22) and roll the

FIG. 22—Rolling the canoe from the capsized to the swamped position.

canoe to the upright position. Take paddles and other gear out and put them in the bottom of your canoe. Pull your canoe ahead or astern, grasp the end of the swamped canoe and lift it slowly in not more than 2 or 3 feet across your canoe (Fig. 23). Then roll the canoe bottom-up and draw it across your canoe till it is resting empty on the gunwales in a balanced position (Fig. 24). Now roll it rightside-up (Fig. 25) and slide it back onto the water.

To get the crew back into their canoe, place both canoes side by side, holding their gunwales tightly together with the

FIG. 23—The canoe end has been lifted in over the rescue canoe and is about to be rolled bottom-up across the gunwales.

FIG. 24—Empty and in balanced position across gunwales of rescue canoe.

FIG. 25—Rolling the canoe rightside-up before sliding it back onto the water.

FIG. 26—Holding gunwales of canoes tightly together so that victim may climb in.

outwale of the rescued craft under that of the rescuing craft
unless excessive tumblehome prevents. Have the victims climb
aboard (Fig. 26) one at a time. The first one in may help you
hold the two canoes together while the other climbs in. When
both are aboard, return paddles and other gear.

CANOE-OVER-CANOE RESCUE WHEN BOTH CANOES ARE CAPSIZED

It is possible that conditions causing one canoe to capsize
might also cause an accompanying canoe to capsize (Fig. 27).
If no additional craft are near enough to help, one of the canoes
will have to be emptied over the other capsized canoe. Once
this is done, the emptied craft can be used to rescue the other
by employing the normal canoe-over-canoe rescue technique.

When the two canoes capsize, there will be at least two persons at the scene, one for each canoe. Both should hold onto
their canoes (Fig. 27). Decide which canoe is to be emptied;
select the lighter one if there is a difference in weight. Roll this
one over from the capsized to the swamped position, remove
all gear, and allow it to float nearby on the surface of the water
or put it under the other canoe. Maneuver the canoe to be
emptied into a position so that one end can be lifted gently up
onto the bottom of the other canoe a short distance (Fig. 28).
At this point, roll it over and slowly draw it across the bottom
canoe (Fig. 29). When it is at a balanced position, each man
in the water supports himself with one hand on the bottom
canoe while lifting the upper canoe with his other hand (Fig.
30). The canoe is in this way flipped over to the upright position empty. It is then slid off the bottom canoe (Fig. 31) and
boarded by its crew, who will then rescue the other craft.

Although not essential, it may be of some advantage to trap
air under the bottom canoe so that it will form a slightly firmer
base for the rescue.

FIG. 27—Two canoes capsized.

FIG. 28—Lifting the end of one canoe up onto the other.

FIG. 29—Upper canoe rolled over and drawn across the other.

Fig. 30—Empty canoe being lifted for a flip-over.

Fig. 31—Sliding the empty canoe off the bottom canoe.

TOWING A CANOE

Towing a canoe is not a common practice, but once in a while it may be helpful and wise to do so. For example, a strong headwind may make it impossible for children of camp age to make much headway by paddling. If their ultimate objective is to windward and if overall program-planning calls for them to arrive within a reasonable length of time, towing would be sensible. The motorboat should be handled by a skilled operator who handles his craft safely. A hitch like that shown in Fig. 32 should be used. This provides from waterline level a pull that will keep the canoe riding with its bow slightly higher than its stern, thus eliminating the possibility of its burying into a wave and being swamped, or running off course and being capsized. If more than one canoe is being towed, they should be towed in single file using the *towing bridle* on each canoe. The motorboat operator should proceed at moderate-to-slow speed, in accordance with how rough the water is. Towing speed should be no greater than paddling speed.

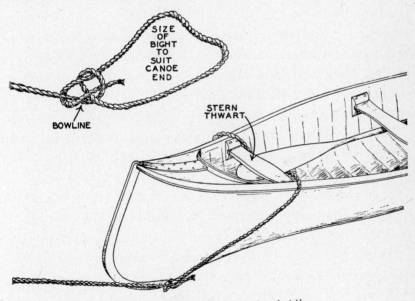

FIG. 32—Quick-release towing bridle.

CHAPTER IX

CONTESTS AND SPECIAL ACTIVITIES

CONTESTS AND NOVELTY EVENTS

Contests and novelty events are fun, and they stimulate interest in canoeing. Most of them actually test basic skills learned. They tend to speed up learning since they contain the element of competition that motivates the participant to improve his performance.

Fun and informality prevail when these events are staged. Those in charge, however, should keep matters well in hand, conduct all events fairly, match canoes evenly, enforce rules, judge fairly, and observe safety precautions. A course of about 100 to 200 yards is satisfactory for the events that involve racing. The chapter on canoe racing contains information on laying out a course and the titles and duties of officials needed to efficiently conduct races.

The activities described in this chapter are some of the more commonly known. Imagination and originality may devise others.

1. *Hand-Paddling Race* (Fig. 1): Crews are one to four men, paddling only with their bare hands, in any position or manner they desire. (This event illustrates the extreme stability of the craft if crew members are sitting in the bottom.)

2. *Shingle-Paddling Race:* This is the same as the hand-paddling race except that a small piece of board is held in each hand or attached by straps. An old table-tennis paddle would be excellent.

3. *Broom Race:* This is the same as a regular single-blade paddling race except that brooms are used instead of paddles. One of the several kneeling positions should be used.

FIG. 1—Hand-paddling race. Note that one crew is in a sitting position and the other in a kneeling position.

4. *Standing Race* (Fig. 2) : Crews are one to four men, paddling with single-blade paddles, in standing position in the canoe.

5. *Canoe-over-Canoe Rescue Race:* Each team consists of two canoes, A and B, one or two men to a canoe. All A's line up on the starting line, with B's close behind. On the starting signal, A's race off the line and B's move onto the line. When A's are about halfway to the finish line a second signal is given, at which time all A's capsize and B's race off the starting line, paddle to A's, and do the canoe-over-canoe rescue. As rescues are completed, A's get under way again for the finish line; B's remain at rescue site.

FIG. 2—Standing race; with proper stance this is a powerful and efficient way to race for a short distance.

6. *Gunwale Paddling Race* (Fig. 3): Crews are one-man or tandem, paddling while standing on the gunwales with single blades or double blades.

Fig. 3—Gunwale paddling race. This activity develops agility and "at home-ness" in the canoe.

7. *Tail-End Race* (Fig. 4): This race is run *downwind* and with single-blade paddles. One man kneels or squats in the bottom of the canoe, as far forward as is possible so that behind him the tail end of the canoe is high in the air. He may not move aft of this extreme position during the race. On the starting line, contestants face into the wind, with the tail end of the canoe toward the finish and with sufficient interval to allow for turning. On the starting signal, canoes are turned and competitors endeavor to paddle straightaway to the finish. Backwater strokes are prohibited under penalty of disqualification, but any other stroke may be used and sides may be changed. To win, a contestant must cross the finish, facing in

FIG. 4—A tail-end race.

the direction of the race, with the tail end of the canoe high behind him. Collisions and bumping do not constitute fouls.

8. *Kangaroo Race* (Fig. 5): This race is always run *downwind*. Crews are one-man or tandem. Canoes take position on the line. Upon the starting signal, competitors mount the gunwales, near the stern, and propel the canoe toward the finish by alternately bending and straightening their knees to bounce it along. Paddle may be held in the hands for balance but it may not be used for stroking, bracing, or steering. Contestants falling overboard may board their canoe and continue.

9. *Upset Race:* One-man or tandem crew; single blade or double blade. Start as in an ordinary paddling race. Upon the

FIG. 5—Kangaroo race.

Fig. 6—Canoe tilting. A (left)—The platform and proper stance. B (right)
—When no platform is available, the poleman may stand on the gunwales but should beware of injury to his toes by the bow of the other canoe.

c (left)—Canoes approach head-on.   D (right)—Canoes engaging.

second signal, when about halfway, each crew immediately capsizes, then empties the canoe by the shakeout method, boards it, and continues to race to the finish line. To qualify at the finish, a canoe shall not have more than 1 inch depth of water in it, measured amidships, with the canoe dead-level. (Only contestants who have complete mastery of the shakeout should be entered in this event.)

10. *Numbered Shingle Race:* Crews are one-man or tandem. Single blades are used. Shingles, or similar pieces of light wood, are prepared with a number, not over ½ inch high, marked on one side, and then are scattered widely, fanwise, on the course. By lot, crews draw numbers corresponding to those on the shingles. On starting signal, crews race out and endeavor to find the shingles with their numbers, and return with them to the starting point. Upon picking up an incorrect number, it may not be secreted but may be thrown as far as possible in any direction.

11. *Canoe Tilting* (Figs. 6A, 6B, 6C, 6D): This is conducted as an elimination tournament. Two-man crews; one man as "spearsman," and the other to paddle with a single blade. A platform, not over 42 inches long, nor extending beyond the gunwales, is attached on the forward third of the canoe, for the spearsman to stand upon. Tilting poles should not be less than 7, nor more than 9 feet long. One end is fitted with a plumber's 5½-inch-diameter rubber suction-cup into which is cemented a 5-inch rubber ball. The entire end is covered with two thicknesses of heavy unbleached muslin gathered and bound securely to the neck of the pole. The pole is used for thrusting only, above the waist, to push one's opponent overboard as the canoes approach head-on. Tilting may continue until the spearsman is opposite his opponent's paddler, when a "bye" is called by the referee for both canoes to back off and re-engage. Clubbing, swinging blows, attack below the

waist, pushing or pulling opponent's canoe, attack on opponent's paddler, participation by paddler (except by paddling) kneeling, stepping off the platform, and bracing on or touching the platform or gunwales each constitutes a foul. Three fouls disqualify a team, except that in the semifinals, or the finals, five fouls might be granted by agreement. A crew wins when the other crew has been disqualified by fouls, when a member of the other crew has gone overboard, or when the other canoe has swamped.

12. *Bucket-Filling Contest:* This is similar to the tilting, except that the spearsmen are armed with buckets with which they throw water into their opponent's canoe to swamp it. Buckets must be dipped overboard. Bailing of one's own canoe is prohibited. If galvanized buckets are used they should be attached to the canoe by a long lanyard, so that they will not be lost if dropped.

13. *Tug-of-War:* Tandem or four-man crews; single blade or double blade may be used. Secure canoes stern-to-stern and about 10 feet apart by means of a double bridle, and station them in the center of the course with the bow of each canoe the same distance from a point designated as its goal. Winner is the canoe whose bow comes up to or passes its own goal while dragging the opponent's canoe stern-first. See Chapter VIII, Fig. 32, for drawing of a way to rig a bridle.

14. *"Tired Swimmer" Rescue Race:* Crews are tandem or one-man. Canoes line up on the starting line or on the beach. "Tired swimmers" line up 100 yards away. On the starting signal, canoes race to "tired swimmers," help them aboard, and return to starting place. First canoe there wins.

15. *Overboard Race:* Crews are one-man or tandem. On the first signal they race off the starting line as in an ordinary paddling race. On the second signal they stow paddles, vault overboard, climb back in immediately, and paddle for the

finish line. The "go-overboard" signal may be given more than once during the race if desired.

16. *Bang-and-Go-Back Race:* Crews are one-man or tandem. All crews race forward on the starting signal. On the next signal, each canoe must stop and go back, by having paddlers change direction or by stopping and backing or by doing a pivot turn. There may be several such signals given and the race may finish back at the starting line as the official finally decides.

17. *Hurry-Scurry Race:* This is run like an obstacle race, such as: A short dash to end of pier, dive in, swim to a moored rowboat and board it; row to a moored canoe, exchange craft; paddle back to dock, tie up canoe.

18. *Dipper Race:* Four-man crews, three men to paddle and fourth man armed with a tin dipper, are used. Dipper-men ride in bow position in an opponent's canoe and endeavor to fill and swamp the canoe before the paddlers can drive it across the finish line. Paddlers and dipper-men cannot unduly interfere with each other's operations.

19. *Pickup Relay Race:* Crews are four men. Two men of each crew are in the water at the far end of the course, one man is in the canoe at the start, and one is in the water. The first lap is paddled by one man. He picks up a second man and paddles tandem for a return lap. Then he picks up a third man for next lap, the fourth man for the final lap. Canoes may be turned at each end of the course or paddlers may merely reverse their own positions.

20. *Swamped Canoe Race:* Crews are one, two, or four men. The race may be run as a hand-paddling event or with single-blade paddles. Crews are seated in bottom of canoe, legs beneath the thwarts, at the start. Upon signal, they lean sideways to fill the canoe until completely swamped and then proceed to race swamped to the finish line.

21. *Backwards Race:* The crew is one-man, with single blade. Crews are lined up and started as for a regular straight-away race, only backwards. The paddler who is most skillful doing a reverse J stroke will win, for he will be able to maintain a straight course. This also could be staged as a tandem race.

22. *Canoe-Emptying Contest:* This is purely a contest of speed in accomplishing the shakeout. Each canoe is manned by a crew of one, who is seated on the bottom. When the signal is given, the canoes are capsized, rolled over, emptied, and boarded again. The first contestant to be again seated in the bottom of his canoe wins, provided he does not have more than the allowed amount of water remaining in his canoe.

23. *Eskimo Roll with Hands:* The Eskimo roll is related to the technique the Eskimos use to right their closed-in water-tight kayaks, when the rough seas overturn them. To the Eskimo it is a survival measure; for us it is just a stunt. It does give additional emphasis to the fact that a canoe filled with water does not sink.

It is generally easier to learn the Eskimo roll using the hands first, and then graduating to the use of the paddle. At the start, the canoe is rightside-up, filled with water. You are seated in the bottom, near midships, with your thighs braced under a thwart. To start the roll, shift your hips sideward in the direction of the roll, pulling the far gunwale over. Keep your head up and close to this gunwale until the canoe starts to turn bottom-up. Then drop your head and trunk to the vertical and finish the roll, using swimming strokes of your hands. Sculling strokes are best. Keep your head down in the water until the roll is nearly completed. If the canoe is wide, it will help to shift your hips over near the following gunwale during the last half of the roll. A noseclip should be worn while learning this stunt.

24. *Eskimo Roll with Paddle* (Fig. 7) : The same principles are involved as when the hands are used. Shift your hips to the side in the direction of the roll. Hold the paddle in the normal manner and start your first stroke well under the canoe. Apply a little pressure to turn the canoe bottom-up. When upside down, reach for the surface on the other side with your paddle and do sculling strokes until the roll is completed. Wearing of a noseclip is recommended.

25. *Surface-Dive Eskimo Roll*: This is essentially a swimming rather than a canoeing skill. The canoe is turned bottom-up. Take a position abeam of the canoe, 20 to 40 feet away. Swim a smooth crawl stroke toward the canoe and when about 2 yards away, do a surface dive. When leveled off 6 feet or more below the canoe, look up. The canoe will be plainly visible. Swim up and grasp the gunwales near midships. Raise your buttocks toward the surface until they are in contact with the bottom of the canoe. Thrust your legs in between the midships thwart and the canoe bottom. Let go of the gunwales, drop head and trunk to near vertical, and with sculling strokes of your hands roll the canoe to the upright position.

The stunt may be performed by two persons, one swimming in from each side. As prearranged, they select thwarts nearer the ends and avoid working in opposite directions when rolling the canoe. This activity is most spectacular when performed by four or six persons with the canvas-covered war canoe found in many camps. *Noseclips are recommended for learners.*

26. *Eskimo Roll with Shift (Only for Good Swimmers)*: Three canoes—each manned by one person—are lined up abreast, facing the audience. One person is the leader. Upon his signal, all three capsize and do a few Eskimo rolls in unison. On another signal, they go around another half-turn and stop, with the canoes bottom-up. They swim down out of their canoes to a depth of about 6 or 7 feet. The man at the right

FIG. 7—Eskimo Roll with Paddle.

A—At the start, shift hips toward the direction of the turn and press upward with the opposite knee.

B—The paddle is sliced deep under the canoe, and pressure is applied to turn the canoe upside down.

c—The paddle is then extended to the surface on the other side and pressure applied to complete the roll. With experience will come the ability to use a sculling stroke from the time the roll starts until it is completed.

d—Completing the Eskimo roll.

swims to the center canoe. The man at the center canoe swims to the canoe at the left. The man at the left swims all the way over to the canoe at the right. All enter the canoes and do a half-roll to sit facing the audience.

27. *War Canoe Shakeout:* The war canoe shakeout is spectacular. It is done in the regular shakeout manner except that added hands make the task lighter. It is effective as a followup to a surface-dive Eskimo roll done by a crew of four or six.

28. *Formation Paddling:* There are various possibilities for an effective formation-paddling demonstration in conjuction with an aquatic show. Fifteen- or sixteen-foot canoes with shoe keel or no keel are most desirable. The paddlers must be skilled. Waltz music might accompany the activity. Canoeists must stroke and do all movements in unison and in reasonable timing with the music.

Following are some suggested maneuvers and activities. Many others may be developed. Four canoes, one-man, single-blade, are used. One man is leader and controls all that is done.

    a. Approach demonstration area in single file about a canoe-length apart. Keep spacing uniform.

    b. Go into a circle with all paddling on outside of circle.

    c. Shift to inside circle paddling.

    d. Break circle and go into single file parallel to shoreline or grouped audience.

    e. Do a 90-degree flank movement and come to a momentary stop, line abreast, facing audience.

    f. Scull sideward in pairs; the two canoes at the left go to the left, the two at the right go to the right. Scull back together, leaving 3 feet of space between canoes.

    g. Left-flank canoe sculls sideward to the left. Right-flank canoe sculls sideward to the right. Inside-right canoe paddles ahead. Inside-left canoe paddles astern, using reverse J stroke.

h. Change to circle paddling as in b, above.

i. Change paddling positions from kneeling to standing on the gunwales, and continue circle paddling.

j. Change to positions standing in the bottom and continue circle briefly. Then all turn abruptly to face the geometric center of the circle. Paddle slowly toward the center, checking speed as the bows converge. Stop the canoes in this cloverleaf position.

k. Stow paddles and do headstands on the bow thwarts. (Or take some effective pose.)

l. Resume kneeling positions. Back out of cloverleaf formation and resume circle paddling. Break into single file. Do flank movement into line abreast, facing audience.

m. Do simultaneous overboard entry into the water in good form.

n. Board canoes in unison and with good form.

29. *"Charles River Paddling"*: Races, maneuvering contests, or just plain paddling with the canoe heeled over so that the water is almost coming in is fun. The canoe is very maneuverable and quite different to paddle than when trimmed on its regular lines (Fig. 8). This style of paddling was popular in earlier decades on the smooth waters of the Charles River near Boston, hence the localized term.

30. *One-hand Paddling:* In some areas of the country, paddles rather than oars are frequently used to propel boats of the "fishing boat" variety. The technique of holding the paddle with only one hand while paddling has developed presumably because the other hand has held a fishing pole. Most everyone who has paddled a canoe very much has at one time or another maneuvered the canoe with one hand, but few have developed the skill very much. Interesting contests can be developed involving skill in maneuvering or speed on a straight-

Fig. 8—Paddling with the canoe heeled over almost to the point of taking in water. Kneel sitting on your heels.

Fig. 9—Paddling with one-hand control of the paddle. Note the shaft position behind the forearm to provide leverage.

Fig. 10—One-hand control of paddles. The shafts are in front of the forearms for leverage to paddle forward.

Fig. 11—One-hand control of paddles. The shafts are behind the forearms to provide leverage for going backward.

away course using one paddle in one hand (Fig. 9) or two paddles in two hands (Figs. 10 and 11).

CANOE CATAMARAN

A canoe catamaran (Fig. 12) can be assembled for use in a pageant as part of a water show. It has often proved excellent for carrying a load too heavy for one canoe and not divisible among separate canoes.

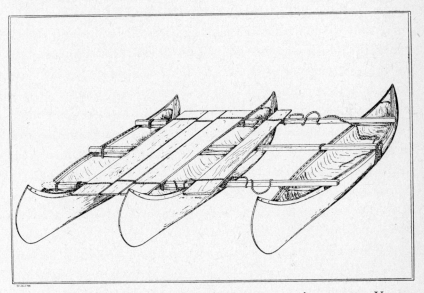

FIG. 12—Canoe catamaran for all utility purposes and pageantry. Use two or more canoes. Canoes must be absolutely parallel. Lash center beam first; if thwart is missing, pass lashing around the hull. Lash the center canoe and the two other beams when lashing the platform. With heavy loads and choppy water, leave canoes open for bailing, otherwise platform can be solid.

WAR CANOE ACTIVITY

Canoes currently made in lengths from 20 to 26 feet are suitable for use as war canoes in recreational programs. In earlier years longer canoes were made. For example, some American Canoe Association regattas featured races in 30-foot-long war canoes of rib-and-plank construction, set up

with crews of nine men. War canoe races in Canada were conducted in canoes somewhat longer and manned with crews of
fifteen men. A popular war canoe in summer camp programs
is one 25 feet long. Typical activities are war canoe cruising,
racing of informal type, formation paddling, and mass instruction drills.

The principles of careful handling apply to war canoes with
added emphasis. War canoes are larger and heavier and consequently more easily damaged if not carefully handled. It is
important to have sufficient persons carry the canoe and launch
it because of its weight. The usual procedure is to have the
entire crew carry and launch it. It is mandatory to have the
war canoe waterborne alongside a dock, bank, or in shallow
water parallel to shore before boarding it. The crew members
should board one at a time beginning at the amidships section
and proceeding toward both ends, and from side to side, to keep
the canoe on even trim from side to side as well as fore and aft.

In a war canoe, whether manned by a crew of nine, ten,
twelve, fifteen, or whatever number, coordination of action is
of importance. The paddler at the bow is the *stroke*. All others
coordinate their paddling with his, except in special situations.
The paddler at the stern is called either *sternman* or *coxswain;*
the better name is probably *sternman*. The sternman is in
charge of the war canoe; for example, in war-canoe racing he
alone may talk. He is in command; others must do as he says.
That is because racing, although recreational in nature, is com-
petitive and hence a serious activity for its participants. Certainly in activities other than racing in formal regattas, this
command by the sternman should be far less rigid. It ought
to be just sufficient for efficiency in handling the war canoe.

A minimum of commands that all crew members understand
are necessary:

"Out, *paddles*"—All crew members take their paddles out of their positions in the canoe, and prepare for paddling. Often crew members will man their paddles individually as they take their positions in the canoe, in which case this command is not necessary. This is probably a more natural and more seamanlike method.

"Get set"—All crew members prepare to move the canoe ahead by putting their paddles in position for the catch of a bow or crew stroke.

"Give way together"—All paddle ahead, keeping in stroke with the *stroke*. This command is for unhurried forward movement.

"Go"—All crew members paddle ahead rapidly for a racing start. By agreement, the command may also be used for other than racing starts; for example, when said slowly and quietly it could mean to get under way at slow-to-moderate speed, but if said sharply it would mean a racing start.

"Let her run"—Crew stops paddling and rests paddles across gunwales, letting the canoe run on its own momentum.

"Hold her"—All crew members hold with the backwater type of holding stroke until the canoe comes to a stop. If the canoe is being backed and the order to "hold" is given, all crew members hold with the crew (bow) stroke.

"Weigh all"—Crew members finish the stroke they are doing and let paddles trail or rest across gunwales. Some sternmen may prefer to use the simpler command "Enough" as an alternative.

There are other commands used for maneuvers, such as moving sideward and turning. The sternman simply tells specific crewmen which strokes to use; for example, "portside—sweep"; "starboardside—*reverse sweep*."

In earlier years paddle drills and salutes from war canoe for-

FIG. 13—War canoe crews engaged in a paddle drill. (Courtesy of Luther Gulick Camps)

mation were popular in summer camp and other programs. It is still an occasional activity (Fig. 13). W. Van B. Claussen[1] describes these as follows:

"Paddle drills and salutes form a very interesting part of war canoe work, and in addition to the standardized commands and movements given below, offer a fertile field for originality in devising distinctive camp programs. They should start and finish with the position of 'Rest paddles.'

"Up, BLADES—Paddles are swung to a vertical position with the blade uppermost and front of the blade facing forward; grip held in the hand in the lap.

"Side, BLADES—Paddles are swung to a horizontal position athwartships overhead with both arms straight; blade outboard and facing forward.

"Quarter forward, BLADES—Same position as 'Side, BLADES' except that blades are pointed at a forty-five-degree angle forward instead of directly athwartships.

"Quarter aft, BLADES—Same position as 'Quarter forward, BLADES' except that blades are pointed at a forty-five-degree angle astern.

"Cross, BLADES—Paddles are swung through the

[1] *Waldemar Van Brunt Claussen*, Canoeing (*New York, Boy Scouts of America*, 1931), *p. 92. Out of print.*

vertical with the grip in the hand in the lap, until the blades are at a thirty-degree angle toward the opposite side of the canoe, so that viewed from a position dead ahead the blades form a 'V' just above the alignment of the paddlers' heads.

"Passing, SALUTE—Used as a salute under way. At the second word of the command, paddlers complete the stroke and instead of feathering through the ordinary recovery, they toss paddles to the position of 'Side, BLADES' and immediately drop them into the beginning of the next stroke without breaking the paddling cadence."

CANOE SLALOM

"Canoe Slalom," as its name implies, arose out of the idea of the ski slalom (zigzag, downhill ski race). It is conducted on a moderate-to-fast stream over a course roughly $\frac{1}{4}$ to $\frac{1}{2}$ mile long. White-water canoeing problems are simulated by the placement of poles that outline in numerical sequence a specific course. Black-and-white-banded poles are passed on either side. Color markings of green or red bands on the poles indicate whether the canoeist will pass them on his starboard side or his port side, respectively. A solid red or green color denotes complete encirclement in the required direction; a solid white color, in either direction. Pairs of poles comprise a "gate" to pass through. Placement of the starboard and port poles may require a sharp lateral maneuver without headway in the swift water. Several poles (painted yellow) side by side at right angles to the current represent a large barrier, such as a log or rock, which would require a greater degree of sideward movement.

A judge is stationed on shore opposite each obstacle. In accordance with a point scoring system, he records points against the competitors; for example, 10 points for minor difficulty such as touching a pole, and so on up to 100 points for complete failure to do a required maneuver. A judge at the finish line records in seconds the time for completion of the course. Contestants start at intervals in order not to interfere with one another. Points scored on elapsed time of passage are added to those given by the course judges. Low point scorer is the winner.

Because this activity is conducted in "white water," it is particularly important for a *safety committee* to be on guard. Members of this committee should be stationed at recognized hazard spots with long bamboo reaching poles and/or heaving lines. The latter should be provided with ring buoys or "monkey's fists" (see Chapter XII under "Equipment") to ensure more effective heaving.

The poles are suspended by means of overhead wires or ropes spanning the stream bed, with their lower ends close to water level. Where the stream is too wide for such spanning, it may be possible to suspend the "gates" or poles along one shore with special rigging ingeniously devised.

When canoe slalom (an international sport) is conducted at a formal regatta, the entries are usually divided into five categories:

1. One woman, double blade, folding kayak　(F-1)
2. One man, double blade, folding kayak　(F-1)
3. One man, single blade, canoe　(C-1)
4. Two men, single blade, canoe　(C-2)
5. Mixed tandem, single blade, canoe　(C-2)

At such regattas the course must be obviously feasible; however, a competitor may not try the course previous to his race. Each contestant goes over the course twice; his better score determines his final standing.

In the United States of America *canoe slalom* is conducted

on a formal basis by the American Canoe Association. Its quarterly publication, *The American Canoeist*, contains articles on the activity and indicates where detailed information is obtainable.

CANOE SAFETY DEMONSTRATIONS

Canoe safety demonstrations have been conducted over a period of many years. Their content has been planned to show safe methods of handling canoes, how to use them for self-rescue in case of mishap, and how to use them to help or rescue others in trouble in or on the water.

Thousands of people have witnessed these demonstrations. They have learned from them, and in many cases doubtless passed on information to others. Thus it can be assumed that many lives have been saved.

Since the close of World War II, the volume of activity afloat in small boats has increased to a remarkable degree. In many cases, newly created lakes are involved with their low percentage of experienced boatmen. These facts indicate a need for more frequent use of the demonstration method of teaching small-craft safety to large numbers of people. The greatest need lies in the area of outboard motorboat safety, but there is also much good to be done by conducting canoe safety demonstrations.

It is often easier to conduct a canoe safety demonstration than one on boating because of the relative ease of getting a canoe into an indoor pool and certain types of outdoor pools. For this reason, small-craft safety demonstrations have been given more often with canoes than with boats. Another reason perhaps equally as significant is the fact that a canoe is easy to put on and take off the roof of an automobile. It must not be overlooked, however, that the currently popular prams (approximately 8 feet long by 4 feet wide) and other types of car-top boats are light, easy to handle, and very suitable for boating demonstrations.

Types of Groups for Whom Demonstrations Might Be Given.—It may be assumed that nearly everyone would profit by observing a well-presented demonstration of safe canoe-handling, for the principles of safe handling apply to all small craft, not just to canoes. Experience, however, indicates that certain groups make more or less natural audiences, some readymade and some assembled. They are as follows:

Swimming Classes	State Park Programs
Lifesaving Classes	Public School Programs
Aquatic Shows	Youth Groups
Summer Camp Groups	Recreation Department Programs
Picnics	Hunting and Fishing Clubs
Schools and Colleges	Boat and Canoe Liveries and Clubs
Sportsmen Clubs	Country Clubs
	Others

Time Allotment for Demonstration According to Type of Group.—If the demonstration is but one of many activities on the program (for example, at an aquatic show or sportsmen show), it should probably take from 10 to 20 minutes, as prearranged in accordance with scheduling of other activities. If the demonstration is being featured, 30 minutes might be prearranged. If it is being conducted for a special-interest group and is the only event on the program, a longer period will generally be desirable.

Some General Suggestions.—(These are intended as helpful reminders of varying importance when giving demonstrations.)

1. For the one-man demonstration especially, the following are important:

    a. Avoid having the sun in the audience's eyes.

b. Get the wind behind you if possible, if it is blowing hard.

c. Center your demonstration so that all the audience will see it.

d. Remember that out-of-doors, before large audiences, you may move farther out from shore to the focal point of all eyes, because your voice will carry well over water.

e. Face toward your audience when talking.

f. In an indoor pool, if acoustics are poor, experiment with speed and volume of your delivery to get best results. If results are poor, do less talking and get to the parts of the demonstration where you are in and out of the water. You will find that when you are down close to the water your problem with acoustics will be less acute.

g. Whenever you can, use the wind to your advantage in a demonstration. Skillful performance in this respect will be an important part of your demonstration, so capitalize on it. Explain and demonstrate the principles as part of your demonstration.

h. Similarly, use current and eddies to your advantage, working wind and current in opposition when possible.

i. It is an element in showmanship (without seeming to show off) to take advantage whenever you can of boats and moorings, buoys, ends of piers, as objects to work close to and avoid, to make your canoe-handling seem more skilled because of the hazards all around you.

j. Your canoe ought to be in good repair and properly equipped. A broken or loose thwart or a tangled painter will detract from the finesse a demonstration should have.

k. Remember that even though your skill is not outstanding, you can still give effective demonstrations as long as you do not pose as an "expert." Your sincerity in presenting important safety information and skills will impress the audience. They will be grateful and appreciative.

l. If you are very skilled, it will be a delight to watch you perform. However, as a hobbyist one must guard against giving the impression that great skill is indispensable, or that any one way of doing a thing is in all cases superior to other ways. The majority of people watching a demonstration will never become superior in their skills, but they can learn to do them passably well and safely. That is sufficient for our objective of saving human lives.

2. If the demonstration is of the novelty-event type, have preliminary rehearsals and be sure that events take place in rapid succession. The audience will lose interest if there are periods of waiting. Have the events take place exactly on time if they are scheduled among other show activities. When selecting events for a program, be sure that among them will be one that shows a self-rescue skill and another that shows a skill used to help or rescue someone else.

An Adaptable Canoe Demonstration Routine.—Suitable items in the following demonstration routine may be selected with respect to the time allotted and the type of audience. It is difficult to estimate the amount of time the entire routine will take. The degree of efficiency with which the action takes place and the conciseness of the explanations will influence this. The type of group will influence the amount of detail included in the demonstrations and the explanations. Usually, detail can be expected to slow up the action and dull the interest of the viewers. It should ordinarily be avoided.

If you have been allotted plenty of time, try the entire routine. Carry on a running explanation and commentary to fit the action. If you have a brief time allotment, you may wish to use the "Suggested Short Canoe-Demonstration, with Key Comments," which follows the longer routine given here.

The Demonstration Routine

1. Launch the canoe, using one or more methods.

2. Board the canoe at dock and/or beach.

3. Show several positions for paddling. Stress importance of keeping one or both knees in contact with bottom of canoe.

4. Maneuver the canoe with several paddling strokes. Paddling relates to safety, but one should avoid giving the impression that great skill in canoe-handling is indispensable. These are for one-man handling. Some demonstrators may wish to do a tandem routine.

 a. Paddle the canoe in a straight line, using the J stroke.

 b. Move it sideward with the draw stroke, using over-water recovery followed by underwater recovery.

 c. Move it sideward in the opposite direction with the pushover stroke, using both types of recovery.

 d. Move the canoe sideward with the sculling stroke and immediately in the opposite direction with the reverse sculling stroke.

 e. Do an inside pivot turn, and then an outside pivot turn.

 f. Do a stationary draw maneuver and a stationary pushover maneuver.

 g. Show a couple of smooth landings at the dock or pool edge.

5. Vault overboard and reenter the canoe from deep water.

6. Capsize the canoe and hold onto it for support and self-rescue. "Swim" it along toward shore.

7. Roll the canoe over to the swamped position and board it. Stress the self-rescue factors.

8. Empty the canoe in shallow water or over a dock, using canoe-over-canoe principle.

9. Rescue a tired swimmer.

10. Use the shakeout method of emptying a canoe in deep water. Be sure to emphasize that this skill is a swimmer's rather than a canoeist's, and not of particular importance in canoeing. Mention, however, that it is a great convenience under certain circumstances.

11. Make the canoe-over-canoe rescue.

12. Make a closing summary statement, such as: "It has been a pleasure to present this safety demonstration. We hope your canoeing will be enjoyable and safe. Tell others about these things. You may in that way save a life."

Suggested Short Canoe-Demonstration, with Key Comments.—The demonstrator, or his narrator, if a public-address system is being used, should carry on a running explanation of the action. In addition, it is suggested he include the key comments given opposite each action-item in the outline below.

Introduction

A master of ceremonies or someone in charge of the program or the group will introduce the demonstrator. It will be helpful to provide him with concise information on which to base his introduction.

Demonstrator's Opening Comments

1. Acknowledge introduction.

2. Set the stage for the demonstration with comments such as: "Each year many drownings occur because many people out in small boats and canoes lack skill in handling them and lack knowledge of self-rescue measures to employ when they fall overboard, swamp, or capsize. Skill in paddling a canoe, rowing a boat, or safely and courteously operating an outboard motorboat are best acquired by combining capable instruction with much practice. Fortunately, self-rescue skills are relatively easier to learn for anyone who swims well enough

to be at ease in the water. Anyone who does not know how to swim should wear a lifejacket at all times while afloat. These demonstrations will emphasize self-rescue skills as they apply to a canoe. The principles apply equally to rowboats, outboards, and small keelless sailboats."

The Demonstration

Action	Key Comments
1. Launch the canoe smoothly—parallel to the dock or pool edge.	1. "When carrying or launching a canoe, handle it carefully."
2. Board the canoe slowly and smoothly.	2. "When getting into a canoe, step into the center and hold onto the gunwales."
3. Take the normal one-man cruising position on both knees. Then show a contrasting position by sitting on a thwart with knees high and both feet flat on the bottom.	3. "Canoes are more stable when you kneel in them. Sitting on a seat without at the same time kneeling on one or both knees invites a capsizing and makes skilled paddling difficult."
4. Vault over the side into deep water. (If you are working in a shallow pool, simulate deepwater conditions throughout the demonstration.)	4. "One reason for going overboard is to practice the self-rescue skill of boarding a canoe from deep water. Vaulting—rather than diving—enables you to keep contact with your canoe, which otherwise might be blown away—especially if there is a good breeze."
5. Board the canoe from deep water.	5. "When boarding the canoe, remember to keep kicking

your legs until you get the elbow at the far gunwale high. When you have reached the position of balance, do a quarter turn and sit in."

6. Go overboard again and show an alternate method: place both hands in the bilge, press on them and kick your feet until the canoe is under you and you can roll in; or use a thwart as an aid.

6. "This is a good method for youngsters and some adults who find the other method difficult, especially with a large canoe."

7. Capsize the canoe and hold onto it for support.

7. "In the event of a capsizing, remember that a canoe or a boat will float. Hold on for support and 'swim' the canoe to shore if the shore is near."

8. Roll the canoe over gently to the swamped position and board it smoothly, demonstrating that it can be hand-paddled in comfort to shore.

8. "If you are some distance from shore, it will be easier to get in the canoe and hand-paddle it to shore, or rest while waiting for an approaching rescue craft."

9. Empty the canoe in shallow water.

9. "This is how to empty the canoe in shallow water."

10. Do the canoe-over-canoe rescue. (When working in an artificial pool, have someone stand by on each side of the pool to prevent either canoe from hitting the sides of the pool.)

10. "It is neither difficult nor dangerous to help when another canoe capsizes. Come alongside parallel to the capsized canoe. Instruct the person in the water to hold onto the end of your canoe to support himself. Roll the canoe

over gently to the swamped position. Take out all gear and put it in the bottom of your canoe. Move to one end and raise it slowly, sliding it out of the water rather than lifting it, and bring it in a couple of feet over your canoe in front of you. Then roll the canoe bottom-up once more and slide it in this position until it balances across your gunwales. Roll it upright and slide it out onto the water. Swing it around parallel to your canoe. Hold the gunwales of the two canoes close together with your hands close together. Instruct the person in the water to climb back into his canoe. Give him his paddle and other gear."

11. Make a closing summary statement.

11. "It has been a pleasure to explain and demonstrate safe canoe-handling, self-rescue, and how to help others. We hope your canoeing will be enjoyable and safe. Tell others about these things. You may in that way save a life."

Novelty Events.—Boat and canoe novelty events are sometimes staged as part of the program of an aquatic show for the
primary purpose of attracting and entertaining the crowd.
During the conduct of the events, the announcer makes appropriate comments relating elements of the activities to
safety knowledge and skill. Thus, through entertaining comes
the opportunity to educate. When selecting events for a program, be sure that among them will be one that shows a self-
rescue skill and another that shows a skill used to help or
rescue someone else.

CHAPTER X

CANOE RACING

Canoe racing is an organized sport headed by the American Canoe Association, which conducts divisional and national championships annually and, as a member of the United States Olympic Association and the International Canoe Federation, selects an Olympic team to compete in the Olympic Games when they are held. Canoe clubs have crews that train under the supervision of volunteer coaches, who are usually former outstanding crewmen. These crews compete in regattas indicated above and in other intradivisional regattas.

Other informal canoe racing is done in summer camps and in other recreational areas. It is for these groups who do not have affiliation with the organized sport that this chapter is included. It is assumed that little or no special training will be done for participation in regattas and that they will be largely informal. The illustrations in this chapter, however, are of the formal type of racing in order to more clearly present efficient conduct of the sport.

Events.—Any or all of the events listed below could be scheduled for a regatta. The order in which they are listed is a good order in which to conduct them.

1. One-man, single-blade (Figs. 1, 8, 11)
2. Tandem, double-blade (Fig. 4)
3. Fours (four-man crew), single-blade (Fig. 7)
4. One-man, double-blade (Figs. 3, 12)
5. Tandem, single-blade (Fig. 2)
6. Fours, double-blade (Figs. 5, 6, 9)
7. War canoe race (nine-man crew), single-blade (Fig. 10)

If there is a wide range in age and size, as might be the case in a summer camp, events 1 through 6 could be repeated on a class basis, as, for example, junior class, intermediate class, and senior class. This would give broader participation and tend to neutralize the age and size factor. Study Chapter V, "Positions in Canoe," for information on trim of craft, methods of kneeling, and related information.

THE RACING COURSE

Reasonable care should be taken to lay out a racing course that will be fair to all contestants. The diagram on page 319 shows a suggested layout including an indication of regatta officials and their duties. The following information will be helpful in laying out the course markers.

1. Lay out buoy No. 1 near shore where the finish line is desired. In place of a buoy it would be better to nail a board or pole vertically to the end of the pier where the finish line judges will be located. If there is no pier, but the water is reasonably shallow, a pole or stake could be driven into the bottom with enough of its length above water to permit attachment of a flag to make it more visible and more distinctive.

2. Lay out buoy or stake No. 2 downshore a couple of hundred yards, more or less, according to the length of the course desired. No. 2 should be far enough offshore so that an imaginary line between No. 1 and No. 2 is outside shallow water and waterfront structures. It might be the end of another pier.

3. Hold the angle of a carpenter's square at No. 1 and aim the edge of one arm at No. 2. Have a second person sight along the corresponding edge of the other arm of the square while a boat crew stands by and lays out buoy or stake No. 3 on his line of sight.

Racing Course Diagram, Indicating Officials and Their Duties

Patrol boat stands by as a safety measure. (Referee's boat also is a rescue boat when necessary.)

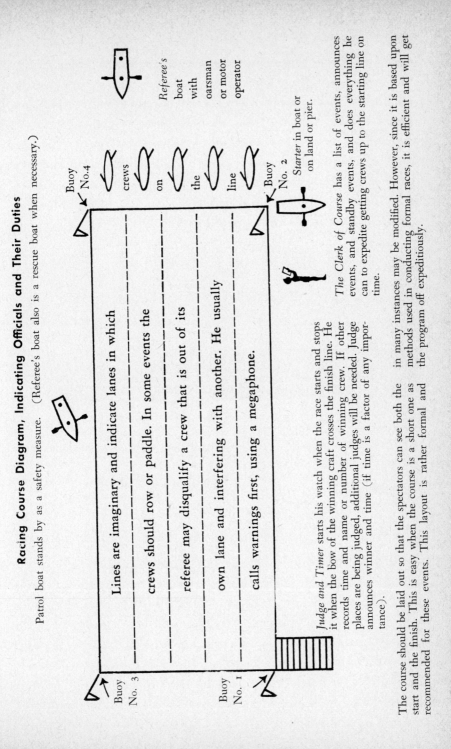

Referee's boat with oarsman or motor operator

Buoy No.4

crews on the line

Buoy No. 2

Starter in boat or on land or pier.

Buoy No. 3

Buoy No. 1

Lines are imaginary and indicate lanes in which crews should row or paddle. In some events the referee may disqualify a crew that is out of its own lane and interfering with another. He usually calls warnings first, using a megaphone.

Judge and Timer starts his watch when the race starts and stops it when the bow of the winning craft crosses the finish line. He records time and name or number of winning crew. If other places are being judged, additional judges will be needed. Judge announces winner and time (if time is a factor of any importance).

The course should be laid out so that the spectators can see both the start and the finish. This is easy when the course is a short one as recommended for these events. This layout is rather formal and

The Clerk of Course has a list of events, announces events, and standby events, and does everything he can to expedite getting crews up to the starting line on time.

in many instances may be modified. However, since it is based upon methods used in conducting formal races, it is efficient and will get the program off expeditiously.

4. To lay out buoy or stake No. 4, hold the angle of the carpenter's square at No. 2 and aim the edge of one arm at No. 1. Have the second person sight along the corresponding edge of the other arm of the square while the boat crew stands by and lays out the stake or buoy on his line of sight. You can guess at making the distance of No. 4 from No. 2 equal to the distance of No. 3 from No. 1. It does not have to be accurate. It is only essential that the starting and finishing lines are parallel and that the angles of No. 1 and No. 2 are right angles.

FIG. 1—One-man crew with single-blade paddle in an official Olympic Canadian racing canoe, called C-1. It is about 17 feet long, with a beam of approximately 30 inches, and a weight of approximately 45 pounds. It is generally of molded plywood construction. See Chapter V, "Positions in Canoe," for a detailed description of this high kneeling, or racing, position for paddling.

CONDUCTING THE RACE

Starting the Race.—The starter should locate himself at one end of the line so that he can sight along the line. He instructs the crews to move onto the line, keeping proper spacing. With instructions to each as necessary, to move up or move back, he gets all craft lined up with their bows on the line (Fig. 11). Then the starting signal is given. A perfect lineup will rarely be possible. A fair start should be the objective (Fig. 12). A good starter will not start the race with a crew in motion, either ahead or astern, but will wait until all craft are practically motionless.

In singles (one man) (Figs. 1 and 3), the control of the craft on the starting line and the necessary alertness is entirely up to the individual. He is on his own. In a one-man single-blade race, the canoe should not be pointed directly toward the finish line when on the starting line. Its bow should be headed off toward the paddling side about 30 degrees. This is because the first three or four strokes required to get it rapidly under way will be fast ones with no steering, and will consequently throw the canoe over as much as the allowed 30 degrees before the steering begins. This will not be a consideration in the one-man double-blade race, because the strokes alternate on both sides.

FIG. 2 (left)—A tandem crew with single-blade paddles in the same craft shown in Fig. 1. When manned by a tandem crew, it is called a C-2. Chapter V, "Positions in Canoe," gives information about setting up a tandem crew for this style of paddling.

FIG. 3 (right)—One-man crew paddling with double blades in an official Olympic Racing kayak, called a K-1. This kayak measures approximately 17 feet long by 20 inches wide, and weighs about 26 pounds. Its cockpit is about 37 inches long by 15 inches wide. There is a low platform for the paddler to sit on and a stretcher against which he braces his feet. Its hull is usually of molded plywood construction (for example, 4 layers of mahogany veneer and plastic glue). Its deck is waterproof fabric—except for the cockpit area, which is mahogany.

In tandem crews (Figs. 2 and 4) the task of keeping the craft on the line and ready to go is primarily that of the sternman and only secondarily that of the bowman. The latter's task is to watch the starter to be sure that his crew gets the best possible start. The sternman shares in this concern and does as much watching as he is able. The canoe is pointed directly toward the finish line.

In fours (Figs. 5, 6, 7, and 9) the sternman is in command. It is his task to keep the craft on the line. Usually he will ask

FIG. 4—A tandem crew with double blades, paddling in a two-seater kayak, known as a K-2. This craft is about 21 feet long by 21 inches wide, and weighs about 40 pounds. See Fig. 3 for additional information.

FIG. 5—A four-man crew in a four-seater kayak, called a K-4. It is used in kayak racing in Europe. It is 36 feet long, 24 inches wide, and weighs about 78 pounds.

Fig. 6—A four-man crew paddling with double blades in the traditional four-man racing canoe used in the United States. This craft is of plank-and-rib construction, 20 feet long, 30 inches wide, 12 inches deep amidships, and of a minimum weight of 65 pounds. The bowman (stroke) uses a seat like the one on page 227, in Chapter VI, "Paddling." The other three use the same type of seat minus the attached footbracing. Each of them braces his feet against the seat of the paddler in front of him.

Fig. 7—A four-man crew paddling with single-blade paddles in the 20-foot racing canoe described in Fig. 6, above. In setting up a four-man crew, single blades, put the heavier men in the middle ordinarily, and make minor adjustments of positions of all four to get the canoe trimmed even, fore and aft, and so that each will have room to paddle without hitting the man in front of him. They counterbalance each other and may kneel off center in the direction of their paddling sides in order to get nearer the side of the canoe so they can paddle more efficiently.

the help of number 3 man, if it is needed. The stroke and number 2 man keep their eyes on the starter in order to get the best start possible. The canoe is headed directly toward the finish line. These principles apply also to the war canoe (Fig. 10).

FIG. 8 (left)—Before the adoption of the official Olympic Canadian type canoe, C-1, used for both one-man and tandem single-blade racing, and the kayaks, K-1 and K-2, for double-blade paddling, the craft in use in the United States for all one-man and tandem races, both single and double blades, was this racing canoe of rib-and-plank construction commonly called a "peanut" by some and a "single" by others. It had a maximum length of 16 feet, a minimum beam of 30 inches, a minimum depth of 10 inches, and a minimum weight of 45 pounds.

FIG. 9 (right)—A four-man double-blade crew, paddling in the high kneeling position. This style is rare now but formerly was popular among some canoe-racing clubs and occasionally produced championship crews.

FIG. 10—This is a nine-man crew manning a war canoe of the traditional type used in the 1-mile war canoe races of the American Canoe Association regattas. This craft is 30 feet long, 36 inches wide, 17 inches deep amidships, and has a minimum weight of 120 pounds. It is of plank-and-rib construction, the planking usually of cedar and the ribs and gunwales of hardwood. (Courtesy Samoset Canoe Club, Boston, Mass.)

Under Way.—Maintaining a straight course throughout the race is necessary in order to avoid fouling other crews and to paddle the shortest distance to the finish line. The best way to assure a straight course is to select an object beyond the finish line, such as a tree or distant building that lines up with your lane, and keep your eyes on it from the start to the finish of the race. In tandems, fours, and war canoes, only the stern-man need do this, except in adverse wind conditions when teamwork will be necessary to keep a straight course.

In the case of single-blade racing, when the gun goes off, stroking begins rapidly. The first stroke is a long, strong pull,

FIG. 11—On the starting line, one-man crews in the C-1's waiting for the starting gun to go off.

FIG. 12—The start of a K-1 race.

followed by a very rapid recovery. The next half dozen or so strokes are taken as rapidly as possible and are consequently shortened. The speed of stroking is progressively built up during these initial strokes and then the strokes are lengthened out into long, steady pulls. It is attempted, however, to maintain a rapid recovery throughout the race. The paddler must try to maintain good form, striving always to reach forward for a long pull, cutting the stroke off at the hip each time, minimizing body motion, maintaining a rapid but relaxed recovery, keeping in perfect timing with the paddler in the stroke position. As the finish line is approached, a spurt is expected. This spurt will be very obvious in the case of a poorly trained or poorly coached crew, for the paddlers will break out of their steady smooth form and "dig" for the finish line. Their craft, already moving nearly as fast as it is possible for them to paddle it, will pick up speed only a little, if any. The roughness of their paddling and its accompanying excessive body motion will nearly always bounce the canoe along and consequently inhibit the maximum attainment of speed. The only occasions when rough paddlers with inefficient form come through for a win is when they have been paddling a long time together and have mastered timing so perfectly that they are truly "in stroke." To the untrained eye, paddling in stroke is a thing accomplished when the members of a crew are observed to put their paddles into the water and take them out of the water at the same time. This of course is absolutely necessary, but there is more to it. The members of the crew must have the same style of paddling so that the length of stroke will be the same for all and so that the power application comes at the same time for all, rather than near the beginning of the stroke for one, at the middle portion for another, and steadily from start to finish for still another. The spurt for the finish line by the trained crew will not have the inhibiting factors indicated above. It will be effected simply by increasing the tempo of the recovery and maintaining the same smooth, unbroken stroke. To the unskilled eye, this crew will appear to move ahead without seeming to be trying hard, when in reality they may be exerting all their energy.

The Referee.—The referee should locate himself back of the starting line before the start of the race. From this position he can watch the racing crews. He should call to them by name or number, warning of impending fouls. Some may not keep a straight course. However, if they have not interfered with another crew's chances of winning, he should overlook it. But if the craft off-course strikes another; causes another to strike it; causes another to slow up to avoid striking it; or, coming close across the other's bow, throws a handicapping wash; then such a craft off its course should be ruled out of the race. The referee should announce this immediately to the offending crew. The referee's decision should not be altered.

Judges.—See racing course diagram.

TIMING

Timing may be done if desired. It may add interest and importance to the races. Timing canoe races, however, is largely of little value, even in formal official races. Because of their disinterest, canoe-racing men often are not able to tell anything about their times. This is because time is but little indication of performance, in view of the fact that every racing course is different in terms of depth of water, smoothness of water, direction of wind, and—very often—accuracy in measurements of the standard-length course. Conditions, in fact, may vary so much from day to day on the same course that local times may be of little importance. It is not rare that conditions have changed so in the space of an hour that the times for the junior races have been faster than those for the senior races in the same regatta.

CANOE MARATHONS

A classic event in canoe racing is a one-man single-blade marathon conducted on a river in conventional stock-model (ordinary pleasure-type) canoes. Other long-distance races, both shorter and longer than the marathon (26 miles, 385 yards) have been conducted with both one-man and tandem crews. Some of the most highly refined styles of single-blade paddling have developed through the years as products of the study, analysis, coaching, and training applied to producing winners of these races. Their accomplishments in terms of sustained-speed paddling over many miles have been remarkable. Fig. 13 shows a superior paddler in a typical "marathon canoe" on the Charles River, in Massachusetts, where many marathons have been conducted.

FIG. 13—A canoe marathon champion on the Charles River.

River! that in silence windest
    Through the meadows, bright and free,

* * *

I have felt my heart beat lighter,
    And leap onward with thy stream.

* * *

'Tis for this, thou Silent River!
    That my spirit leans to thee;
Thou hast been a generous giver,
    Take this idle song from me.[1]

[1]*Selected lines from* To the River Charles *by Henry W. Longfellow.*

CHAPTER XI

CANOE TRIPS

The typical canoe trip is a form of itinerant camping in which the canoe is the means of transportation. Thus the canoe camper must not only employ canoe-handling skills contained in other chapters of this book, but also possess a knowledge of how to live in the wilds, away from the facilities and conveniences of civilization. In other words, he has to learn to be a good camper as well as canoeist. This may be done by going on a canoe trip with an experienced person, friend or hired guide, or by going on short trips near home to gain experience, and reading some of the many fine books written on camping. Some writers have combined canoeing and camping. Carle W. Handel in his book *Canoe Camping*[1] gives the subject detailed treatment. Robert E. Pinkerton's *The Canoe*[2] has several chapters from the viewpoint of the camper.

In the space available here, essential topics will be given consideration to provide enough information to guide the canoeist in planning and going on his canoe trip. Further reading and practical experience will round out the individual as a canoe camper.

THE FOREST AND ITS CONSERVATION

It is important that a person who plans to go into forest areas, whether nearby or remote, for a day or for extended periods, understand the importance of the forest and its conservation.

[1]*Carle W. Handel,* Canoe Camping (*New York, A. S. Barnes and Company, 1953*).

[2]*Robert E. Pinkerton,* The Canoe, Its Selection, Care, and Use (*New York, The Macmillan Co., 1946*).

"The forest itself is beautiful and useful, and has played a vital part in the development of the human race. . . . The history of the United States is staged against a forest background. . . . As the country expanded . . . communities sprang up subsisting mainly upon the bounty of the forest. Each decade saw more and more forests cut away with an extravagance born of the idea that the forests of America were inexhaustible.

"The forests have been and still are one of the nation's most important natural resources. Not only do they play a leading part in the economic and industrial life of the nation today, but they also serve us in many other ways. By checking the rains and melting snows, they help to prevent erosion and floods and to insure a steady flow of water for power and domestic use; they are the source of many products besides lumber; they produce forage for domestic livestock; they are the home of much of our game and wildlife; they furnish innumerable opportunities for recreation; and they make this country a more pleasant and beautiful place in which to live. If we were deprived of forests, we would suffer economically, physically, and esthetically. It is therefore important that we handle our forest wealth so that it may be used to fill our countless needs and at the same time continue as a permanent natural resource."[3]

A review of the literature, including government pamphlets, dealing with the use of our forests for recreation reveals quite uniform rules for conduct. These rules are for the conservation of the forests in the light of the foregoing definition of their broad and indispensable character.

1. Build your campfire close to the water's edge and on a spot where all leaves, moss, lichen, deadwood, or other flammable matter has been scraped away in an area 10 feet in

[3]Our Forest Resources, *Agriculture Information Bulletin No. 131, U. S. Department of Agriculture, Forest Service, pp. 1 and 2.*

diameter. Drown the fire with water before leaving camp—even if you're to be away for a few minutes. Mix the ashes thoroughly with water. Merely pouring water on top of the fire is not sufficient since live coals may not be reached and may start a forest fire after you are gone. The U. S. Forest Service states that nine out of ten forest fires are started by man,[4] so remember you cannot be too careful. On a dry and windy day it might be best not to light a fire, unless at the very water's edge, and perhaps with a stone barrier at the onshore side of the fire. Under normal conditions, build fires where others have built them before you. This is generally a specific rule in national forests and national parks. Be aware of and abide by local regulations that pertain to campfires.

2. Dispose of garbage and trash by burning it in your campfire. Bury unburnable refuse, including bottles. Tin cans should be burned in the campfire, then crushed or flattened, and buried or put out of sight in rock crevices or in a space under a stump or boulder. Leave the campsite clean, cleaner than when you arrived if necessary. A National Parks folder of information expresses outdoor cleanliness and good manners as follows: "Let it not be said, and to your shame, that all was beauty here, until you came."

3. Be sure you know the regulations about smoking. Generally smoking is restricted to times when you are afloat, or in the cleared campsite area. When in doubt, consult a ranger, or use your best judgment.

4. Don't pollute the ground or the water. Never throw any refuse of any kind into the water, and do not clean fish in the water. Latrine area should be a good distance away from the water and from the open campsite area. Excreta should be buried promptly.

[4]The Work of The U. S. Forest Service, *Agriculture Information Bulletin No. 91, U. S. Department of Agriculture, Forest Service, p. 13.*

5. Abide by applicable regulations regarding cutting wood. Usually only dead and down wood should be cut, and trees and shrubbery should not be defaced. On the other hand, this is a matter of location. ". . . Where hundreds of square miles are a solid mat of trees, it isn't a crime to thin out the branches of a few evergreens to make a bed, and a blazed trail isn't the mark of a tenderfoot with an itchy new axe. A live tree can even be knocked over for a useful purpose. But it's just as wrong to damage a tree needlessly in the wilderness as it is in the park. . . ."[5]

The Boy Scouts of America have expressed these rules of conduct in a document entitled *Outdoor Code*. This code was developed not only for Boy Scouts but as a guide to conduct for all Americans. It is quoted here with permission:

OUTDOOR CODE

Boy Scouts of America

As an American, I will do my best to:

—BE CLEAN IN MY OUTDOOR MANNERS—

I will treat the outdoors as a heritage to be improved for our greater enjoyment. I will keep my trash and garbage out of America's waters, fields, woods and roadways.

—BE CAREFUL WITH FIRE—

I will prevent wild fire. I will build my fire in a safe place, and be sure it is dead out before I leave.

—BE CONSIDERATE IN THE OUTDOORS—

I will treat public and private property with respect. I will remember that use of the outdoors is a privilege I can lose by abuse.

[5]Cal Craig, *"Blueprint for a Bush Trip,"* Boats and Canoes (*New Brunswick, N.J., Boy Scouts of America, National Council*). *A reprint from* Boys' Life.

—BE CONSERVATION-MINDED—

I will learn how to practice good conservation of soil, waters, forests, minerals, grasslands, and wild life; and I will urge others to do the same. I will use sportsmanlike methods in all my outdoor activities.

(Reprinted from *Boys' Life* magazine)

YOUR SAFETY

On extended canoe trips you may be far from the types of emergency services available to you at home. You will have to be far more self-reliant and avoid foolish or unwise acts, for an accident in the wilds may prove serious or even fatal. Some recommendations for your safety are as follows:

1. Be trained in first aid before going on a canoe trip. Such training will give you an appreciation of the possible seriousness as well as the needlessness of accidents, make you accordingly less likely to be accidentally injured, and equip you with the skill and knowledge necessary for giving proper first aid to others and yourself. You can obtain information on first aid courses from your local Red Cross chapter.

2. Learn to swim well enough to float, tread water, and be relaxed and at ease in the water. Become familiar with the principles of water safety particularly as they pertain to personal safety. It would be of great value to you to take a course in lifesaving. The local Red Cross chapter can give you information on lifesaving courses.

3. Know how to paddle your canoe reasonably well before undertaking a canoe trip. Also practice the self-rescue and rescue skills beforehand.

4. Don't go on a canoe trip alone. In an emergency, your life might very well depend on the help of another person. A good setup is a party of four in two canoes. Be sure to let ap-

propriate persons know your planned approximate day-to-day location and your expected time of return.

5. Take along a first aid kit. Readymade kits are available in sporting goods stores, drug stores, and from distributors of Boy Scout equipment. The automobile-type kit sold in drug stores is satisfactory. At less expense, you can make up your own. You can stuff several items into an inexpensive transparent waterproof pouch or plastic bag that will pack well with your other personal gear. The following minimum items are recommended for a kit:

a. Adhesive compresses of assorted sizes in a small metal can.

b. A package of 3-inch sterile gauze squares.

c. A small bottle of antiseptic (in aqueous solution) or a package of individual applicators.

d. A 1-inch roll of adhesive tape.

e. Two triangular bandages, which you can make from a square piece of cotton cloth. Fold and pack them as cravats so they will be ready for immediate use as pressure bandages in the event of serious bleeding.

f. Tweezers.

g. 1- and 2-inch roller bandages.

h. Small tube of castor oil or mineral oil.

i. Tablets for water purification.

j. *American Red Cross First Aid Textbook.*

6. The danger of tetanus is present in any type of wound. Therefore, if you are going far from civilization it is strongly recommended that you have a tetanus shot before you leave. In addition, it's wise to have an examination by your family physician to make certain your health is adequate for the trip. He may wish to recommend additional first aid supplies and other items relating to maintenance of good health.

7. In sections of the country where poisonous snakes are

common, take along a snakebite kit—and be sure ahead of time that you understand exactly how to treat a bite.

8. Observe health routines.

    a. Eat properly prepared and balanced meals.

    b. Be sure that drinking water is pure. Water purification tablets used according to instructions may be advisable, or the water may be boiled and allowed to cool.

    c. Wash dishes and utensils in hot soapy water; then rinse in water at or near the boiling point.

    d. Follow your normal habits of personal hygiene and cleanliness.

9. Unless you have a guide who thoroughly knows the river, it is unwise to run any but the mildest rapids. Injury to yourself and your canoe are both serious when you are far from civilization. Carry around all bad stretches of water, and be sure to stop soon enough when approaching such places.

10. Have more than one compass in your party. If one is lost or broken, it may be difficult to keep from getting lost in lake country even with a good map. The compass is often necessary in order to identify physical features that may be clear on the map but from your position look like and blend with other features.

11. Stay off large bodies of water when the waves are large and when the wind is strong. In lightning storms, get off the water. Underwriters Laboratories, Inc., provides the following information: ". . . any isolated object in an open area tends to attract lightning. Therefore, a person in a boat or canoe, on a lake or other large body of water should make for the shore rather than remain exposed in the open. . . . It is recommended that the person keep away from . . . isolated trees, wire fences, hilltops or open spaces. Shelter in a cave, depression in the ground, a deep valley or canyon, dense woods or grove of trees is recommended."

12. Usually, employing a guide will be required or recommended for trips into wild country. This is particularly important to your safety.

13. Take the best available maps with you unless you thoroughly know the waters.

14. Whether you're afloat or on portage, don't become separated from your companions. And don't wander away from camp. Carelessness and inattentiveness in these respects present a danger of getting lost.

15. Select your campsite 2 or 3 hours before darkness. A variety of hazards lies in not getting settled down for the night by the time darkness comes.

16. If your swimming ability and water safety knowledge are only minimum, it is wise to take along a lifejacket for each person. These may be carefully tied in the canoe so that they will be readily accessible for wearing whenever turbulent water conditions develop. In fact, if large bodies of water must be crossed or if rapids are to be negotiated, it would be best for anyone to have a lifejacket under some conditions, as, for example, when the water is very cold as it is in the spring or the fall or even in the summertime in the far north. Normal self-rescue procedures are difficult to perform in very cold water and fatigue sets in quickly due to rapid loss of body heat. A lifejacket will give the lift needed, even to the most experienced waterman, under these conditions.

SOURCES OF INFORMATION ABOUT SPECIFIC CANOE TRIPS

There are many thousands of lakes and rivers in the United States and Canada on which to take canoeing trips. Obtain information about trips that may be taken locally from local people or the Chamber of Commerce. Information about other trips is available from agencies in both countries.

In the United States.—Every state capital has a department that provides information on request about vacation and recreational opportunities within its borders. These departments or offices do not have names common from state to state, but it should be possible to obtain the name of such a department for a specific state. Therefore, space is not devoted here to listing departments state by state. Some typical names of such departments may be helpful as a guide: *State Development Commission, State Tourist Bureau, State Publicity Bureau, Development and Publicity Commission.* Such offices in states where canoe trips are a popular recreational activity will have information to provide or will know where to direct you for information. For example, the Maine Development Commission, State House, Augusta, Maine, publishes a folder entitled *Maine Canoeing.* It has illustrations, a map of canoe routes, general information about canoeing in Maine, and 35 popular canoe trips listed and described. The information given includes the distance in miles, the time required in days, whether or not a guide is required, where the trip starts and finishes, portages to be made, map references, if there are any, and other information. Other states in canoeing country have similar material.

The Map Information Office, United States Geological Survey, Washington, D.C., will upon request provide a free information folder entitled *Topographic Maps* and *Topographic Map Symbols.*

It will also answer specific questions regarding availability of maps, and provide free an *Index to Topographic Mapping in (name of state).* This index contains an outline map of the state showing quadrangles bearing a name of a prominent city, town, or prominent natural feature. These quadrangles represent topographical maps available for 20 cents each from United States Geological Survey, Washington 25, D.C., for portions of all states east of the Mississippi. For states west of the Mississippi, maps should be ordered from Geological Survey, Federal Center, Denver, Colorado. The index of state maps contains additional information about the availability of special maps and sheets and a list of local agents who sell topographical maps at a slightly increased price but providing the convenience of not having to wait for the mails. For example, in Maine, topographical maps may be purchased in 23 different cities and towns.

In Canada.—The Canadian Government Travel Bureau, Ottawa, Canada, will provide free on request a booklet entitled *Canoe Trips in Canada,* which lists canoe trips by provinces, giving a short description of each. Available also are additional information and sketch maps of specific trips. Detailed topographical maps of specific localities are available from Maps Distribution Branch, Department of Mines and Technical Surveys, Ottawa, Canada. The cost is usually 25 cents each.

When writing to the Travel Bureau, give complete details about the information you desire. Specifically designate the section of the country in which a canoe trip is planned. In this way, one may obtain complete information, including unpublished facts about a region.

Additional information may be obtained from the specific province you plan to visit. Names and addresses of offices in each province are as follows:

Newfoundland: Tourist Development Office, St. John's

Prince Edward Island: Prince Edward Island Travel Bureau, Charlottetown

Nova Scotia: Bureau of Information, Dept. of Trade and Information, Halifax

New Brunswick: New Brunswick Travel Bureau, Fredericton

Quebec: Tourist Branch, Provincial Publicity Bureau, Quebec City

Ontario: Department of Travel and Publicity, 67 College St., Toronto

Manitoba: Bureau of Travel and Publicity, Department of Industry and Commerce, Legislative Building, Winnipeg

Saskatchewan: Tourist Branch, Legislative Building, Regina

Alberta: Alberta Travel Bureau, Legislative Building, Edmonton

British Columbia: Chief Forester, Forest Service, Parliament Buildings, Victoria, Attention: Parks & Recreational Division

Local councils of the Boy Scouts of America may arrange for canoe trips in the canoe country of Superior National Forest in Minnesota and the Quetico Provincial Park across the international boundary in Canada. These arrangements may be made through the Boy Scouts of America, Region Ten, 238 Minnesota Building, St. Paul 1, Minnesota. The trips are based out of the Sommers Wilderness Canoe Base, Ely, Minnesota. A similar opportunity for qualified Scouts is available through Region Seven, Boy Scouts of America, 9 W. Washington Street, Chicago 2, Illinois. The Region's canoe base is located on White Sand Lake, 5 miles east of Boulder Junction, Wisconsin. The canoe trips are taken in the heart of the lake country of northern Wisconsin and upper Michigan.

Members of the American Canoe Association engage in canoe cruising and camping. The association has a cruising committee interested in promoting this form of recreation. Its chairman will provide information about its activities. Members of the American Canoe Association receive a quarterly magazine, *The American Canoeist*, which contains names and addresses of current committee chairmen for the Association's various activities. Since the organization has no permanent headquarters, contacting a member is a logical first step in getting in touch with the officials or in obtaining a current publication address for *The American Canoeist*.

EQUIPMENT

The selection of equipment for a canoe trip should be done with care. Only essential items should be taken in order that the task of carrying them over portages will be no more difficult than necessary. On the other hand, certain luxury items that will add to the pleasure of the trip may be worth the additional effort of carrying them.

Canoes.—Typically, there should be one canoe for each two persons. If, however, children are going along, this rule will be modified. For example, one adult and two children with their gear would be the indicated load for a canoe; so would two adults and one child or even two children if the canoe is large. The size of canoes would ordinarily range from 16 to 18 feet. The canoes should be rigged with bow and stern lines and have an extra 50-foot coil of ¼-inch manila or similar line.

Paddles.—If the crew is tandem, each person should have two paddles: a softwood, lightweight paddle for use in deep water, and a hardwood paddle for use in shallow or rocky areas. If a child is along, he should have a special paddle of suitable size and weight.

Kneeling Pads.—Each person should have a kneeling pad. It should be comfortable but of a size that would permit jamming it into the end of the canoe during portages. It could also double as a pillow.

Repair Kit.—Chapter XIII, "Canoe Repair," contains information on which to base selection of items for a canoe-repair kit in accordance with the type of canoe being used. For example, a kit for a canvas-covered canoe might contain the following: a tube of waterproof liquid cement; one or two square feet of unbleached muslin for repairing damage to the canvas covering of the canoe; a roll of 1-inch plastic, electrical tape for covering tears in the canvas on an emergency basis until camp is made and the canoe can dry sufficiently to make a permanent repair; a small can of plastic resin cold-water glue for making repairs to broken paddles, thwarts, or gunwales; three lightweight 1½- or 2-inch C-clamps for applying pressure when gluing the latter parts; four 1-inch rubber bands cut from an automobile tire inner tube for use in applying pressure when gluing a split paddle blade; a screwdriver and a pair of pliers. Additional items that would be useful under some circumstances are a canvas needle (sailmaker's needle), size 14, 15, or 16; sewing twine or machine cord; a small piece of beeswax for waxing the twine or cord; and a sailor's palm. These additional items would be useful also in making repairs to moccasins, packs, and tents. A spool of button-and-carpet thread and a couple of suitable needles could be added for use in repairing clothing. All these items could be placed in a small bag made of strong canvas. This could be secured under the deck, well up into one end of the canoe.

A Carry Yoke.—If you are going into canoeing country where portages are many and long, it will add to your comfort to have a yoke. (See Chapter IV.)

Team Items (one to each canoe).—

A canteen—for drinking water.

Axe—a single-bitted axe, 2 to 3 pounds, with an overall length of 24 to 28 inches. It should be kept sheathed always when not in use. Include also an axe file and sharpening stone. (A good substitute for an axe is a surgical saw.)

A trench shovel—for digging and covering latrines.

A tarpaulin (small size) for use as a cooking shelter in rainy weather, and other uses.

A tent—a lightweight one. In the spring and fall, when insects are not a problem, the canoe may be rigged as a satisfactory shelter (see Chapter III) unless the weather is wet and cold, in which case a tent will be desirable. Tents with sewed-in floors and special insect-proof netting are best, but of course more expensive than simpler types.

Insect bomb—for use in tent.

Lifejackets—one for each person if large bodies of water or rapids are to be negotiated during the trip or if the individual's swimming ability and water safety knowledge is deficient. They should be worn when turbulent conditions develop. Keep them tied in the canoe at other times.

Maps—an inexpensive oilskin or plastic case will keep the maps dry and protect them from wear.

A canvas or plastic bucket—for carrying water and to hold lunch.

A pair of canvas gloves—for the cook.

Cooking and eating gear—lightweight, compact nest-type is most suitable.

First aid kit—See page 335.

Personal Equipment.—It is easy to take more equipment than is needed, and equally easy to leave out an essential item through oversight. To guard against both possibilities, it is wise to read carefully the recommendations of those who have had experience. The following is a suggested list:

Insect repellent

Matches in a waterproof container

Toilet articles, floating soap, and two towels

A small sheath knife or jackknife

Flashlight, two-cell type, with two extra batteries; or a pen light

Pocket compass

Sleeping bag, or two to four blankets

Chapstick

A large pack (Duluth, rucksack, or other large packs)

A groundcloth

Water-purifying tablets (halazone)

Notebook and pencil

Sunglasses (optional)

Camera (optional)

Tissue paper

Sunburn lotion or olive oil

Binoculars (optional)

Fishing tackle (optional)

Sewing kit (optional)

Candles (optional)

Air mattress (optional)

Clothing.—The items suggested are for the summer months.

A pair of heavy shoes for portages and a pair of moccasins or similar soft shoe for use in the canoe

Two pairs of trousers of strong material, like dungarees (wide-bottom type). A heavy belt is desirable.

Two sets of underwear

Two pairs of wool socks; one heavy and one medium weight

Two long-sleeved shirts; one wool, the other strong cotton

A hat; preferably an old felt hat, but a cap will do.

A poncho or raincoat. A sou'wester may be needed if you have only a cap.

Handkerchiefs

Swim trunks

A waterproof windbreaker. If it isn't wool lined, include also a sweater.

FOOD

Selection, packing, and preparation of food require careful consideration by those who plan to go on a canoe trip.

Selection should be based first upon the important need to provide well-balanced meals under environmental circumstances that usually induce more than ordinary appetite. This will require menu-planning, meal by meal, during the trip-planning period, in order to know what food items to buy and in what quantity. This is assuming, of course, that the trip will be taken where resupplying will not be possible during the canoe trip. If the canoe trip will involve any portaging, it is particularly desirable to purchase food in forms featuring lightness and diminished bulk. It will in this way pack better and be less laborious to carry. Dried foods and dehydrated foods are excellent in these respects.

Packing the food so that it will fit neatly with other things in the canoe and be easy to carry on portages is a task requiring thought and knowledge of methods. Consideration must also be given to its arrangement in the pack in respect to accessibility so that food for a specific meal may be found without handling the entire supply of food.

Preparation of the food into tasty meals is the objective. The beginning camper should practice outdoor preparation of food at home or on short trips near home so that he will have experience behind him when he goes on his carefully planned canoe trip.

Space does not permit going into detail here regarding the many aspects of the subject of food. The Boy Scouts of America *Handbook for Boys*[6] has sufficient information in Chapter 16, "Fire Building," and Chapter 17, "Camp Cooking," to enable one who studies it to handle the food situation satisfac-

[6]Handbook for Boys (*New Brunswick, N.J., Boy Scouts of America*).

torily. Handel's *Canoe Camping* contains two chapters with excellent information on food and cooking: Chapter 2, "Plans and Preparations," and Chapter 6, "Wilderness Cooking and Food." In addition, there is a wealth of written material on food preparation, including ordinary cookbooks and books on camping and campcraft.

PACKING AND PORTAGING

It is desirable to efficiently pack the various items to be taken on the trip. Food should be packed in small cloth bags. Other items such as clothes, toilet articles, mess kit, and canteen should each have its separate cloth or lightweight canvas container. These many small bags, along with such other items as blankets, tent, raincoat, and first aid kit should be systematically arranged in one large pack to eliminate loose items that clutter up the canoe and are a nuisance on portages. The *Handbook for Boys* gives helpful details about how to pack efficiently and tells how to make food bags inexpensively.

Packs should be placed in the amidships section of the canoe. By trial and error, adjustments may be made so that the canoe trims even fore and aft and from side to side. If the weather is damp, the packs may be covered with one groundcloth or tarps. Two or three straight sticks an inch or more in diameter and 5 or 6 feet long placed under the packs will keep them out of water that may accumulate in the bottom of the canoe if it rains. It may be a nuisance to regard these sticks as permanent equipment and carry them day after day over portage after portage. You may prefer to discard them when they are not needed and pick up others when next the weather is threatening. It should not be necessary to lash packs into a canoe. Every precaution should be taken to assure no capsizings, but even if a capsizing occurred the packs would float, if they did not contain a lot of canned food, and could be picked up by another canoe, or later when the capsized canoe was emptied. It is wise to tie loose nonbuoyant items, such as an axe, to the canoe.

A knowledge of the methods of carrying a canoe presented in Chapter IV will be the basis for efficient portaging. The easiest methods will be those using the commercial-type yoke, or the improvised paddle yoke properly padded. It will be important not to hurry on portages: doing so may cause an accident, such as a bad fall, and will cause unnecessary fatigue and discomfort. A too-heavy load is also dangerous and unnecessary, though of course one should be willing to do at least his share of the work in keeping with his capacity for heavy work. Frequent stops for rest should be taken if they are needed and time out taken for recreation. A portage should not be a contest of speed and strength under the typical present-day circumstances in which canoe trips are taken.

CAMPSITE

Some features to consider in selecting a site and setting up camp are as follows:

1. Avoid making camp near tall trees, which may be struck by lightning or blown down in a strong wind. In the mountains be sure you are not in the path of rocks, which a rainstorm might set loose.

2. Select a spot that is relatively open but not a hilltop.

3. In cool weather look for shelter from the wind. This might be provided by a grove of small trees or a hollow, or by camping on the shore in the direction from which the wind is blowing (windward shore).

4. In warm weather, a breeze in camp may be desirable to keep insects away. In this case you would seek a campsite on the leeward shore or on a peninsula.

5. Avoid lowland along either a river or lakeshore as a camp-

site. Not only the insect problem but the discomfort of the mist or low-lying fog over the water at night will be present. It is better to seek a campsite with an elevation of at least 10 feet above the surface of the water when possible in order to be dry and comfortable at night.

6. Be sure that your campsite is not where a rainstorm in the night will flood you out. For example, a gully might become a small stream in the event of rain. In some regions it will be necessary to camp far enough above high-water mark to be out of reach of a flash flood.

7. Do not pitch your tent or make your fire on a portage or game trail, and avoid camping too close to such natural hazards as cliffs and waterfalls.

A copy of the Boy Scouts of America *Handbook for Boys* is a good thing to have in your pack, for ideas helpful on your trip, both in camp and on the trail. Other books you will find helpful include:

Bernard S. Mason, *Woodcraft* (New York, A. S. Barnes & Company, 1939).

Bernard S. Mason, *The Junior Book of Camping and Woodcraft* (New York, A. S. Barnes & Company, 1943).

George W. Martin, *Modern Camping Guide* (New York, D. Appleton-Century Company, Inc., 1940).

Dillon Wallace, *The Camper's Handbook* (New York, Fleming H. Revell Company, 1936).

CANOE SONG

Melody from a German Pilgrim Song of the 15th Century. As so much of the pioneering in Canada was done by canoe along waterways, this seemed to be an appropriate tune for the lyric, which should be sung as if to the rhythm of a paddle.

John Murray Gibbon   Old German Pilgrim Song

FROM NORTHLAND SONGS NO. 1

CHAPTER XII

CANOEING ON SWIFT RIVERS

If you're already a proficient canoeist on deep and quiet waters, you may quickly learn skilled canoe-handling on rivers with swift currents. You must, however, become familiar with some of the characteristics of swift rivers and with the safety procedures to heed when on them. It is desirable also to consider the type of equipment wise to use, and to practice the special techniques for handling a canoe on swift rivers.

RIVER CHARACTERISTICS

The downhill slope, or fall, of a river conforms to the general lay of the land. Sometimes the river is relatively steep and swift. At other times, fairly flat and slow moving. But always it seeks out the lowest land and easiest path downward. In general, a river flows rapidly—though irregularly—near its source, and gradually more slowly but more steadily as it reaches the broad valleys near the sea.

When a river narrows, as for example when it flows from open country in through a gorge, its speed increases, then decreases when it leaves the gorge and widens out again. When it flows from a deep bed into one more shallow, the river speeds up, then slows down as it deepens again.

The water in a river flows fastest near the surface and in the middle because friction with the bottom, the sides, and even with the adjacent slower-moving water is least there. (The upper ⁹⁄₁₀ths moves faster than the water beneath it. The latter moves slower and slower as it nears the bottom.) Thus, when two rivers of different sizes have the same fall, the larger river flows more swiftly because it is retarded less by friction than the smaller river. When two rivers of the same size have the same fall, the one with the smoother bottom and sides will be the swifter because of less friction. It follows logically, therefore, that a smooth-bedded river of lesser fall than a river with a rocky bed might flow the faster of the two. On the other hand, it will be far less turbulent and hence safer.

The speed of flow varies from river to river and from week to week in the same river, but the range is generally from less than 1 mile per *hour* in broad valleys to usually not more than 10 miles per *hour* in turbulent rapids. Some rapids, of course, flow faster than this, but they are rarer than one would think. Often their great turbulence gives the impression of greater speed. For many years the engineers of the United States Geological Survey have been instructed to report maximum stream velocities in excess of 20 feet per *second* (f.p.s.)[1] as measured at their thousands of gauging stations. From 1929 through 1954 only six reports were received in their headquarters at Washington. They are as follows:

Speed	Date	Location
22.11 f.p.s. (15 m.p.h.)	April 5, 1929	Little Colorado River, Grand Falls, Arizona
22.4 f.p.s. (15.2 m.p.h.)	May 14, 1932	Potomac River at Chain Bridge, Washington, D.C.
22.26 f.p.s. (15.1 m.p.h.)	Sept. 27, 1936	Brazos River near Waco, Texas
24.59 f.p.s. (16.7 m.p.h.)	Feb. 4, 1939	Caney Fork near Rock Island, Tennessee
20.23 f.p.s. (13.76 m.p.h.)	Jan. 18, 1953	North Santiam River below Boulder Creek near Detroit, Oregon
23.98 f.p.s. (16.3 m.p.h.)	April 26, 1954	Iron River near White Pine, Michigan

[1] *20 feet per second = 13.6 miles per hour.*

On a long, straight stretch of river, the deepest water is usually in midstream. If one bank is considerably higher than the other, the deep water and strong current will be closer to the high bank. If the other side of the river is bordered by lowland, there will be shallows quite far out along the shore.

On bends in the river, the deep water and main current will be nearer the outside of the bend. Water near the inside of the bend may be shallow—especially if the adjacent land is low. If the bend is sharp and the inside shore is peninsular rather than a smooth curve, the shallows may take the form of a bar extending quite far out.

In general, the main channel of a winding river flows from the outside of one bend to the outside of the next bend. Downstream from points of land, islands, rocks, logs, and other obstructions, there are areas of slack water and eddies, places where portions of the current turn and head upstream. The current of these eddies will be quite noticeable if the main current is swift, but barely perceptible if the main current is slow. In either case, however, the eddy is easily recognized because of its contrasting smoothness (Fig. 12).

Shallow places with an even but gravelly bottom cause a lot of tiny waves, often called "sandpaper." If the shallow place is "slick," the bottom is smooth, possibly a flat ledge of rock.

The presence of a large submerged rock in the bed of a river is revealed by a surface disturbance. The typical form of this disturbance is a "boil," the swirling upheaval of water downstream of the rock. The water right on top of the rock is smooth and higher and is tumbling down into the swirling water (Figs. 1 and 5).

A rock that projects above the surface splits the current so that a wall of water flows by each side of the rock. Below such a rock is a distinct eddy.

When fast water running through rocks and shallow areas

hits deeper water moving much slower, its momentum is checked so abruptly that a standing wave, called a "haystack," is caused (Fig. 1). This wave stays in the same place, and changes only its size and shape in conformance to significant changes in the volume of water flowing in the river. Haystacks, usually in groups of several to many, are spaced at fairly equal intervals (Figs. 5 and 10) and designate the deepest water in that part of the river.

The rock-caused disturbance and the haystacks create rapids, or "white water."

FIG. 1 (left)—In the foreground is a "boil," a swirling upheaval of water caused by a large rock directly under the smooth water upstream (left foreground of picture) of the boil.
In the background is a standing wave called a "haystack," caused by fast-moving water striking deeper and slower-moving water.

FIG. 2 (right)—An iron shoe, or socket, on the end of a river pole protects it from damage. These were each made by cutting off the end of a boat hook just above where the hook joined the body of the socket.

EQUIPMENT

Canoes.—Swift-water canoeing is easiest with a canoe that has either a shoe keel or no keel at all. The standard keel makes canoe-handling sluggish in rapids, where quick maneuvering is imperative. A keel also increases the likelihood that the canoe will swamp or capsize if it gets momentarily out of control and strikes a rock while not in line with the current. A keelless canoe or one with a shoe keel will in many cases slide off a rock without mishap, but a standard keel will catch on the rock that is not extremely smooth.

If a keelless canoe is not available, a keel canoe that has considerable rocker to its bottom line will prove satisfactory with skillful handling and greater vigilance. Although such a canoe is quite maneuverable in spite of its keel, the danger of hanging-up on a rock is still present.

The size of a canoe for white-water canoeing should be determined on the basis of this principle: when maximum maneuverability is required and when obstructions are present just beneath the surface of the water, it is good to have a canoe that rides lightly on the water ("like a yellow leaf in autumn"). The 15- and 16-foot canoes are suitable for solo handling in rapids. Manned by one person, such a canoe will draw only a little water. But with two persons aboard, it will draw enough to risk damaging the canoe. This, of course, is a generalization. Obviously, the combined weight of two men might be about the same as the weight of one heavy man. Or, the width and general fullness of the canoe bottom often make one 15-footer draw much less than another. Generally, 17- and 18-foot canoes are the most suitable for tandem crews.

Paddles.—In rapids it is often necessary to "claw" along from rock to rock, or push on the rocky or gravelly bottom with the paddle. It is therefore desirable to have hardwood paddles for this type of canoeing. (See Chapter III for information on paddles.)

Poles.—Although poling upstream and even "setting" downstream may be done with a long hardwood paddle in shallow sections of a river, it is better to have a pole especially prepared for these tasks. Ash and spruce are commonly used for poles. Some canoeists prefer ash because of its strength; others favor spruce because of its lightness. Poles are an inch or more in diameter and range from 9 to 14 feet or more in length; a 10-foot pole is quite common. They can be purchased from some canoe manufacturers or made at home. The end of the pole is protected with a pointed iron socket, often called a shoe, or pike. These shoes may either be purchased from a canoe manufacturer or made by a blacksmith. A quick way to obtain both pole and shoe, if you live near a marine hardware store, is to buy a boathook pole of ash and a galvanized malleable iron boathook. These may be purchased separately or already assembled. If you buy the hook separately you can put it on a pole you can make yourself. First, convert the hook into an iron shoe by sawing off the end of the boathook just above the point where the hook joins the body of the socket (Fig. 2). Then, thin down the shaft of the pole to make it lighter. Finally, if the pole doesn't have a knob at the other end, you can shape one. The knob keeps the pole from slipping out through your hand.

Bow and Stern Lines.—An efficient way to rig bow and stern lines so that they will be out of the way when not needed and yet always ready for instant use is shown in Chapter III.

Tracking Line.—An extra piece of line, for example 50 feet of ¼-inch manila, is a good thing to have along for tracking or lining purposes. The regular bow and stern lines are not always sufficient.

A Lifesaving Heaving Line.—The tracking line may double as a lifesaving heaving line, especially if it has a monkey's fist at one end. Recently, heaving lines of a new material called polyethylene have come on the market. Unlike heaving lines of manila, nylon, sisal, or cotton, they float. With a monkey's fist[2] worked into the end of such a line to increase throwing

[2]*For information and diagrams explaining how to make a monkey's fist see: Clifford W. Ashley,* The Ashley Book of Knots *(Garden City, N.Y., Doubleday & Co., Inc., 1944), pp. 353–355.*

accuracy, this becomes an excellent rescue device. The strength of the line is adequate for rescue work but not for heavy hauling. The ⁵⁄₁₆-inch size has a test strength of 500 lbs. For comparison, sisal is rated at 800 lbs., manila at 1,000, and nylon at 1,950.

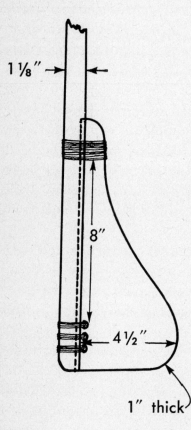

1 ⅛"

8"

4½"

1" thick

FIG. 3—A hardwood "crowfoot" attached to the end of an ash pole 10 to 12 feet long for swamp use or for elementary practice of the technique of poling, before attempting it on a swift river. The other end could be ironshod. The "crowfoot" is bound into a groove in the pole with wire serving.

WHITE-WATER SAFETY

Negotiating the rapids of swift rivers is exciting and often dangerous. The danger exists for any canoeist in water of violent turbulence. Less turbulent water, quite safe for the experienced canoeman, is dangerous for those inadequately prepared for it.

The first thing in being prepared is knowing how to swim, the more skilled the better. Minimum swimming skill should be sufficient to make the individual at home and at ease in the water when fully clothed and when he is suddenly plunged under water.

Learn the skills of tandem and solo paddling, self-rescue, and rescue in smooth water before you try swift rivers. Even the special skill of using a pole may be practiced alongshore on quiet streams or on lakes. For practice in places where the bottom is soft, a "crowfoot" may be attached to the end of the pole (Fig. 3).

Experience in running rapids and poling up against them should be acquired by starting on easy ones and gradually seeking out more difficult water as you master techniques. There is a limit beyond which it is foolhardy to go in testing one's ability to run white water. Always stop far short of risk to life and limb.

Follow these safety procedures—they're all recommended by canoeists skilled in white-water canoeing:

1. Undertake only rapids of a difficulty for which you are prepared. Always work with a skilled canoeist whenever possible.

2. If the rapids are heavy, wear a lifejacket (Fig. 9) even if you're a good swimmer. This is particularly important when the water is cold; one becomes fatigued quickly in cold water.

3. Wear soft-soled canvas shoes or the equivalent. If both the water and the air are cold, wear suitable clothing. Wool is best: if you get wet, it will keep you warmer than will other types of material. Take along a change of clothing packed in a waterproof bag.

4. Begin on moderate rapids—even if you are experienced —at the start of the season. Don't try canoeing on heavy water until you are again in condition for it.

5. Group activity is safer than that done alone. Two, and preferably more, canoes assure that someone will be able to help in an emergency. Canoes should stay together, but not bunch; a single-file arrangement is best. Upon reaching a difficult run, all should put into shore and then one crew at a time should go through while the others stand at strategic points alongshore, prepared to throw heaving lines to effect a rescue in case of an upset. In some cases it may be advisable for one crew to remain afloat at the foot of the rapids or to station their canoe in an eddy. Then they'll be ready to paddle out into the stream if a rescue operation is necessary.

6. When coming to an unknown stretch of rapids or to rapids you haven't run recently, put in to shore and walk along the bank the entire length of the rapids. Examine them carefully to determine if they are safe to run, making mental notes of special hazards. It is also wise to take a good long look from the head of the rapids, standing up to do so if necessary, before starting down. This same alertness to what lies ahead should prevail throughout the run. You can move sideward or backward into eddies for a rest and examination of the river ahead; or you can slow the canoe almost to a stop above each pitch to look ahead and select the best course down.

7. When you're doubtful about the safety of running a heavy stretch of rapids, don't gamble; carry around it or line the canoe down through it.

8. Broadly speaking, there are three speeds at which rapids may be run: the speed of the current, faster than the current, and slower than the current. In moderate water, the speed of the current is appropriate. Where the current is very swift and turbulent, safety dictates a speed much slower than the current to prevent the canoe from burying into large waves and to give the needed time to observe the water and select the best course. Traveling faster than the current is wise only

in easy-to-moderate rapids with which one is very familiar. If you know the rapids well, hazards are minimized and the exhilaration of traveling down at higher speed is not foolhardy.

9. Keep the canoe in line with the current when running rapids or poling up through them. Move into eddies broadside or from a downstream direction, keeping the canoe in line with the direction of the main current. When alongside the shore or bank, keep the upstream end of the canoe closer to the bank than the downstream end so that the current will hold the canoe against the bank rather than catch it and pull it broadside out into the stream.

10. If you should fall overboard and the canoe goes on out of your reach, and the current is too strong to permit you to stand up and wade to shore, get on your back immediately with your feet pointed downstream (Fig. 4). Kick your legs enough to keep them up near the surface and directly out in front of you so that they will protect your body from injury by rocks. Scull with your hands in such a way that you work diagonally out of the main stream into a nearby eddy or gradually in to shore.

11. If your canoe capsizes or swamps, follow the universal principle of staying with the canoe, holding onto it for support and protection. You should, however, quickly move to its upstream end. This will keep you from getting caught between the canoe and a rock. You will serve as an anchor to the upstream end, so that the canoe will swing into line with the current. In this position you are protected and your canoe is most easily guided gradually out of the main stream into an eddy or in to shore where it may be emptied. If your swamped canoe is in an athwartstream position, keep the upstream gunwale high while swinging the canoe into line with the current; for if the open part of the canoe is upstream and the canoe

FIG. 4—If you fall overboard and the canoe gets away from you, get on your back with your legs pointed downstream. This is the best way to protect yourself from bodily injury when the current is too strong to permit you to stand up and wade ashore. Scull with your hands in such a way that you move diagonally out of the main stream into an eddy or in near shore in quieter water.

is held by a rock, the canoe may be broken in two or at least badly damaged by the great force of the water against its inside. In very turbulent streams it may be dangerous to hold onto the canoe because it may be pulled under and hurled about violently. In such a case let it go, and concentrate on your own rescue as mentioned in 10, above.

12. Learn to recognize the nature of the stream by the appearance of the surface of the water. You will then be able to avoid hitting rocks or other underwater hazards. If the "haystacks" are large and foamy, avoid their centers; instead, go through their lower portions to the side (Fig. 5). If standing waves are very foamy it is because a lot of air is mixed with the water. Since this type of wave will not support your canoe like regular water, you will bury deeper into it and take in water. Enough of these waves could swamp you.

13. The current will tend to carry you toward the outside

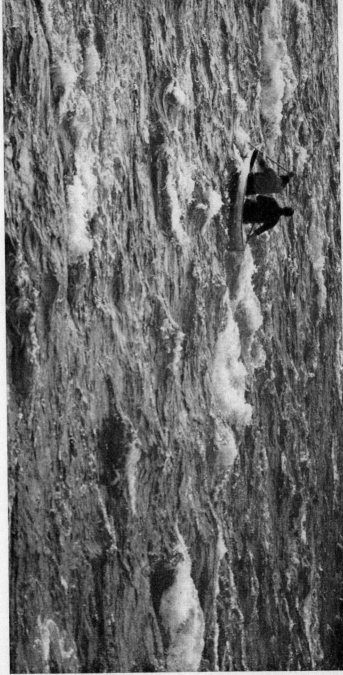

FIG. 5—Choosing a safe course down through rapids. This crew followed a course just to the left of the row of heaviest haystacks back of them and then moved sideward enough to pass to the right of the heavy one ahead. Note the single foamy wave formation below a relatively smooth place in the left foreground. This combination indicates rocks projecting up near the surface of the water. The wise thing is to avoid such places.

of bends. This may be dangerous in very swift water because of low tree limbs, undermined banks, logs, rocks or ledges, or even fallen trees. Size up the situation; if it seems wise, hug the inside of the bend, staying only far enough out to avoid bars and eddies.

14. If you hang-up on a rock in a moderate current, you may be able to slide off or back off by shifting position in the canoe. If the current is sufficient to present immediate risk of being rolled over, the wisest thing to do is to quickly vault overboard in the most favorable direction, free the canoe, and then step back in again if possible, or move the canoe to where you can reboard.

15. Stay off swift water in darkness, and away from falls at all times. Put in to shore a safe distance above falls, carry around, and launch again well away from the foot of the falls.

CANOE-HANDLING TECHNIQUES

Trim of Canoe.—For solo handling using a paddle, a position at or near amidships permits maximum maneuverability and shallow draft. It also permits maximum rise and fall of the ends of the canoe as the waves work upon it (Fig. 6). These are all desirable features.

When a pole is used in solo handling, for poling upstream or "setting" downstream, it is usually best to trim the canoe so that its downstream end is lower than its upstream end (Figs. 7 and 8). In this way the upstream end rides lightly on the water and escapes the grip of the current, while the downstream end is firmly gripped by the current. This results in keeping the canoe in line with the current. Sometimes, however, a strong wind may be blowing directly downstream. This will call for putting the canoe on even trim (Fig. 9) so that the wind will not blow the upstream end around with more force than the current grips the downstream end.

FIG. 6—When running rapids solo it is advisable to take a position at or near amidships as shown. This permits shallowest draft, maximum maneuverability, and maximum rise and fall of the ends of the canoe as the waves work on it. The latter is important in keeping out water when waves are large.

FIG. 7—Poling upstream. Note that the canoe is trimmed so that the stern is deeper in the water than the bow. In this way, the force of the current will grip the downstream end and hold the canoe in line with the current.

For downstream work in tandem handling with paddles, the best way to trim the canoe is even. If the rapids are rough, requiring that the canoe be held back slower than the current, there is a theoretic advantage in having the downstream end lower than the upstream end to help keep the canoe headed with the current. But if the downstream end is lower in the water,

FIG. 8—Setting downstream by snubbing the canoe. The canoe is trimmed with its downstream end deeper in the water than its upstream end so that the force of the current will hold it in line with the current.

FIG. 9—Poling upstream against current and wind. When a wind is blowing downstream it is best to trim the canoe even, fore and aft; otherwise, the force of the wind striking the upstream end may be greater than the current's grip on the downstream end and will turn the canoe broadside to the current. Note lifejacket, which should be worn in hazardous circumstances.

it will not rise as readily. Therefore, it is doubtless best to trim the craft even, moving the crew closer together for negotiating heavy rapids so that the ends will more readily rise and fall with the waves, thus keeping out water (Fig. 10).

A tandem crew going upstream, using either paddles or pole (Fig. 11), should have the downstream end lower than the

FIG. 10—In heavy rapids it is wise for the members of a tandem crew to locate close together so that the ends of the canoe will rise and fall with the waves to keep the water out. Chapter III contains information on thwart placement in a canoe, and Chapter V explains efficient positioning of crew members in respect to location of thwarts.

FIG. 11—A tandem crew poling upstream. The canoe is trimmed so that its downstream end is deeper in the water than its upstream end.

upstream end because in going against the current the canoe
is constantly being gripped by its force. If this grip is firmer
at the upstream end, the canoe will run off at an angle and
finally be turned broadside to the current. With the downstream end low and firmly gripped by the current, the canoe
is held in line with it. These principles also apply when a tandem crew uses a pole for "setting" downstream, for the canoe
is being continually brought to a stop in the current.

Fig. 12—Upstream paddling: getting a fast start out of an eddy.

Upstream Paddling.—Upstream paddling generally is not
as popular as going downstream; it is more difficult. It is sometimes necessary, however, and it reveals the nature of a stream
quickly because to progress the paddler must constantly study
the water and try to set his course where the current offers the
least resistance and provides the most help. It is not possible
to enumerate in detail the exact course to follow on a typical
river, for there is no really typical river—and the same stretch
on a river will vary according to water level.

There are, however, principles that are common to all rivers
on which you would paddle upstream. Paddle near shore where

the current is more moderate than in midstream. On most rivers, one shore will be better than the other in this respect. A quick recovery with extra attention to relaxation during the recovery will prove better for most persons than attempt-- ing to paddle with greater power. Rest in the eddies if neces-- sary. Pick up speed in an eddy in order to hit the current hard at the outside of the eddy (Fig. 12). This will enable you to fight your way up through a steep place to a flatter place above, to a similar eddy on the same side, or to quarter across the current to an eddy on the other side or below a large rock or small island. Keep in mind that there are many slack places and eddies that are small, and hence not obvious without close examination of the surface of the water. They will often give that small amount of help that is just enough to carry you through.

When rapids are not present, but a strong current must be overcome, paddle near the shore that has the slackest water. On a winding river this will be on the inside of the bend. Stay on this side until you can see ahead that the river bends in the other direction. When you feel the current getting stronger where you are, head diagonally across the river to the other shore where you should find slower water.

Downstream Paddling.—When the river has a fast current but no rapids, it will be most satisfactory to paddle in the main current. You will go along at a pleasantly rapid speed and be always in the deepest water the river provides. This latter fact will assure as much as possible that you will not run onto a rock.

When the river has rapids, proceed in accordance with the recommendations in the previous section on "White-Water Safety." Some of the specific canoe-handling techniques in- volved in following these recommendations are as follows:

1. When maneuvering a canoe off its course in rapids for

the purpose of avoiding a rock close ahead or setting a better course in respect to the general pattern of rocks for some distance ahead, move it sideward. To avoid a single rock you often need to move the canoe only a foot or two. Missing a rock by a few inches is sufficient: when the canoe is in line with the current, the water—deflecting at a slight angle from the rock—will keep the canoe away.

In solo paddling, the draw and pushover strokes and sculling and reverse sculling strokes are best to use. Rudder-type strokes, including the stationary draw and stationary push-over, are ineffectual unless the canoe is moving faster than the water. When the direction to move is opposite the paddler's paddling side, he will find that the reverse sculling stroke is surprisingly effective because of the automatic emphasis on the forward-press portion. This holds the canoe back and moves it sideward, thus giving the desired result. This is mentioned as an example of the fact that many of the paddling strokes described in Chapter VI and practiced in quiet water are readily adaptable to swift water.

In tandem paddling, moving sideward is a simple matter of alert teamwork. If the bowman sees a rock directly ahead, he should move the bow of the canoe out of line with that rock. The sternman should immediately move the stern of the canoe in the same direction the same distance so that the canoe is still in line with the current. The bowman could use any of the strokes mentioned above, plus the cross-bow draw, as needed. The sternman could also use any of those mentioned plus a reverse quarter sweep. Although it is expected that because of the bowman's better ability to examine the water he will initiate nearly all emergency maneuvering, the sternman may also take this initiative at times, especially if he is more experienced or more alert than the bowman. He will move his end of the canoe sideward. An alert bowman will then move the bow as required to maintain alignment with the current. He would be helped by the tendency of the current to swing the downstream end of the canoe into line. In most cases, it is necessary for the crew to have some agreed-upon voice signals to assure teamwork. For example, some canoeists use the word "right" or "left" to mean that the partner should move his end of the canoe in that direction.

2. Slowing the canoe down in fast water may be done by any type of back-paddling movements. The two most efficient ones are back sculling, done aft of the paddler's position, and the simple backwater stroke. The sculling stroke, though not as effective as repeated backwater strokes, can be developed with practice to the point where it may be used to actually bring the canoe to a stop in reasonably fast water (Fig. 13). The backwater stroke as done by a solo paddler may be refined to a reverse J stroke in order to keep the canoe in precise control while slowing it or stopping it. A tandem crew doing

FIG. 13—Back-sculling in moderately fast current (between 6 and 7 miles per hour). With this technique the canoe may be slowed up or even stopped to give you time to select the best channel or to prevent the canoe from knifing into large waves.

back paddling will usually combine it with whatever draw or pushover strokes are necessary to keep the canoe in line with the current. In streams where the water is fast and turbulent enough to require that the canoe be kept at a pace slower than the current, there may still be intervals when the canoe may be allowed to go along for short distances at the speed of the current since steep sections of the rapids often alternate with relatively level stretches. Often in moderately severe white water the slowing down will be done only by the sternman while the bowman devotes his attention entirely to assuring a collision-free course and to avoiding heavy portions of the haystacks.

Once again, remember that when the current is fast and the water turbulent, you will get along nicely if you hold the canoe back slower than the current (Fig. 14); if you do not, you will bury into wave after wave (Fig. 15), taking in water and possibly swamping.

Poling Upstream.—Going upstream is much easier with a pole than with a paddle. In fact, streams that are impossible to climb with a paddle can be climbed with only moderate expenditure of energy by a canoeman who has become adept at using a pole, provided the water is shallow enough. Water over 3 feet deep gets increasingly difficult. Usually, fast water is shallow—if not in midstream, then nearer shore.

In solo handling, the canoeist takes his position so that the canoe trims with the downstream end lower in the water than the upstream end (Fig. 7). His stance is essentially the same as that used for *standing paddling* (Fig. 8 in Chapter V), namely, facing diagonally toward the side with feet apart in the fore and aft direction and about on the line of the keel. He presses one leg against a thwart (which leg will depend upon the location of the thwarts and factors that might affect trim, such as a pack or other gear). Whenever possible, the

FIG. 14—When the canoe is held back at a speed slower than the current, in a fast and turbulent river, it does not bury into the waves, but rises and falls with them, keeping the canoe dry as long as the centers of larger haystacks are avoided. Note that the paddlers are dry and that the bow is rising with the wave.

FIG. 15—In a fast and turbulent river a canoe will bury into large waves if not held back to a speed slower than the current. Note the bow burying into a wave. The bowman's wet clothing indicates that the canoe has hit other waves too hard, upstream of its present position.

forward leg should be the one to brace against a thwart because, in addition to helping the poleman keep his balance, it is also something to push against with his leg while poling.

Before considering the details of the poling technique, it will be helpful to reflect on the essential thing that happens when a canoe is maneuvered with a pole. The poleman sets the point of the pole on the bottom of the river and by applying force to the pole moves *himself* along. This is possible because the canoe supports his weight and at the same time moves easily on the surface of the water. The canoe, however, would move in a general sort of way without specific direction except for the fact that the poleman's points of contact with the canoe, namely his two feet and the leg that presses against a thwart automatically apply a constant controlling pressure against the parts of the canoe rather than merely seeking support in it. It is helpful, therefore, to the beginning poleman to think in terms of steering and of generally controlling the canoe with his feet, working them in unison or in opposition as the situation demands.

The detailed description of poling upstream is as follows:

1. Drop the point of the pole to the bottom just about even with where you stand in the canoe. Hold it firmly, with both hands a comfortable distance apart (Fig. 16).

2. Using the proper foot-pressure, get the canoe headed in exact alignment with the current.

3. Thrust backward with the pole in a direction parallel with the keel of the canoe (Fig. 17). For additional power, "climb" the pole hand-over-hand.

4. Recover the pole for the next thrust by reversing the hand action, or with a tossing action that slides the pole back through the hands. If your thrust was a single action, that is, with no "climbing" of the pole involved, and you are in quite shallow water, you can make the recovery by simply lifting

FIG. 16 (left)—Poling upstream. The pole is set, the canoe is in line with the current, and the thrust is just starting.

FIG. 17 (right)—Poling upstream. The poleman has "climbed" to the end of the pole and is giving a final thrust.

your bottom hand and swinging it forward and upward enough to clear the surface of the water with the point of the pole. As the swing gets under way, you can grasp the pole a couple of feet lower down with your other hand and help guide it to a forward position from which its point may be dropped and set firmly on the bottom for the next thrust. If the end of the pole should get caught between two rocks so that it cannot be readily recovered, ease the canoe back until recovery is possible; but guard against losing control of the situation. It is better to drop the pole and reach for your paddle than to be knocked out of the canoe by the pole or to be swamped or capsized.

5. In addition to getting the canoe in proper alignment before the thrust, the canoe may be steered as the thrust takes place by modifying the direction of thrust as necessary. For example, to turn the bow slightly toward the poling side, the stern would be pushed slightly toward the opposite side. This would be done by bringing the upper end of the pole in over the canoe and thrusting backward at an angle of 5 or 10 de-

grees with the stern, rather than directly astern. Conversely, to turn the bow slightly away from the poling side, the upper end of the pole would be held out away from the canoe more than is normal. The thrust would be made so that the stern of the canoe would be pulled over in the direction of the poling side.

6. Poling is ordinarily done continuously on one side of the canoe, but this need not be regarded as an ironclad rule. There may be times when the poler would prefer to pole occasionally on the other side. Constant changing from side to side should not be necessary.

7. Moving the canoe sideward in the direction of the poling side is done simply by setting the point of the pole on the bottom out away from the side of the canoe, abeam of the poler, and pulling the canoe over to it. Move the canoe in the other direction by setting the point of the pole in the same place and pushing the canoe away from it.

8. In working upstream, work continuously but do not hurry as much as you at first may think you need to. Each thrust will give your canoe enough forward momentum to give you ample time to recover for the succeeding thrust.

In tandem handling, the bowman often uses a paddle while the sternman poles. The poling technique is the same as above. The bowman concentrates on keeping the bow of the canoe headed upstream. The bowman may, of course, also use a pole. In the ordinary recreation-type of canoe, it is usually wisest for him to remain in the kneeling position, using a shorter pole. Because a bowman in a light canoe cannot see the action of the sternman and accommodate his balance to it, it is easy for him to lose his balance and fall out from a standing position. Some canoeists, including some using large, heavily loaded canoes, pole in tandem from opposite sides of the canoe as in paddling. The majority with experience in poling apparently favor having both pole from the same side. With practice a tandem crew can go upstream in fairly heavy water. This requires teamwork and involves the added power provided with two poles and the fact that both can thrust together but recover separately so that one is always holding. The reason that poling on the same side works out so well is that although the typical thrust of the bowman's pole has an effect on the canoe similar to a typical stroke with the paddle, that is not the case with the sternman. A typical paddle stroke by the sternman tends to throw the bow over in the direction opposite his paddling side; a typical thrust of the sternman's pole would tend to push the stern over in the direction opposite his working side.

"Setting" Downstream.—A fast but shallow stream may be run with care and precision by using a pole. The unique feature of this method is that the canoe may be brought to a full stop, or "snubbed" (Fig. 8), with relative ease as often as

FIG. 18 (left)—Slowing the speed of the canoe going downstream by dragging the pole. The lower hand presses down on the pole and the other hand exerts counterpressure upward.

FIG. 19 (right)—When the canoe has been snubbed (Fig. 8), the poleman may change his pole to the other side to aid him in moving the canoe sideward toward his normal poling side, while at the same time keeping its forward movement checked.

necessary in order to maintain careful control. Hand-in-hand with this technique of "setting" is that of "dragging" the point of the pole on the bottom (Fig. 18) in order to slow the canoe in fast water. These two techniques may also be used in conjunction with one another.

The technique of dragging is quite simple. The pole is held aft of the poler at an angle of about 45 degrees. Its end is pressed firmly against the river bottom. The poler does this by applying downward pressure on the pole with his lower hand, while at the same time exerting counterpressure upward with his other hand (Fig. 18). This will keep the canoe going slow enough for good control in water that is only moderately fast. When the canoe must be moved sideward, one direction or the other, in order to follow the best channel, the pole is brought forward and its point set on the bottom abeam of the poler out away from the side of the canoe a comfortable distance. The canoe is then pushed or pulled sideward as necessary.

Setting the canoe downstream by "snubbing" is done as follows:

1. The stance of the poleman is the same as used when poling upstream, but his position is nearer the bow. This puts the down stream end of the canoe lower in the water than the upstream end. This is necessary in order to utilize the force of the current for keeping the canoe in line with the current.

2. The poleman holds the pole so that it is angled forward (Fig. 8) rather than to the rear as when poling upstream. This puts his forward hand low on the pole and his other hand high. It is helpful to visualize the relationship of the stance and position of the pole in poling upstream to the same in snubbing downstream. If the poleman in the former situation were to pivot on both feet and face to the rear without changing position of either pole or hands, he would be in a position for

snubbing. Some polemen will do this; others prefer to work on the other side of the canoe.

3. The pole point is set against the bottom with the pole held firmly. The poleman's arms and legs are braced for resisting the force of the current and the momentum of the canoe as it is brought to a stop. The stop should be abrupt but not necessarily jerky; that is, there may be some give to the arms and legs to smooth the action. As the canoe comes to a stop, it has a strong tendency to remain in line with the current because of the firm grip the current has on its deep downstream end. The poleman uses his feet to control the alignment of the canoe as he firmly holds it in position in relation to the pole. If he wishes to move the canoe sideward, he can move the point of the pole to a position a little farther to the side and push the canoe over in the direction opposite his working side. If he wishes to move it sideward in the direction of the working side, he can move the point of the pole to the same respective position on the other side of the canoe (Fig. 19) and push. In both cases he will return his pole to the snubbing position.

4. To let the canoe go on slowly downstream, the poleman lets it move forward until his pole is nearly vertical. He then lifts his pole, and positions it to snub again. He will do this immediately if the speed and turbulence of the stream so demand, or he may first let the canoe drift for some distance under moderate conditions.

5. When there are two in the canoe, the snubbing is done in the same manner, if one is a passenger. The only change would be that of the position of the poleman. The canoe would be trimmed the same but because of the weight of the passenger, the poleman would locate himself farther aft in the canoe. If the second person is a crew-mate, he should kneel in the normal bow position, use a paddle, and concentrate on helping

to steer a safe course. The poleman would concentrate on
dragging or snubbing as necessary (Fig. 20).

Tracking, Lining, and Wading.—When a stream is too fast
for successful upstream work, it will be necessary to carry
around the difficult places or tow the canoe upstream. Towing
the canoe is called "tracking," often done with a long line tied
to an upstream thwart and another to a downstream thwart.
It is better that the upstream line be rigged bridle-fashion to

Fig. 20 (left)—Tandem crew going downstream. The sternman has snubbed
the canoe to a temporary stop, and the bowman is using his paddle to help
hold the canoe in line with the current.

Fig. 21 (right)—Tracking the canoe upstream, using the bow and sternlines.
This keeps the canoe away from the logs and rocks and permits the crew to
wade in shallow water.

lead out from the forefoot of the canoe. This will assure that
this end of the canoe will at all times ride lightly, free of the
grip of the current. One canoeist working both lines—or two
canoeists, one on each line—tows the canoe along in deep
water while walking along the bank or wading in shallow water
along an obstacle-cluttered shore. This is accomplished by
letting the current hit the inshore side of the canoe at a slight
angle, keeping it headed away from shore as it is pulled upstream. The canoe is kept at this desired angle by adjusting

the relative lengths and pulls on the two lines. In mild circumstances the same task may be done with the regular bow and stern lines (Fig. 21). Sometimes only the upstream line is used and the second person keeps the canoe offshore with the tip of his paddle.

When water is too dangerous to run, the canoe may be carried around the bad stretch or lined down through. Lining is the opposite of tracking, in respect to the direction you are moving the canoe, but the rigging of lines (e.g., upstream line leading from forefoot) and the handling principles are the same. Work the lines, one against the other, to put the canoe in the right position in respect to the current so that it will be carried downstream clear of the alongshore obstructions, but under control at all times.

If when going upstream you encounter rapids against which progress cannot be made and yet shallow water makes wading possible and safe, it is an easy matter to step out and wade up through, towing the canoe along. It is necessary to tow from the upstream end and helpful to lift lightly on the end rather than lean on it so that the current will not catch it. When you encounter very shallow and rocky stretches while going downstream, follow the same procedure. Wade, holding the upstream end, and guide it down with the current.

The Song My Paddle Sings

by

E. Pauline Johnson

(1862–1913)

August is laughing across the sky,
Laughing while paddle, canoe, and I
Drift, drift,
Where the hills uplift
On either side of the current swift.
The river rolls in its rocky bed,
My paddle is plying its way ahead,
Dip, dip,
When the waters flip
In foam as over their breast we slip.

And oh, the river runs swifter now;
The eddies circle about my bow:
Swirl, swirl!
How the ripples curl
In many a dangerous pool awhirl!
And forward far the rapids roar,
Fretting their margin for evermore;
Dash, dash;
With a mighty crash,
They seethe and boil, and bound and splash.

Be strong, O paddle! be brave, canoe!
The reckless waves you must plunge into.
Reel, reel,
On your trembling keel,
But never a fear my craft will feel.

We've raced the rapids; we're far ahead:
The river slips through its silent bed.
Sway, sway,
As the bubbles spray
And fall in tinkling tunes away.

And up on the hills against the sky,
A fir tree rocking its lullaby
Swings, swings,
Its emerald wings,
Swelling the song that my paddle sings.

CHAPTER XIII

CANOE REPAIR AND RELATED INFORMATION

Canoe manufacturers list in their catalogs or brochures replacement parts and other materials available for purchase. Some manufacturers also have instruction sheets explaining how to make repairs to their specific canoes. This informational material is usually available on request, and will prove helpful. In addition, the contents of this chapter should help you to successfully care for your canoe and make satisfactory emergency and permanent repairs. It must be kept in mind, however, that methods vary greatly among canoeists and obviously many excellent and equally satisfactory procedures have been omitted.

CARE

A canoe, if handled with consideration, will remain in good condition for many years and require only a minimum of routine maintenance. Most of the time the average canoe will be *out* of the water where general deterioration can be rapid unless proper preventive measures are taken. The following practices will increase the useful years of your craft.

1. Between periods of use, rack the canoe *inverted, off the ground,* and *in the shade.* If it is not practicable to put it on a rack, turn it over, in the shade if possible. Great damage results from long exposure to the sun. Protect the ends and the gunwale where they come into contact with the ground by placing flat boards or stones under them. Dry rot, particularly at the ends of the deck, is the result of neglecting drainage and ventilation when the canoe is left in this position too often. If the canoe is unattended, provision should be made to lash

it down to protect it from high winds. Obviously, no one should be permitted to sit on or get into a canoe that is resting on the ground. It should not be left rightside-up for long either on shore or at a mooring, since rainwater left in the canoe for long will damage it.

2. Handle the canoe with care when carrying, launching, or lifting it out of the water. Avoid contact with the ground or the dock.

3. Observe proper techniques of boarding and debarking.

4. Wear soft-soled shoes while using the canoe.

5. While under way, avoid contact with fixed or floating objects. Hitting them may seriously damage your canoe.

6. Avoid dragging the canoe through shallow water.

7. Properly rack the canoe *inside* during the off season. Carefully employ the principles used in the canoe storage racks illustrated in Chapter III. If the canoe remains without even support over a long period, it will twist out of shape. A cover to protect the finish from dust and light is desirable. The canoe should be cleaned thoroughly before storage. No weight should be permitted on the canoe and measures should be taken to prevent anything from falling on it. Racking it securely overhead with lines is very satisfactory. If it is to be refinished before the next season, it would be better to plan this work for early spring.

GENERAL ROUTINE MAINTENANCE

Keep a good coat of marine or exterior spar varnish on all wooden parts of the canoe. Wherever there is a bare spot, moisture can enter the wood. The absorption will add weight and cause general deterioration. However, avoid varnishing the whole canoe when only a few spots need touching up. If succeeding coats of varnish are built up, before long the entire finish will begin to crack or "alligator." These cracks penetrate to raw wood, and there is no cure for the condition but to remove all the old varnish and start over.

The first rule in the general painting or varnishing of a boat or canoe could well be: always sand off as much as you plan to put back on. However, if the whole interior is to receive a coat of varnish, sand and touch up the worn spots first. When dry, sand the entire interior (a fine garnet paper is recommended) and apply one coat, or two if needed, sanding well between coats. *Follow* the directions on the can for best results. Always sand with the grain of the wood. When the old varnish is to be completely removed from the interior, it can best be done with a remover. Use a type that will not retard drying of new varnish as traces of the remover are bound to remain in the seams. Directions for using the remover will be found on its container.

The same general rules apply to maintenance of the exterior finish of the canoe. Although the interiors are usually varnished, several types of finish are commonly found on the canvas. To reduce the dangers of blistering, peeling, cracking, and tackiness, determine the type of the original finish and use the same for renovation. For example, use enamel on enamel, varnish base paint (deck paint) on varnish base, and airplane dope only on dope. This general rule has its exceptions. For example, aluminum powder paint is often applied over dope, and *then* paint of other colors applied. When uncertain as to the original finish, test your selection on a spot about a foot square and after a reasonable drying interval, check for "tack," adhesion, and the like.

Old cracked finishes on the canvas can be removed, but in most instances it is better to recanvas the canoe. The cracks that develop in heavy coats of paint penetrate through the filler into the canvas and if the condition has existed for some time it is likely the canvas has rotted under these cracks. Of course, the weight of the canoe has been increased by water absorption and the result is a heavy, waterlogged craft, difficult to handle. However, if the canvas proves to be good under the accumulation of paint, it can be prepared for refinishing by removing the old paint with a remover (same type as recommended for the interior) or with a blowtorch. On very heavy layers of paint, the latter method is preferable. Some workmen report that to facilitate the removal of the finish, they soak the canoe by submerging it under water at least 24 hours. The moisture in the canvas when vaporized by the torch will help to loosen the old paint and filler and at the same time lessen the danger of severely scorching the canvas. Remove the outwales, stem bands, and keel, and invert the canoe over supports where there is good ventilation and no danger of fire. Use a blowtorch with a muzzle attachment that will give a fanlike flame, and a broad knife (2½ to 3 inches) for peeling off the paint. Start at the forefoot of the canoe and work toward your left if you are right-handed. Peel off the blistering paint immediately behind the flame as it is passed slowly over a small area 8 or 10 inches long parallel to the keel line. The torch and knife must move across the surface in unison because the paint will rebond if it cools. Successive strips are peeled off with the knife lapping the cleared area above as you progress down toward the gunwale. The next 8- or 10-inch section is cleared in the same way and so on until the job is finished. CAUTION: When the outwales have been removed there is always a chance that the edge of raw canvas might catch fire and smolder unnoticed. Burns beyond the gunwale line could necessitate recanvasing. Remove as much of the filler as possible as you burn and peel off the paint, because the cracks are there even though nearly impossible to see. Before repainting, use a commercial canvas-filler thinned down for deeper penetration, and build up a smooth surface before applying the first coat of paint. If you have decided to use dope, this can be applied without using a filler, but a more thorough removal of the old filler before application of the dope is necessary.

REPAIR OF CANVAS-COVERED CANOES

Torn Canvas.—Holes in the canvas vary in size from a small puncture to a tear many inches long. The puncture and very small tears can be repaired by filling them with waterproof liquid cement, letting it dry, and applying a second coat. Larger repairs require a patch put over or under the hole, or both.

A. Outline of tear on patching material   **B.** Patch inserted between canvas and hull

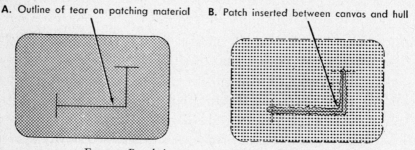

FIG. 1—Patch between canvas and planking.

Be sure the canvas and hull are dry when making the repair. Prop open the lips of the cut for better ventilation and faster drying of the area. Use a lightweight piece of cloth with a close weave (broadcloth, muslin, etc.) and cut a patch that will extend an inch beyond the ends of the cut and about the same distance on each side. Place the patch on top of the tear and trace with a pencil the contour of the tear, which can be felt through the patching material (Fig. 1). If the cut in the canvas is too small to permit working in a patch of this type, slightly enlarge the tear with a sharp knife. Impregnate the patch with a coat of waterproof liquid cement and allow to dry, for the slight stiffness given to the material by the cement will make it easier to work the patch into position. Trim the edges and round the corners of the patch before inserting it under the canvas. If the cut is on the turn of the bilge, spring in the hull by applying pressure a few inches from the tear in order to get more working room between the canvas and the planking. Line up the tracing on the patch with the tear in the canvas and carefully cement in place (Fig. 1). Most water-proof liquid cement will "lift" the paint or varnish, so try to avoid getting any on the exterior finish. A moderate amount of pressure should be applied to the repair while the cement is setting. Place a piece of wax paper over the repair to prevent sticking. In repairing large rips of a foot or more in length use

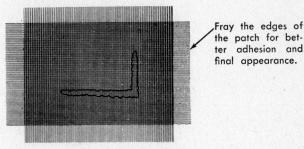

Fray the edges of the patch for better adhesion and final appearance.

FIG. 2—Patch on the outside.

the same technique. However, it may be advisable to take a few "stitches" every 3 or 4 inches to help draw the lips of the cut together again. After the repair has dried completely, fill in the voids between the edges of the cut with canvas filler or additional liquid cement. When this is dry, sand and "touch up" to match the original finish if you desire.

In certain instances it may not be possible to use the foregoing method. Cuts close to the stem or keel are hard to fix in this manner. When a patch can't be placed beneath the canvas, apply one on the outside (Fig. 2).

Occasionally, a portion of the canvas may be torn or worn off completely. This is repaired by filling in the void with canvas of about the same weight as the original (Fig. 3). To

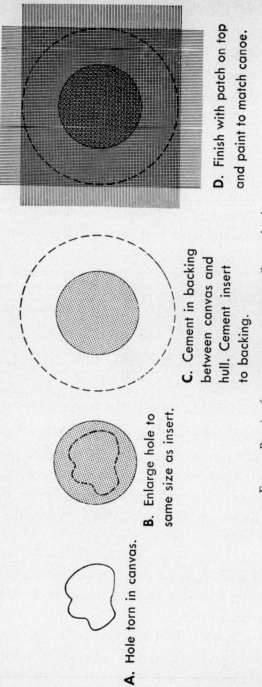

A. Hole torn in canvas.

B. Enlarge hole to same size as insert.

C. Cement in backing between canvas and hull. Cement insert to backing.

D. Finish with patch on top and paint to match canoe.

Fig. 3—Repair of canvas torn or worn off completely.

ensure a perfect fit, prepare the filler piece by first giving it a priming coat of waterproof cement. Allow this to dry and then trim with a razor blade or scissors to a size slightly larger than the hole. Place the material over the hole, mold it to fit the contour of the canoe, and then with a razor blade enlarge the hole to fit the contour of the material. After the hole has been altered to fit the insert, cement a backing of light, strong material between the canvas and the hull. Cement the insert to the backing and finish with a lightweight patch on top.

Repairs to the canvas on a trip are usually of a temporary nature because thorough drying of the canvas is seldom practicable. However, the surface can be dried enough to permit some sort of an emergency repair. Waterproof adhesive tape, especially the newer type of plastic electrical tape, applied over the tear makes a good temporary repair, and makeshift jobs have been done with chewing gum, pitch from certain trees, wax from a dripping candle, and so forth. Chapter XI contains suggestions for a canoe repair kit to be taken along on a canoe trip.

Hull Repairs.—The ribs and planking of canvas-covered canoes occasionally may need repairing or replacing. Repairs to thwarts, decks, gunwales, and stems are sometimes necessary. This is particularly true of old canoes being rebuilt. Repairs that not long ago were considered impossible by the average person are now practicable using laminations (thin strips of wood) bonded with easy-to-use, waterproof glues.

Rib replacement (with canvas on): First, determine if the rib or ribs must be replaced. If they are merely cracked and not more than two or three are adjacent to one another, it may not be necessary to remove them. On the other hand, when just one rib has broken and has caused a marked bulge on the hull (usually at the turn of the bilge), it should be replaced before excessive wear occurs to the canvas immediately over the "bump."

To take out the rib, first remove any screws at the gunwale and keel, then carefully split out the rib with a screwdriver. The tacks are then worked up through the planking using a pair of pliers. If small pieces of the planking are pulled through with the tackhead, press them back in place or fill the voids (when larger than $\frac{1}{4}$-inch diameter) with plastic wood so that they will not be felt through the canvas after the new rib has been put in. With a hacksaw blade, clip off the nails that held the old rib in place at the gunwale if the canoe is of open-gunwale construction. On closed-gunwale canoes, the top and side molding strips are removed first and the nails securing the rib to the gunwale can be pulled. Clean the area thoroughly, taking care that no old varnish ridges, splinters, and the like, remain to prevent a good contact between the planking and the first lamination. The laminations should be of straight-grain white cedar, although good spruce, basswood, cypress, or other tough, nonbrittle wood may be used. Have the laminations sawed from a piece about 60 inches long, and the width of the rib (usually $2\frac{1}{4}$ inches). If they are made by a cabinet-maker, using a fine saw blade with little or no set to the teeth, more laminations of about $\frac{1}{16}$ inch will result. The smooth surfaces made by a saw of this type will require less glue and permit better contact between laminations. Place the canoe on a flat surface and block it in an upright position so that the bottom (or keel) directly under the repair area is in full contact with the supporting surface.

Bend the first lamination into a horseshoe shape and with the ends pointing toward the end of the canoe, slip it into place, working the ends up through the gunwale slot. Wedge it at the gunwale with a couple of screwdrivers after pressure is applied *downward* at the *tips* of the lamination to ensure contact with the hull. If the wood was well selected and the laminations not much over ⅟₁₆ inch thick, it will not be necessary to steam or soak the strips to get a good fit without danger of breaking. Cut off the ends about 2 inches above the gunwale and mark for a taper that will match the taper of the adjacent ribs. This taper is usually only on the amidships side of the rib. Remove the lamination and cut the taper with a sharp knife and block plane, then use the first as a pattern for the two or three additional laminations that will make up the thickness of the rib. Do not attempt to bevel the edges or cut the ends to the finished length at this time.

Coat the planking and the bottom surface of the first lamination with a well-mixed plastic resin glue. Slip the lamination into place as before and wedge temporarily at the gunwales. Avoid pressing it in with the hand at the turn of the bilge; there is less danger of breaking the lamination if pressure is applied downward at the tips. Moving the ends slightly forward or back may be necessary to secure a perfect fit. Next, coat the top surface of the first and the bottom surface of the second lamination, and slip it into place in the same manner. Thinner wedges will be necessary at the gunwale each time a lamination is added; they are inserted between the inwale and the last lamination. A small C-clamp can be used on open-gunwale canoes at the end of the adjacent rib to prevent the outwale from springing out if there are no screws through it at that point. (On closed gunwales use a C-clamp to hold the laminations in place and taper the *flat* side of the ends *after* the glue has set.) If the last lamination results in a rib slightly thinner than the original, build out the rib with a thin wedge between the inwale and the last lamination to maintain a uniform gunwale slot. When all the laminations are in place and wedged, cut the ends to within an inch of the gunwale and tap them with a mallet or hammer to reconfirm contact with

here is little danger of forcing them in too tightly

canvas cover serves as a backing and, too, having

esting on a smooth, supporting surface will prevent

rom forming on the bottom. If the rib is wedged
in too tightly, a bulge would first be noticed at the turn of
the bilge. A tap on the gunwale next to the ends of the rib
before the glue has set will correct this.

Wipe off the excess glue with a moistened cloth. Cut a temporary thwart or crossbar to hook under the inwales next to
the ends of the new rib and also one that will just catch the
turn of the bilge (Fig. 4). Pad the ends of the lower one to

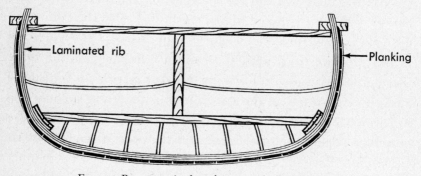

FIG. 4—Pressure rig for gluing up laminated ribs.

prevent scarring the rib, and force an upright between the
two that will exert sufficient pressure to hold them firmly in
place. Now fan out wedges between the lower cross member
and the rib, using scrap pieces of the laminating material for
this purpose. The slight spring from these strips will give
enough pressure for a good glue joint.

If more than three ribs in one section have to be replaced,
it is advisable to remove and replace every other one in the
first operation and then repeat the process on the broken ribs
that were skipped, after the first ones have set. In this way
there is less danger of losing the original shape of the hull.

Allow 24 hours for the glue to set thoroughly and then trim the ends flush with the gunwale and straight-bevel the edges with a sharp knife. A final sanding will slightly round the edge of the bevel and the rib is ready for varnishing.

If the canoe is to be recanvased as well, it is best to replace the ribs before removing the old canvas; but instead of pulling the tacks through the planking, clip them off flush with a pair of diagonals. After the canvas has been removed they can be easily pulled out.

When the canoe is to be recanvased, it is doubtless more practical to send to the manufacturer of the canoe for new ribs that can be put in while the canvas is off. Record the serial number and size of the canoe as stamped on the inside stem. Designate each rib needed by counting from the end nearest the break toward amidships. If the serial number has been obliterated, measure the canoe, determining its overall length, its width at widest point, and its depth amidships. Send this information with any other descriptive data to the manufacturer. He may be able to fill your order satisfactorily on the basis of this information. An alternative is to make and bend the whole ribs yourself, or with local help. Clear, straight-grained spruce or cedar is recommended. Soak the ribs in boiling water if a steam box is not available, then bend them around the outside of the canoe and clamp them to the gunwales, not where they will be finally placed, but two ribs closer to the end of the canoe. When they are dried to shape, put them inside in correct position.

In some cases it may be desirable to save the time and expense of putting in new ribs. If so, proceed as follows: 1. Remove the planking and tacks around the break (Fig. 4A). 2. Force the rib back to its original contour and hold it there with a strip of copper as shown in Figure 4A. 3. Replace the old planking with new.

F‌IG. 4A—A broken rib repaired with a ⅝-inch by 4-inch strip of roofing copper (flashing). The edges of the copper strip are trimmed and filed smooth. Ten holes are punched at random in the copper to accommodate the ¹¹⁄₁₆-inch *canoe tacks,* or suitable substitute. The latter are clinched against a backing iron held inside of the rib. Waterproof glue is worked in the break beforehand. Afterward, the edges of the copper strip are tapped into the wood of the rib, carefully supported with the backing iron. The tack heads are filed flat before the planking is replaced. (*Note:* A ball peen hammer and a small hand dolly [for backing iron] of the *cart rack* or *mushroom* type available in automobile supply stores are good tools for this project.) (Courtesy of Thomas Costello and Roy Sanders)

Planking Repair.—Broken sections of planking between ribs can be repaired with two-ply laminations without removing the canvas. Remove any loose pieces of the planking and trim the broken ends even with the edges of the ribs, but with a 45-degree bevel leading back under the rib. Insert a thin metal strip between the plank and the canvas while cutting the bevel to prevent accidental puncturing of the canvas. The same type of laminating material recommended for the ribs is used for the repair. Sand two small pieces until their total thickness equals that of the original planking. After planing the edges down to the width of the space to be filled, cut a 45-degree bevel on one end and insert the lamination under one of the ribs so that the beveled ends are matching. Cut at right angles even with the edge of the other rib so that the first strip will fall in place. The second piece is prepared in the same way but with the beveled end locked under the rib opposite the first. Check for a final fit; then remove the top piece and coat the contact surfaces with waterproof glue and fit the top piece back in again and apply pressure until dry. Do not glue the bottom lamination to the canvas. This procedure locks the patch in place (Fig. 5).

When the canvas is off the canoe, replacing planking is a simple procedure of nailing on a new piece so that it evenly abuts adjacent planking at the midpoint of a rib at each end. If two new pieces go on side-by-side, avoid having their joints fall on the same ribs.

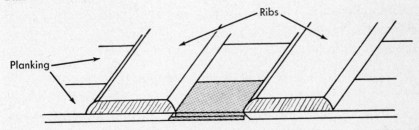

FIG. 5—Laminated planking patch.

Gunwale Repair.—Repairing a gunwale may involve one or more of a variety of possible procedures. An entire outwale or inwale strip might need replacing. These are easily milled, taking measurements from the old pieces. A split, or "hogged out," gunwale can be strenghtened or repaired by straightening or compressing the gunwale with a Spanish windlass around the canoe until the gunwale line is nearly straight, and then gluing and screwing a hardwood lamination to the underside of the inwale. One or two strips will correct a weak spot or hogged condition; more may be needed to effect a stronger repair for cracks or breaks. The laminations should extend a foot beyond the damaged area and can be up to $\frac{1}{4}$ inch in thickness. C-clamps are used to hold them in place, and the windlass is not released until the glue has set. Unless the gunwale has been badly splintered, it is seldom necessary to splice in a section. However, this can be done by lapping the joints (length of lap should be at least six times the thickness of the joint) and splinting with laminations beneath the gunwale (Fig. 6). If the break occurred at a seat or paddling thwart location, it is advisable to reverse the ends of the canoe by relocating the cross members.

In some cases, when a canoe is quite "run down" and appearance not an important consideration, repairs to broken gunwales are made with angle stock of aluminum or brass. For details, see c of Fig. 6.

Stem Repairs.—(*Note:* When removing old brass screws, especially at the stems of a canoe, beware of getting small particles of brass into your eyes.)

A cracked or broken stem that hasn't lost its original contour may be repaired without removing the stem band or opening up the canvas cover of the canoe. Laminations the length and width of the stem and about $\frac{1}{16}$ inch thick are glued to the inside face of the stem. They are firmly pressed up into place, and a tack or small nail at the end of the stem will hold them there. When the glue has dried, remove the nail and "feather" the lamination into the stem (Fig. 7).

If the break altered the contour of the end, additional work will be necessary to effect a permanent repair. After the inside curve of the stem has been reinforced with laminations, remove the stem band, open up the canvas and reshape the outside edge of the cracked or broken stem, using the ends of the planking as the contour guide. Work down small defects in the curve with a wood file; but on sharper breaks, plane the outside length of the stem down somewhat smaller than the original size. For a guide, scribe with a pencil the original curve $\frac{1}{8}$ inch back from the ends of the planking, and plane down to this mark, feathering out at the forefoot. Now build

FIG. 6—Repairing a gunwale.

A (above)—Inwale splice secured with glue and screws.

B (below)—Lamination glued under splice.

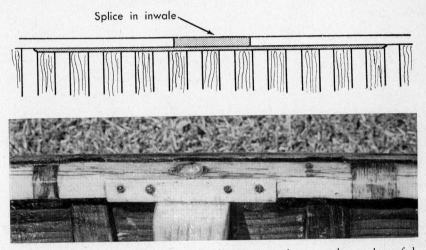

c—An inwale break is repaired with aluminum or brass angle stock as follows:

1. Take a 6-inch piece of angle stock of aluminum or brass measuring about ¾ inch vertical and the same horizontal and lay it against the broken inwale so the bottom side is under the inwale.

2. Mark and trim the vertical side about the same height as the inwale.

3. Spring inwale back in place at the break until it resumes its normal contour.

4. (a) Center the angle stock over the break, clamp it, and bore four or five horizontal holes through the metal and inwale (*only*). These should accommodate thin brass stove bolts ⅛ inch by about 1½ inches in length. Bore to miss the ribs.

(b) Work waterproof glue into the inwale break.

5. Set the bolts. Nuts and brass washers pull up against the outside edge of the inwale (between inwale and outwale). Tighten the nuts with a small wrench and then trim the bolts flush.

6. Round off all sharp edges and corners with a file. (Courtesy of Thomas Costello and Roy Sanders)

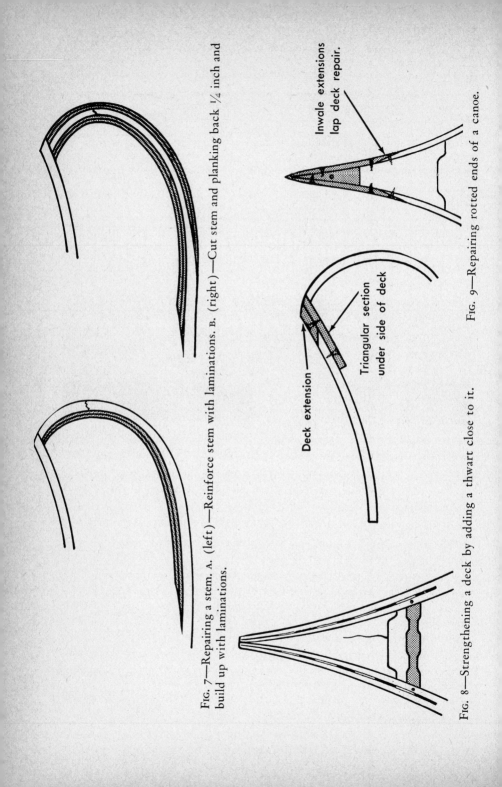

FIG. 7—Repairing a stem. A. (left)—Reinforce stem with laminations. B. (right)—Cut stem and planking back ½ inch and build up with laminations.

FIG. 8—Strengthening a deck by adding a thwart close to it.

Deck extension

Triangular section under side of deck

Inwale extensions lap deck repair.

FIG. 9—Repairing rotted ends of a canoe.

up the stem to the original size by gluing on several thin laminations. The laminations must be wide enough to cover the ends of the planking. After the glue has set, feather the laminations into the forefoot and taper the edges accordingly before resecuring the canvas. In recanvasing an old canoe, the stems are often found split and rotted along the tack line. Follow the directions above for building up a new solid surface to which the canvas can be securely fastened.

Deck Repairs.—The decks are very important structural parts of a canoe and are subject to considerable stress and strain. To repair a cracked or split deck, first release the out-wales 3 or 4 feet from the tip of the deck. Pour waterproof glue down into the crack and draw together with a large C-clamp or carpenter's clamp until the glue has set. The deck area should be further strengthened by adding a short, narrow thwart a few inches back from the base of the deck (Fig. 8). The thwart will prevent further outward strain on the deck and also provides a good hand grip for short carries.

Rotted or otherwise damaged deck tips are trimmed off carefully to provide for a lap joint and built up with sections properly shaped and fitted. Since some inwale work is usually involved, they are cut back beyond the deck repair. The prepared extensions of the inwale are then secured to the deck; and by lapping the deck joint, a stronger and neater repair is achieved. All sections should be secured by screws as well as glue (Fig. 9).

Repairing Thwarts.—If a thwart breaks, remove it, and use it as a pattern to make a new one. Identical reproduction is not necessary, but length, angle of end cuts, and location of bolt holes should conform accurately to assure a precise fit. The curved surfaces of a typical canoe thwart are not necessary. A thwart 3 inches wide with straight edges is suitable. When unfastening the old thwart, bear in mind that diamond-headed bolts used on some canoes have an under flange and cannot be screwed out. They should be tapped up ¼ inch carefully (with nut on tip of bolt) to clear the flange from the gunwale.

RECANVASING A CANOE EASILY AND QUICKLY

With the adoption of airplane dope (clear nitrate dope) as a canvas filler, recanvasing a canoe has become a simpler task than it used to be. Special canvas-stretching tackle is no longer needed. Any person reasonably handy at ordinary handicraft projects can do the job with a helper. Each needs a hammer, a pair of ordinary pliers, a sharp pocketknife. If eventually more than one canoe will be recanvased, it will be worth while having the jaws of the pliers widened to resemble webbing pliers. This may be done easily by having a ⅛-inch steel strap, about ¾ inch by 1¾ inches, welded to both sides of each jaw (Fig. 10).

Tackle is not needed because, although the canvas is put on only hand-tight, the dope filler shrinks it to a very snug fit. In fact, some persons have put the canvas on by using their

Fig. 10—Pliers with pieces of strap-iron welded onto each jaw.

hands, without pliers. Several coats of this quick-drying dope may be applied in rapid succession on a good drying day. This means the filling job that used to take many days now takes a few hours at the most. Adding aluminum powder to the dope, bringing out the desired shade on the final coat, takes care of the coloring and finishing. The canoe could be used afloat the same day. (Clear nitrate dope and the appropriate thinner are available in gallon cans from aircraft supply companies and from some paint suppliers. It is not economical to buy it in smaller containers.) The following steps outline how the job is done:

1. Remove the outwales, brass stem bands, outside stems (if any), and the keel (if there is one). Save all these parts. If some are broken or damaged beyond repair, replacements will be necessary. With advance planning you may have already made new parts, purchased these parts from the company that made the canoe, or had them made locally. If the screws are brass and in good condition, save them; otherwise replace them with new brass or bronze screws of the same size.

2. Clinch, or remove and replace, all loose tacks in the planking. Use copper canoe-tacks of the same kind and size. They are available from canoe manufacturers. If you wish, you may safely omit replacing these nails as long as enough remain to hold the planking in place. The doped canvas will hold the planking tightly against the ribs, making excessive nailing unnecessary.

3. Replace any broken planking. Use cedar of the same thickness if cedar is available. Some canoe manufacturers will furnish it. Substitutes may be improvised from whatever material is available, as, for example, slats from an orange crate.

4. If there are broken ribs, repair or replace them. This will

slow up the total job; but broken ribs will be apparent from the beginning, and time will therefore have been allotted for this task. It is best done before the new canvas is applied.

5. Repair the stems with plastic wood or as described in the section entitled "Stem Repairs," or purchase new ones from the manufacturer.

6. Make any other necessary repairs to the wooden structure.

7. When all repairs are completed, sand the entire exterior surface. Be sure no nailheads are protruding.

8. Lay the canoe, bottom-up, on wooden horses or similar supports. Lay on the new canvas, centered, and with equal overhang at each end. Number 10 white cotton duck canvas, 60 inches wide and 1 foot longer than the overall length of the canoe is recommended, but much thinner material may be used if desired. If your canoe is unusually narrow, 54-inch width may be adequate. Determine this by measurement, allowing a few extra inches to work with.

9. Stretch the canvas lengthwise, by hand, and hold it in this position with one large tack at each end, driven part way into the stem at the forefoot. Do not stretch canvas enough to cause the single tacks to tear the canvas.

10. Start amidships and, working opposite each other, pull the canvas down hand-tight and nail it to the gunwales with large copper tacks (about ⅝ inch) driven part way in at every third rib. Stop within 3 feet of each end. This is a temporary step to hold the canvas in position while the job of permanently tacking it on is undertaken.

11. Turn the canoe rightside-up. Work opposite each other and stretch the canvas carefully with pliers, using the gunwales as fulcrum. Sliding a small piece of angle iron along the inwale under the pliers will protect the inwale from marring. Nail the canvas to the gunwales with two ⅝-inch tacks in every

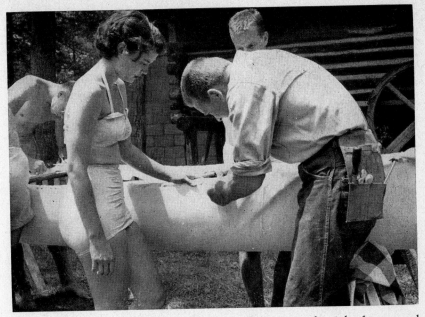

FIG. 11—Putting a new canvas on a canoe. The man in the right foreground is demonstrating to the other two. He is working from amidships toward the end. At the left, two other men are tacking from amidships toward the other end.

rib if the canoe is of open-gunwale construction (Fig. 11). If the construction is closed gunwale, nail continuously at intervals of about 1½ inches. Remove the temporary tacking as you go. Carefully observe the level at which the original nailing was done and duplicate it approximately. If the nailing is too low, the tacks will miss the inwale, coming out beneath it; if too high, the tackheads may be in the way when the outwales are replaced. This nailing should proceed from amidships toward one end, stopping about 3 feet from the extreme end. It should then proceed in the same manner to the other end.

12. Turn the canoe bottom-up. At one end, cut the canvas on the centerline from the end to the place where it has been tacked to the stem (see No. 9). Remove the tack.

13. Lay the canoe on its side. Move the supporting horses closer to the ends of the canoe and it will rest more securely. Pull the upper portion of canvas smoothly across the curve of the stem and start tacking it onto the end of the stem at 1-inch intervals. Use small copper tacks (about ⅜ inch). If they do not hold well, use the larger size used at the gunwales. Tack to about midpoint of the curve and stop. Then bring the tacking at the gunwale along a couple of feet. Alternately work from both directions in this manner to assure finishing smoothly with no wrinkles. Whenever a wrinkle appears, remove the tacks and straighten it out before continuing.

14. With your pocketknife, trim off the surplus canvas at the end, but not along the gunwale. Turn the canoe over on its other side and tack the other portion of canvas to the stem, on top of the first tacking. This tacking, however, should be at closer intervals (¼ inch if you are using the small tacks; ½ inch for the larger tacks). Trim the surplus canvas with care. A waterproof, liquid cement should be used liberally between these tacked portions. As an alternative you could use the airplane dope. If you use the dope, apply a coat to each tacked edge before doing the trimming as an added measure to strengthen the fibers of the canvas so that it will not shred at these edges.

15. Finish the other end of the canoe the same way.

16. If you wish to do a little extra work, you can make a neat job of the ends by adding the following: cut a piece of muslin on the bias, making a strip about 1½ inches wide and long enough to cover the tacking done at the stem. Do the cutting with pinking shears. Glue this strip on with airplane dope. Do the same for the other end of the canoe.

17. Apply several coats of dope, cut as desired with thinner. It is important to get good penetration with the first coat. Remember to color the dope with powder. Changing the shade

with each coat will help to avoid "holidays" or gaps in your brushwork. There is no standard for number of coats. Heavier canvas will take more dope to fill because its fibers are coarser grained. You may keep applying dope till you get a smooth finish if you desire. This is not necessary from a utilitarian viewpoint. Two gallons of dope and one gallon of thinner will provide five or six coats, which is adequate. Sand lightly before the last coat or two. Routine sanding before each coat is probably unnecessary. Flow the dope on with a large brush, working rapidly, because it dries very fast. Stay out of the direct rays of the sun while putting the dope on or it will dry almost too fast to enable you to get on a smooth coat. Save a little thinner to clean your brush when you are done. If you let the brush harden, on the other hand, the dope and thinner will soften it.

18. After the doping is done, trim off the surplus canvas at the gunwales. Cut it exactly even with the top edge of the planking, otherwise you may have some of it in the way when you are replacing the outwales. You could have done this trimming before the doping job, but leaving it on till afterward provides a protection against having the dope get onto the woodwork of the canoe during application.

19. Put on the parts taken off originally, but consider the desirability of not putting the keel back on. If you elect to put it back on, puncture the canvas with an awl at each place where a screw hole appears in a rib along the centerline of the canoe. Put a thick coat of white lead on the canvas at each screw hole. Put the screws in place. Set the keel on, being careful to position it to match and line up with the screws. Tighten the screws. (*Note:* Some people have been successful with leaving off not only the keel, but the stem bands also. With added care in using the canoe no damage resulted.)

REPAIR OF ALUMINUM CANOES

Information and repair materials for use on aluminum canoes may be obtained from the manufacturer or his dealers. Here, however, are some key facts selected from such material:

1. Welding is *not* used in the repair of aluminum canoes, because the heat will leave a brittle area surrounded by a dead-soft area of larger dimension. Neither of these conditions is desirable.

2. *If a rivet loosens,* it may be tightened by holding a heavy hammer against the outside head while striking the inside head with a smaller hammer to further flatten or peen it over.

3. *If a rivet is pulled out,* replace it with a larger one. A rivet can be removed by drilling or chiseling off the outer head, and then punching out the remainder. This procedure must be done with care so as not to enlarge the hole or damage the skin of the craft.

4. *If there is a leak along a rivet joint* and it cannot be exactly located and no rivets are loose, use the marine sealer recommended by the manufacturer or his dealer, or use a known equivalent product.

5. *Large dents* can usually be removed by striking the bulged place firmly with your hand.

6. *Small dents* and creases may be removed by holding a cloth bag filled with sand against the hollow side and pounding carefully on the bulged side with a mallet of rawhide, rubber, or plastic. Work from the outside toward the center and avoid striking too hard. A wooden block may be used instead of the sandbag, especially if a firmer backing is needed. Avoid use of a hard hammer, for too much pounding with it will thin the metal and will also make it brittle.

7. *If keel or gunwales are bent,* block one side and pound the other with a rubber mallet until straight.

8. *To stop extension of a crack*, drill a ⅟₁₆-inch hole at each end of it; then pound out the associated dent as described above. The hole will thus be nearly closed.

9. *Holes may be temporarily sealed* with adhesive tape, rags, a wooden peg, or most any marine glue or cement.

10. *Permanent repair* of a hole may be done by riveting an aluminum patch to the inside, using a gasket-and-seam compound between the patch and the skin of the canoe. The patch should overlap the crack or hole by at least an inch all around. Use ⅛-inch rivets, spaced ½ inch apart and ⅜ inch from the edge of the patch. Permanent repairs are also made with a product referred to as an "aluminum plastic wood." It is available from the manufacturer, or dealer, or some automotive supply stores. For cracks and small holes it may be applied directly to the bare, cleaned, and slightly roughened metal. For larger holes it is probably best to apply it over a fiber patch as indicated in the instructions on the container. It is a paste and should be applied in thin layers. When the job is done, it may be sanded or ground to a bright finish.

Painting an Aluminum Canoe.—If you wish to paint an unpainted aluminum canoe, satisfactory results may be obtained as follows:

1. Clean the canoe with a household abrasive cleanser.

2. Wash it with household vinegar, allowing the vinegar to remain on the canoe for 24 hours. Then wash it thoroughly with fresh water and let it dry.

3. Apply one coat of a good marine metal primer, and allow it to dry according to instructions on the container.

4. Apply two coats of a good marine enamel recommended for metal. Follow the instructions on the container relative to application.

When a canoe is to be used a lot in salt water, it should be purchased factory-painted. Factory-painted canoes receive special protective treatment before painting and a special paint requiring elaborate factory equipment for application. Furthermore, they are primed before being assembled, which gives protection to places that cannot be reached with a normal paint job.

When a factory-painted canoe needs repainting, clean it with a household-type abrasive cleanser and sand it lightly with fine sandpaper. Any chipped or scraped areas should have their edges sanded smooth, but it is not necessary to remove the old paint. Repaint with a good marine enamel recommended for use on metal craft.

RE-COVERING A CANOE WITH FIBERGLASS CLOTH

Within the past few years a synthetic fiberglass cloth has come into use as covering for small watercraft. It is applied to a properly prepared hull with a laminating compound, a synthetic resin. The distributors of these products provide detailed instructions regarding their use; therefore, only a brief consideration will be given here to points that apply to recovering a canoe. This information, based upon one man's satisfactory results, may or may not concur with the findings of others in all respects.

Carefully measure your canoe to determine how much fiberglass cloth is needed. Do not regard the known length of your canoe as necessarily indicating the length of the material needed. A gallon and a half of the laminating compound will be adequate.

In preparing the hull, the old canvas covering must be removed; or if it is an all-wood canoe, the varnish or paint must be removed by scraping or sanding. If the planking on the canvas canoe has been varnished, the varnish must be scraped or sanded off. Replace the keel so that the fiberglass may be put on over it. If you prefer a canoe without a keel, you may leave it off with no misgivings because of the ruggedness of a fiberglass finish. Make all needed repairs and fill the spaces between the planking, if there are any, and all cracks, nail and screw holes, and any other irregularities, with a wood filler. Then sand the entire surface even, rounding any sharp edges for better cloth lay. Use rough rather than fine sandpaper to improve adhesion. Apply, with a brush, one coat of resin to the entire surface. This coat is a filler coat, used to plug the pores of the wood and bind with it. Allow it sufficient time to dry thoroughly, then sand it smooth. For best results follow the manufacturer's recommendations for room temperature and humidity when applying the resin.

Cut a keel-strip of glass cloth wide enough to extend about 3 inches on each side of the keel (or the keel line, if the canoe is to have no keel). Apply resin to the area to be covered by this strip. Allow it to dry until it is sticky or tacky; then apply the glass cloth, working out all bubbles with a lintless rag or cheesecloth dampened in alcohol. Before the resin is thoroughly dry, apply a heavy coat of resin to fill the glass cloth and leave a smooth surface. When the keel-strip is dry enough, sand its edges to remove any rough ridges. The cloth is spun glass and must be handled with care at this time. Wear long sleeves and buttoned collar to protect you from glass particles resulting from sanding. Wearing a respirator or a dust filter, obtainable from dealers in spray-gun equipment, will protect you from throat irritation.

When you are ready to cover the sides, cut the cloth to fit each side and apply in the same way as the keel-strip. Use the selvage edge of the material toward the keel and allow enough material for overlap at each end. Don't try to cover both sides at the same time. In trying to work out the bubbles or wrinkles, you may notice some that just move from one position to another. If you cannot work them all the way out to the

edge, work two or three wrinkles together until they are in
line, then cut the top off with scissors and rub down with your
alcohol rag. Allow material to lap over the stems and cut it in
streamers, sticking each one down independently. Fill the
whole piece as soon as possible, even the streamers that extend
over the stems. When thoroughly dry and hard, sand all edges
smooth. Cover the other side in the same manner.

You are now ready to put the extra strip of glass cloth on
the keel or keel line in the same manner as before. When this
is done, trim the glass cloth surplus at the sheer line, level with
the top edge of the planking.

Three or four additional coats of resin are necessary to
develop a surface of sufficient thickness; however, it is not
necessary to sand between each coat. When the last coat of
resin is dry, sand the entire hull as smooth as possible and, if
desired, apply one light coat with a spray gun. The spray coat
must be thinned about 25 percent with alcohol. This will
leave your hull with a smooth bright surface.

In order to replace any fittings or parts (such as outwales
or stem band) that were removed in re-covering, it is necessary to use a steel drill to bore all holes through the resin. It
is probably unnecessary to replace the stem bands. The new
covering has been put on two layers thick at the stems, plus
the overlappings. This will provide adequate protection. The
outwales should of course be replaced.

The glass cloth appears to be white but when used with the
resin the cloth will become clear. If you wish color, add the
desired color starting with the stick coat, and continue with
color in all following coats. Color applied in this manner will
not fade or streak. Some manufacturers supply the laminator
compound either clear or in standard colors such as red, white,
blue, green.

In the event that you puncture the hull, sand the area

around the damaged spot to a feather edge. Cut a piece of glass cloth slightly smaller than the sanded area. Apply the stick coat, then the cloth, and build up to the surrounding area with resin. When thoroughly dry, sand smooth.

After considerable time in use, or with rough use, your hull may show scratches that you wish to remove. Wash the hull with soap and water to remove any grease or scum, paying particular attention to the scratched areas. Wash with alcohol, then apply more resin to build up the surface to the surrounding area, and sand as necessary.

REPAIRING A DOUBLE-PLANK-CONSTRUCTION CANOE

New pieces of planking and other repair materials are available for purchase from the manufacturer of the canoe. Available on request also is an instruction sheet explaining repair methods. Some information selected from it is as follows:

1. A small gouge in the planking may be repaired with plastic wood or putty. If planking in the area is cracked or broken, but only in minor degree, it may be pressed back in place and secured by putting in some ½-inch copper tacks, clinching them in the same manner as that used in the construction of the canoe.

2. When a section of broken planking must be replaced, the new piece should be only slightly larger than the damaged area and may be only part of the width of a plank to keep the repair as small as possible.

3. If inside and outside are both damaged to the extent of needing replacement of planking, the two pieces should overlap so that an inside joint and an outside joint will not coincide.

4. Cut replacement pieces at angles of 30 degrees across the grain of the wood. Put the replacement piece on the damaged area and, holding it firmly in place, cut deeply around it with

a knife. Remove the copper tacks where the planking is to come out by cutting off the clinch on the inside and carefully pushing the tack out to where it may be grasped by the head and pulled. Finish cutting the old piece out, being careful not to cut the cloth lining. Coat the old cloth lining with slow-drying liquid marine glue. If it has been damaged set a new piece of similar cloth on top of it and apply another coat of glue. Then put the new piece of planking in place and fasten it with ½-inch copper tacks driven through both layers of planking and clinched with a backing iron. An awl hole should be made for each tack through the first layer of planking.

5. When inside and outside pieces are both being put on at a damaged area, the inside piece should be put in place first and nailed to outside planking that it overlaps. Then the outside piece is put in place and nailed to any inside planking that it may overlap and to the new piece.

6. Surplus glue may be scraped off, and washed off with a solvent. When it is dry it should be smoothed with sandpaper or a file. Hammer marks may be removed by applying hot water with a cloth.

7. If there is a leak at a patch it may be stopped by forcing glue into the joints with a glue-saturated cloth. This method of stopping a leak is applicable to any area of the canoe.

It is apparent that bent-to-shape replacement planking from the canoe-maker is especially desirable for inside patching because of the curved surfaces involved due to the transverse direction in which the planking lies. The outside planking, being narrow and running fore and aft, does not need to be pre-bent, but ought to be well wet on the outside when patching is done at a sharp curve. The lamination technique described for replacing ribs in a canvas canoe could be used for inside patching. An effort should be made to get cedar of the same type used in the canoe.

REPAIRING AN ALL-WOOD CANOE

Some of the possible types of damage and suggested methods of repair are as follows:

1. *A split planking.* Apply to the inside of the planking, over the slit, a wooden patch ³⁄₁₆ to ¼ inch thick and about 1½ inches wide (softwood). There should be a liberal coat of marine glue under this patch. Before applying the patch, drill a series of small holes about ½ inch apart along both sides of the split, about ¼ inch from its edge. These holes should be just the right size to admit small brass or copper tacks long enough to go through the planking and the patch and clinch over on the inside. Use a backing iron of some sort held firmly against the patch while the nailing is done, and in such a way that the tacks clinch over as they strike the iron.

2. *A hole.* Remove the broken section of planking, carefully cutting on the centerline of the adjacent rib on each side of the break. The tacks holding the planking to the ribs may be withdrawn by cutting off their clinched ends on the inside of the ribs, with a pair of side (or diagonal) cutters. Fit a replacement piece of planking of the same thickness (and of same or similar wood), and nail it to the ribs. Renail the adjacent plank ends also. Use a good waterproof glue or seam compound at all joints.

3. *A broken rib.* Put in a new rib. Use the lamination method or a pre-bent whole rib. Remove the old one by cutting off the clinched ends of the tacks and backing them out so that they may be grasped and pulled without damage to the planking. If necessary, the rib may be carefully broken up by splitting it with a screwdriver to aid in removing it. Nail the new one in exactly as the original was nailed, using glue or seam compound between the rib and planking to ensure no leaks from the nail holes.

REPAIRING A MOLDED PLYWOOD CANOE

Repairs to gunwales, thwarts, stems, decks, and keel, if any, follow the same general procedures described for the canvas-covered canoe. Repairs to the planking, however, involve somewhat different methods.

Damage such as minor gouging may be repaired with plastic wood, sanded, and varnished. A chipped-out piece of veneer may be glued back in place with plastic resin glue; in fact, several small pieces could be fitted back together like a jigsaw puzzle and glued in place. Pressure must be applied evenly over these pieces. This may be done by placing a piece of flexible board against them and securing it tightly in place with a rope, or clamps if that is possible.

If two or more of the four layers of veneer are broken, it will be necessary to replace one, two, or possibly all layers of veneer. Sometimes a blow on the outside of the canoe will break the inner layer and one or two of the layers beneath it without breaking the outside layer. In this case, carefully cut out the inner layer at the area of the break and make a new piece to fit in its place. Apply plastic resin glue liberally to the inside of the replacement piece and to the underlying parts, working it into the cracks and broken area of the latter. Force these underlying broken pieces into place and insert the replacement piece holding it under pressure with clamps, if possible, or with an improvised rig (Fig. 12). If the outside layer of veneer is also damaged, but there is no definite hole, replace the outside layer also, in the same manner. The intermediate broken layers are in this way locked between the outside and inside face pieces.

When there is a definite hole in the canoe it may be repaired with a piece of 4-layer plywood of the same material as the hull. The edges of the hole must be carefully beveled, and the

FIG. 12—Repairing a plywood canoe. The arrangement of boards and sticks is an improvised method of applying pressure inside and outside the canoe to hold pieces of veneer tightly in place until the glue dries.

edges of the plywood patch also beveled so that it will fit properly into place. Glue it in place under pressure. When the glue is dry, plane and sand the patch flush, as necessary. This type of patch is relatively simple on the flat surface of the bottom, but will be difficult on curved surfaces because of the necessity of molding the patch to the desired shape before fitting it to the hole.

An alternative is to employ the lamination principle used in replacing ribs. This will involve separate replacement of each layer of plywood with a new piece of ⅟₁₆-inch veneer cut to fit snugly in place. These pieces should be purposely cut in different sizes, with the face pieces larger than the underlying pieces, so that when they are all in place they will be glued not only to each other but to adjacent veneer alongside the hole.

In any of the repairs described above, joints that have seams larger than desirable may be filled with plastic wood or a mixture of plastic resin glue and sawdust. A file and sandpaper will smooth the area for varnishing.

CHAPTER XIV

ON MAKING A BIRCHBARK CANOE

"Give me of your bark, O Birch-Tree!
Of your yellow bark, O Birch-Tree!
Growing by the rushing river,
Tall and stately in the valley!
I a light canoe will build me . . ."[1]

Considering the primary purpose of this textbook, very little space seemingly should be devoted to the subject of making a birchbark canoe. We saw in Chapter I, however, the significance of this craft in the white man's exploration and development of the northern portions of North America, and its still earlier indispensable place in the culture of the American Indians of these regions. It is recognized too that the birchbark canoe has disappeared from nearly all the rivers and lakes on which it once was used, and that the art of making one is now known and practiced by relatively few Indians and fewer white men. In light of these facts, this canoeing textbook will contribute to recording information about the art of making this timeless prototype of modern canoes. The book may thus also better pay its respect to a great past, an era in which the canoe was not a plaything but a cultural implement of dignity intimately involved in the lives of people and significantly influencing the course of history.

Before his retirement, Waldemar Van Brunt Claussen, former Assistant Director of Water Safety, American National Red Cross, famous canoeist, and pioneer in small-craft safety, wrote a letter in which he gave the details of making a

[1] *Henry Wadsworth Longfellow,* Hiawatha.

birchbark canoe. He based his notes upon his experience of having assisted a Maine guide several times in this fascinating project. The guide had learned his art from the Indians of Maine. These notes are given almost in their entirety as follows:

In former years the Maine guide would bring a roll of birchbark, roughly riven (split) white-cedar ribs, and "sheathing" (thin planking for insertion between the ribs and bark), and "watap" (cedar, spruce, tamarack, and other conifer roots, thinly split for sewing the bark seams and for sewing the bark to the gunwales, and stems) and during the 10-day period of one of our National Aquatic Schools we would build a 16-foot birchbark canoe as a demonstration. At first we used the ritualistic spruce-gum cooked with tallow and tempered with a little wood-ash for sealing all the seams, but later settled on a roofing compound of pure asphalt with finely shredded asbestos in it. This had the same appearance as the gum but it had the advantage of not softening and running in a hot sun, nor of hardening and cracking in extremely cold weather. The Indians had to always carry a wad of cooked gum with which to touch up the seams of their canoes, as needed; this nuisance we wished to avoid. I still have a birchbark of my own, purchased from a sub-chief of the LaCroix band of the Chippewa in Minnesota, about 1935. This I treated with asphalt, after chipping off the gum when it was cold, and the canoe is still as tight as a birchbark can ever be expected to be (Fig. 1).

The construction method used by the old guide of my acquaintance was that of the Penobscot Indians of Maine. It was quite similar to that shown in the films listed at the end of this chapter.

The bark was taken off the tree in the spring (see Fig. 20 of Chapter I) when the sap was starting to flow, in as large a

FIG. 1—A birchbark canoe purchased in 1935 from a sub-chief of the LaCroix band of the Chippewa in Minnesota. The original gum was chipped off at the seams and replaced with asphalt containing asbestos fibers. The canoe is still tight. Repairs at the gunwales where the dried and brittle watap chipped off were made with rattan of the type used to cane the seats of chairs. The canoe has been preserved by thorough varnishing inside and out. (Courtesy, W. Van B. Claussen)

sheet as possible. Ritzenthaler[2] indicates that the contemporary Chippewa who made his birchbark canoe felled the birch tree across a log cradle to keep it off the ground, drove two nails into the log 18 feet apart and with a string marked a line of cut between these nails. The cut was made with a jackknife and the bark pried loose initially with an axe and then with a long thin pole. He includes an illustration of this procedure on page 68 of the same article.

[2]*Robert E. Ritzenthaler*, The Building of a Chippewa Indian Birch Bark Canoe (*Milwaukee, Bulletin of the Public Museum of the City of Milwaukee, November 1950*), *pp. 67–68*.

After the bark was peeled off, it was kept moist by periodic soaking in warm lake-water, and quite warm water was frequently poured on it to keep it pliable while being worked on. The silvery *outside* of the bark was *innermost* on the finished canoe; it apparently takes the desired shape best in this manner. The thickness of the bark depended on the size canoe desired and to a great extent on the maker's desire for maximum ultimate strength or lightness. I have seen Indian canoes with bark ³⁄₁₆ inch thick; ⅛ inch is probably more normal; my Chippewa is not much over ¹⁄₁₆ inch thick, as it was built for lightness and has to be handled accordingly.

For building, a smooth grassy or sandy level spot was selected and the big sheet of bark unrolled upon it and weighted down with stones. Hot water kept it from splitting during this handling. Two long staves of spruce (any other light wood will do), which ultimately would be used as the gunwales of the canoe, were lashed securely at their ends and then spread to the desired width of the canoe amidships, and held in this shape by temporary "thwarts" lashed in. Staves were about 1 inch by 1 inch and either square or round in cross section; later, before actually being used for the gunwales, some tapering was done at the ends. For the present, however, the lashed and spread staves were laid on the bark, on the ground, and held in place with stones as weights. Some Indians put down some of the thin bottom planking under the stones to protect the bark. This provided a rough "form" around which the large slab of bark could be turned up, with liberal applications of hot water, to obtain the approximate canoe shape. Some Indians used a special frame rather than the gunwale and thwart pieces, and may have saved it for use on succeeding canoes. Speck[3] calls such a frame "false gun-

[3]*Speck*, Penobscot Man, *p.* 59.

wales," and Ritzenthaler[4] calls it a "canoe form." If you look carefully at the picture of the Abnaki canoe in Fig. 22 of Chapter I, you will see a model of such a frame lying on top of the thwarts of the canoe.

As the bark was turned up around the frame, a liberal number of stakes were driven vertically to hold it (see Fig. 2). The stones were then moved to hold the bark on the ground and allow the gunwale staves to be lifted and lashed to the vertical stakes at the desired sheer line curve and giving the desired depth amidships (Fig. 20 of Chapter I). Before the staves were tied to the stakes in position to become the gunwales, the temporary thwarts were removed and permanent thwarts were mortised into slots and secured with watap lashings passing around the gunwale strip and through two or three holes bored in the thwart end. When trade iron-nails became available to the Indians, they quickly adopted these for installing thwarts and for nailing the gunwale strips together. Most birch canoes seen nowadays are built in this manner; the completely sewn canoes, like my Chippewa, are rare.

Additional pieces of bark were then pushed into place outside the gunwale strips and between the edge of the big piece of bark and the vertical stakes, to "piece out" the width needed in the midships section. In more modern times, large birch trees became scarce so that "piecing out" became quite common. A study of the birchbark canoe models in Chapter I reveals that some of the originals were of one-piece construction and some were not. The Penobscot canoe that Hadlock and Dodge[5] describe is 19 feet, 7¾ inches in overall length,

[4]*Ritzenthaler,* The Building of a Chippewa Indian Birch Bark Canoe, *pp.* 75, 77.

[5]*Glendell S. Hadlock and Ernest S. Dodge,* A Canoe from the Penobscot River (*Salem, Mass., Peabody Museum, 1948*). *Reprinted from* The American Neptune, *Vol. XIII, No. 4, 1948.*

3 feet 1 inch at the beam, and made from one piece of bark. This canoe would measure about 56 inches around the bottom at midships, more or less, depending on the depth of the canoe. A tree 18 inches in diameter would yield a piece of bark wide enough for building this canoe of one piece of bark. This canoe was given to the East India Marine Society in 1826, obviously

FIG. 2—Making a birchbark canoe. A large sheet of birchbark is laid on a smooth, level piece of ground and is weighted down with stones laid on a frame made of the gunwales and temporary thwarts, or a special frame for the purpose. The sides are bent up, often with the aid of hot water, and held in place with stakes driven into the ground. (Photograph by the Reverend Louis Roger Lafleur, O.M.I., Rouyn, Quebec)

when larger trees were available. Later, probably due to extensive lumbering operations, fewer large birches were to be found.

Indians sometimes found it also impossible to get one piece of bark for the full length of the bottom of the canoe. When this happened, the largest piece was used in the bottom midships area, and extra pieces were used to fill out the ends (Fig. 3).

The watap having been kept pliable through soaking in water was now used for sewing the overlapping seams of the pieces of bark and for attaching the bark to the gunwale strips. For repairing my Chippewa birch where the dried and brittle lashings chipped off through the years, I have used ordinary rattan such as is used for the "cane" seats of chairs and for commercial canoe seats. When thoroughly soaked, this handles just like the Indian watap; and as it ages, it looks the same. I believe it is considerably stronger and more durable.

Stitching was unbelievably close. It is a marvel that the bark didn't tear along the seams, like perforated sheets of paper. This may have happened occasionally, for Lyford[6] reports: "Stitches of uneven length were often employed, particularly around the ends, to prevent the bark from splitting." Holes were made in the wet bark with an awl; the end of the wet watap was pushed through; but as it was drawn up tight, it was given a slight twist that made its width lie across the length of the grain of the bark. This is probably why the bark doesn't tear at the seams. The stitching pattern was also characteristic of different tribes. My Chippewa is continuously stitched along the gunwales. The Penobscots would stitch closely for about 3 inches and then leave a gap of about 2 inches. Seams however were always closely stitched.

[6]*Carrie A. Lyford*, The Crafts of the Ojibway. (*Washington, D.C., Office of Indian Affairs, U. S. Dept. of the Interior*), p. 54.

When sewing the bark to the gunwales, as one nears the
ends, it is necessary to "lose" material (as in tinsmithing) to
obtain the rise of the ends. This is done by freely making
vertical slits, as necessary, and lapping the edges of the slit in
the vicinity of the gunwale. These slits are closed (and later
pitched with gum) by sewing only the exterior edge of the

FIG. 3—When it was not possible to get one piece of bark long enough for
the entire bottom of the canoe, the largest piece was used amidships and
the ends were filled out with extra pieces, as shown here. These Indians and
the one in Fig. 2 are elderly Tête de Boule Indians of the present day in the
region of the Upper St. Maurice River, Province of Quebec. (Photograph by
the Reverend Louis Roger Lafleur, O.M.I., Rouyn, Quebec)

overlap. No attempt is made to stitch the inner edge of the overlap because this is ultimately hidden by the sheathing and the ribs; these short seams extending downward from the gunwale therefore do not have a "V" appearance externally.

For closing the ends an inside stem is used. In my Chippewa and in the canoe the old guide built, this was a solid strip of wood, slightly wedge-shaped in cross section throughout the curve; this was steamed or thoroughly soaked in warm water and bent to shape. In the films, however, the Crees are shown using an ingenious trick (forerunner of our modern laminated-wood arch-truss construction) wherein they use a series of thin strips that slip on one another as the bend is made. When tightly lashed with watap, while bent, the form is retained. The skill of the Indian is shown by the fact that he bends this curve entirely by eye!

Another method used is as follows: "About two-thirds of the entire length of each stem was made triangular in cross section and the remaining portion was half-round. The triangular part of the stem was split into seven or more parts and wrapped with cedar bark. . . . The purpose of splitting the stem was twofold as it facilitated bending the wood into proper shape, and permitted the builder to pass the split-root lacing of the bow and stern through the stem. The end of the stem was tied in securely with the rails."[7]

The length of the inside-stem is such that its upper end projects sufficiently to be securely lashed to the tapering ends of the gunwale strips, while the lower end finishes inside just where the flat of the bottom begins; it is not fastened to the bark at this lower end, which is merely whittled to a flat taper to blend into the floor line. With this inside-stem in place, the bark is trimmed to a matching curve and watap is then used

[7]Glendell S. Hadlock and Ernest S. Dodge, A Canoe from the Penobscot River, p. :2. Page 8 of same book shows a drawing of this stem.

to sew the ends closed; the sewing completely encircles the inside-stem. Here again, some tribes use continuous close stitching; others use interval stitching.

With the canoe thus completely shaped and sewn, the inside of all seams is pitched with the spruce-gum or other sealing compound.

Meanwhile, long thin strips of cedar are riven out—about ⅛ inch thick by 2 or 2½ inches wide, as available. The Indians apparently do not hesitate to use what might be considered short lengths—3 to 4 feet long; obviously, however, the canoe would be stiffer and stronger with bottom strips that ran almost full length, with the shorter strips reserved for piecing out on the sides above the waterline. These strips, called "sheathing," or planking, are placed longitudinally, covering the entire inside of the canoe and are held in place by the ribs, which are tightly inserted over them. The job of holding them in place while the ribs are being inserted is quite tricky.

Ribs, meanwhile, have also been riven out and held to soak in shallow, warm lake-water, weighted by stones. Ribs are about ¾₆ to ¼ inch thick, by about 2 inches wide at their center, tapering slightly as they rise to the gunwales, and the edges that will be uppermost are slightly beveled. Ribs are set with about 2 inches spacing between them. Initial length of each rib is somewhat longer than when finished.

Here again the Indian shows his skill by bending these by eye with the fine graduation necessary for a sweetly shaped canoe. Even our old guide hesitated to risk this, and we bent them over a 16-foot canvas-covered canoe we were copying.

The trickiest part of the job now comes. Each rib has to be trimmed in curved length, so that when its ends are placed in position beneath the gunwales, it will at first assume an angle of only about 45 degrees with the center of its bow cocked toward amidships; it is then pushed and carefully tapped or hammered to an extremely snug fit vertically in the canoe. This wedging is the only thing that holds the ribs in place in an Indian canoe. The upper ends bear very tightly against the watap sewing that holds the bark to the gunwale strips; these ends are tapered flatwise to give them a good "bite," but not so sharply that they might cut the watap as they are driven into place.

The sharp bend of the ribs near the narrow ends of the canoe is difficult. Since many may be broken in the process, an ample initial supply is advisable. The Indians, however, do not hesitate to thin the rib somewhat in the vicinity of the bend, if necessary. Different grades of cedar bend with varying degrees of facility.

All the outside seams of the canoe are now thoroughly pitched. Whatever is used for "pitch" should have the quality to dry hard to the touch, yet with sufficient inherent flexibility not to crack as the canoe "works" under the strain of use. The pitch also should not run when exposed to a hot sun. I have found the asphalt-and-shredded-asbestos compound ideal for the purpose; it is manufactured for roofing purposes and I have recently noted glaziers using quite a similar compound for setting black-glass slab veneer against brick walls for modernistic shop-fronts. About a pound or two of the compound should "pitch" a bark canoe. Of course, there may be marine caulking compounds having similar qualities, but those I investigated here either dried to too brittle a consistency or their surface wouldn't dry sufficiently to prevent smearing as you handled the canoe.

The "pitch" is liberally daubed on, to completely cover and hide the watap, yet with skill and practice a nice clean edge line can be held. The sewing along the gunwale is not pitched.

Birch canoes are of course "rough." No piece of birch is ever so perfect that the bottom of the canoe will not have some "bumps," even if there are not some seams to roughen it. But the overall lines and the symmetry attained by the Indian builders were marvelous[8]—especially considering the crude materials they had to work with and the fact that everything was done "by eye"! Birch tends to dry out fairly rapidly and then becomes very brittle and subject to cracking—as noted in most museum specimens. When not in use for long periods the Indians would submerge them and hold them down with stones. This prevented the natural oils in the birchbark from evaporating.[9] I unwittingly preserved my Chippewa birch by responding to the modern canoeist's natural tendency to spar-varnish all wood. Shortly after I got it from Chief Burda, I noted the short scraps of sheathing used in the bottom and decided to strengthen the canoe by substituting full-length pieces. When I got all the ribs and sheathing out, I gave the entire inside of the canoe a good coat of spar-varnish; I likewise varnished each rib. Inserting full-length strips cut from a piece of poplar veneer, after varnishing it first, I replaced the ribs and some of the original short-length sheathing up on the sides. The weight was increased from 35 lbs. to

[8]*Canoes were made of other bark, for example, basswood (Fig. 29 of Chapter I) and elm (Fig. 30 of Chapter I). There is little doubt that craft made of these and other barks were inferior to the birchbark and probably in every case represent craft made of substitute materials—usually by Indians who were not the "sailors" that were the Indians of the land of canoe birch with its countless thousands of lakes, ponds, rivers, and streams. An excellent consideration of these aspects of the American Indian canoe industries together with the details of making an elmbark canoe is given in a book entitled* An Elm Bark Canoe in the Peabody Museum of Salem, *by William N. Fenton and Ernest Stanley Dodge, and published by Peabody Museum, Salem, Mass., 1949, 24 pages, with illustrations. Reprinted from* The American Neptune, *Vol. IX, No. 3, 1949.*

[9]*The Indians also often took special measures to protect the vulnerable birchbark when in rapids where sharp rocks might gash the bottom. They lashed thin cedar planks to the bottom. (See Speck,* Penobscot Man, *page 65.)*

slightly over 45 lbs., but the canoe has never dried out through the years. I varnished the exterior too, after re-pitching with asphalt. True, the glossy surfaces are not orthodox for a birch, but it has preserved the craft for use.

Cedar for the ribs and sheathing, spruce for the gunwales and thwarts, was the general Indian practice. However, ribs could be of any wood that would take a sharp bend easily— even thin strips of ash; the difference would merely be in the finished weight of the canoe. I imagine, too, that ash was freely used for gunwale strips and inside-stems and thwarts, where strength was paramount. I have never seen a genuine birch-bark with either a keel or a keelson. Ribs are not installed clear to the ends; about 12 inches at each end was left unsupported by any ribs; but to prevent crushing as the canoe was handled by its ends, a light strip of cedar was curved to a somewhat larger radius than the inside-stem and its width was very cleverly whittled to make a snug fit about 2 or 3 inches in-board of the stem. The upper end was cut with a flat-knob terminus and the lower end trimmed to slip under the first rib. With the lower end in place beneath the first rib, this end-strip was pushed into place so that the knob wedged into the "V" of the gunwale strips. It sealed off a dead space at each end of the canoe (like a curved bulkhead)[10] and its edges supported the birchbark skin somewhat inboard of each stem.[11]

[10]*Speck*, Penobscot Man, *calls it a bulkhead and states that the Indians called it "carrier" or "old woman" for an unexplained reason. Ritzenthaler,* The Building of a Chippewa Indian Birch Bark Canoe, *indicates the Chippewa call it "man-board" because of its shape.*

[11]*In* A Canoe from the Penobscot River, *there is additional information. For example, on page 12:* "The bulkhead was then forced into position by stepping the lower end into a notch which had been previously cut in the stem. The bulkhead fitted tightly against the planking. . . ." *See also page 8 for a drawing of this bulkhead and page 13 for a picture of it in place.*

Thus the Birch Canoe was builded
In the valley, by the river,
In the bosom of the forest;
And the forest's life was in it,
All its mystery and its magic,
All the lightness of the birch-tree,
All the toughness of the cedar,
All the larch's supple sinews;
And it floated on the river
Like a yellow leaf in Autumn,
Like a yellow water-lily.[12]

[12]*Longfellow,* Hiawatha.

Films on Making a Birchbark Canoe

Birch Bark Canoe (English sound track), color, 15 min., free loan. Quebec Publicity Bureau, 48 Rockefeller Plaza, New York, N.Y.

Tête-de-Boule Indians of Upper St. Maurice region build a birchbark canoe.

Portage, sound, 21 min., color or black and white, for sale or loan at rental fee. International Film Bureau, 57 East Jackson Blvd., Chicago 4, Illinois.

A record of the Indian trapper and explorer and of canoe-building. Also available as two separate films: *How Indians Build Canoes* and *Trappers and Traders.*

BIBLIOGRAPHY

"Afloat on Many Waters." *Natural History* magazine (July–August 1929).

The American Canoeist (official magazine of the American Canoe Association, New Haven, Conn.).

American White Water (journal of American White Water Affiliation, Denver, Colo.).

Bearse, Richard H., and Hazelton, Sidney C., *A Camp Aquatic Program*. Hanover, N.H., S. C. Hazelton, 1952.

Bloomster, Edgar L., *Sailing and Small Craft Down the Ages*. Annapolis, Md., United States Naval Institute, 1940.

Bodin, Arthur, *Bibliography of Canoeing* (New York, Arthur Bodin).

Bovey, Martin K., "On Becoming a Back Paddler." *Appalachia Magazine* (December 1936).

Brown, Douglas M., *White Water Canoeing—A Primer*. Meriden, Conn., Douglas M. Brown, 1950.

Brown, Douglas M., *White Water Canoeing—Notes for Experts*. Meriden, Conn., Douglas M. Brown, 1954.

Canoeing Manual. Martinsville, Ind. Developed by New England Section of the American Camping Association, Inc.

Cawley, J. and M., *Exploring the Little Rivers of New Jersey*. Princeton, N.J., Princeton University Press, 1942.

Claussen, Waldemar Van Brunt, *Canoeing* (Merit Badge Series). New Brunswick, N.J., Boy Scouts of America, 1952.

Claussen, Waldemar Van Brunt, *Canoeing*. Boy Scouts of America, 1931. Out of print.

Craig, Cal, *Blueprint for a Bush Trip*. New Brunswick, N.J., Boy Scouts of America. A reprint from *Boys' Life*.

DuBois, Eliot, "White Water Canoeing Technique." *The American Canoeist Magazine* (April 1953).

DuBois, Eliot, "White Water Safety." *Appalachia Magazine*, new ser., Vol. XVI (December 1950).

Eckstorm, Fannie Hardy, *The Handicrafts of the Modern Indians of Maine*. Bar Harbor, Maine, Abbe Museum, Lafayette National Park, 1932.

Ells, S. C., "The Polesman." *Canadian Geographic Journal*, Vol. 32 (April 1946).

Elvedt, Ruth, *Canoeing, A–Z*. Minneapolis, Burgess Publishing Co., rev. ed., 1953.

Fenton, William N., and Dodge, Ernest Stanley, *An Elm Bark in the Peabody Museum of Salem*. Salem, Mass., Peabody Museum, 1949. Reprinted from *The American Neptune*, Vol. IX, No. 3 (1949).

Gibbon, John Murray, *The Romance of the Canadian Canoe*. Toronto, The Ryerson Press, 1951.

Grinnell, Lawrence I., "Canoe Trips within 100 Miles of New York." Boston, *Appalachia Magazine*, 1940.

Hadlock, Wendell S., and Dodge, Ernest S., *A Canoe from the Penobscot River*. Salem, Mass., Peabody Museum, 1948. Reprinted from *The American Neptune*, Vol. VIII, No. 4 (1948).

Handbook for Boys. New Brunswick, N.J., Boy Scouts of America.

Handel, Carle W., *Canoe Camping*. New York, A. S. Barnes Co., 1953.

Leich, Harold M., "White Water on the Potomac." *Potomac Appalachian Trail Club Bulletin*, Vol. XXIII, No. 2 (April–June 1954).

Lewis, Richard Garwood, "Riding the White Water." *The Illustrated Canadian Forest and Outdoors* (August 1929).

Lewis, Richard Garwood, *Small Watercraft*. Toronto, Fullerton Publishing Co.

Lyford, Carrie A., *The Crafts of the Ojibway (Chippewa)*. Washington, D.C., Office of Indian Affairs, U. S. Dept. of the Interior.

Martin, George W., *Modern Camping Guide*. New York, D. Appleton-Century Co., 1940.

Mason, Bernard S., *Woodcraft*. New York, A. S. Barnes Co., 1939.

Mason, Bernard S., *The Junior Book of Camping and Woodcraft*. New York, A. S. Barnes Co., 1943.

McNair, Robert E., "Hints on Reading Fast Water." *The American Canoeist* (October 1953).

Mitman, Carl W., *Catalogue of the Watercraft Collection in the United States National Museum*. Washington, D.C., Smithsonian Institution, Government Printing Office, 1923.

Moore, Phil H., *With Rod and Gun in Canada*. Boston, Houghton Mifflin Co.

Morehouse and Fancher, *Know Your Canoeing*. Chicago, Western Division, American Canoe Association.

Perry, Ronald H., *The Canoe and You*. Toronto, J. M. Dent and Sons, 1948.

Phillips, John C., and Cabot, Thomas D., *Quick Water and Smooth*. Brattleboro, Vt., Stephen Daye Press, 1935. Out of print.

Pinkerton, Robert E., *The Canoe*. New York, The Macmillan Co., 1946.

Pulling, Albert Van Siclen, *Elements of Canoeing*. Ann Arbor, Mich., The Duke Publishing Co., 1933.

Pulling, Pierre (Albert Van Siclen Pulling), *Principles of Canoeing*. New York, The Macmillan Co., 1954.

Quirke, Terence T., *Canoes the World Over*. Urbana, The University of Illinois Press, 1952.

Remy, Joseph, *Canoe Handling*. Teaneck, N.J., American Canoe Association.

Ritzenthaler, Robert E., *The Building of a Chippewa Indian Birch Bark Canoe*. Milwaukee, Bulletin of the Public Museum of the City of Milwaukee, November 1950.

Smith, Ernest F., "White Water Canoeing." *Boys' Life* (June 1954).

Speck, Frank G., *The Penobscot Man*. Philadelphia, University of Pennsylvania Press, 1940.

Swanton, John R., *The Indian Tribes of North America*. Washington, D.C., Government Printing Office, 1953.

Wallace, Dillon, *The Camper's Handbook*. New York, Fleming H. Revell Co., 1936.

Wright, Eleanor L., *An Annotated Bibliography of Books and Articles on Canoeing from 1939 through 1951*. Washington, D.C., American Association for Health, Physical Education, and Recreation.

INDEX